Anne's Cradle

The Life & Works of
HANAKO MURAOKA,
Japanese Translator of
Anne of Green Gables

ERI MURAOKA

Translated from the Japanese
By Cathy Hirano

NIMBUS
PUBLISHING
— NIMBUS.CA —

Originally published in Japan as *An no yurikago Muraoka Hanako no shogai* by Shinchosha, 2008.

Editor: Whitney Moran
Design: Heather Bryan
NB1535

Library and Archives Canada Cataloguing in Publication

Title: Anne's cradle : the life and works of Hanako Muraoka, Japanese translator of Anne of Green Gables / by Eri Muraoka ; translated from the Japanese by Cathy Hirano.
Other titles: An no yurikago. English | Life and works of Hanako Muraoka, Japanese translator of Anne of Green Gables
Names: Muraoka, Eri, 1967- author. | Hirano, Cathy, translator.
Description: Translation of: An no yurikago.
Identifiers: Canadiana 2021009818X | ISBN 9781771089241 (softcover)
Subjects: LCSH: Muraoka, Hanako, 1893-1968. | LCSH: Translators—Japan—Biography. | LCSH: Authors, Japanese—20th century—Biography. | LCSH: Montgomery, L. M. (Lucy Maud), 1874-1942. Anne of Green Gables. | LCGFT: Biographies.
Classification: LCC P306.92.M87 M8713 2021 | DDC 418/.04092—dc23

Nimbus Publishing acknowledges the financial support for its publishing activities from the Government of Canada, the Canada Council for the Arts, and from the Province of Nova Scotia. We are pleased to work in partnership with the Province of Nova Scotia to develop and promote our creative industries for the benefit of all Nova Scotians.

Table of Contents

Author's Note

Some expressions used in this book are no longer considered appropriate but have been used because they are direct quotations from texts written during an earlier time.

Illegible words in excerpts from letters and other written documents quoted in this text have been marked with [...].

Wherever possible, permission was obtained from people shown in the photographs and from the photographer. In some cases, however, people could not be identified. If you recognize any of the people in the photos or know who the photographer is, please contact the author through the publisher.

Hanako at her home in Omori working on the translation of the Anne series, 1958. *The Mainichi Newspapers Co., Ltd.*

Prologue

Translating *Anne of Green Gables* in the Midst of War, April 1945

Although it was already mid-April, a cold snap had turned the day chilly and overcast. Here and there, cherry blossom petals fluttered from branches that were already leafing out.

In the Muraoka residence in Omori, Hanako had finished cleaning up after dinner and was in the study, writing in the dim light of a small lamp shaded with air-raid blackout cloth. She had begun polishing her translation of *Anne of Green Gables*, a novel set in Canada, and was going over the section at the beginning where the orphan Anne arrives in Prince Edward Island and is captivated by its beauty.

Riding down an avenue of apple trees in a horse-drawn buggy, Anne gazes raptly at the canopy of snow-white blossoms arching overhead. As she does for everything she likes, she gives the road a new name: White Way of Delight.

What words, Hanako wondered, would convey to Japanese readers the inner world of this young girl endowed with such a rich imagination?

White Way means *shiroi michi*, she thought. Delight could be *yorokobi*. Or what about *kanki*? *Kanki no shiroi michi*....

Hanako closed her eyes, conjuring up an image of trees adorned with pure white blossoms. The voice of a man singing as he passed by on the street reached her ears.

Cherry blossoms fall.
Those left on the branch
will soon be falling too.

These words from a haiku by Zen Buddhist poet Ryokan Taigu (1758–1831) were sung by Japanese soldiers when they sent their comrades off to the front. The war situation was rapidly deteriorating. Cast into a conflict they had no hope of winning, young men were perishing in foreign lands. Even in Tokyo, air-raid sirens whined frequently, followed by American bombers that sowed destruction. Three and a half years earlier, at the start of the Pacific War, no one had anticipated such devastation.

Canada, the birthplace of the book Hanako was furtively translating, was now an enemy. Slogans denouncing the Allied forces were used to whip up popular sentiment, and distorted accounts of Japanese military exploits had intensified the nation's militaristic fervour with each passing day. What condemnation would society heap upon Hanako should it catch her translating a book from an enemy nation?

In 1942, three years earlier, Canadian missionaries from Hanako Muraoka's alma mater, Toyo Eiwa Girls School, had been interned despite having committed no crime. In the same year, the leaders of the United Church of Christ in Japan had all been arrested for violating the Peace Preservation Law. Hanako and her husband, Keizo, Christians since their parents' generation, were no longer allowed to go to church. Even if Hanako succeeded in finishing her translation, would it ever be published in Japan?

Trying to shake off her gloom, Hanako reached for the porcelain cup on her desk and took a sip of pungent, twiggy *bancha* tea. Lucy Maud Montgomery's[1] story brimmed with hope for the future. Hanako longed to see the book published in Japan to cheer the hearts of Japanese readers. With fresh resolve, she picked up her pen and focused once more on revising the manuscript.

✿

A little over a month earlier, on March 10, a fleet of American Boeing29 Superfortress heavy bombers—what the Japanese referred to as B-29s—had launched a massive air raid on Tokyo, pummelling the city centre with firebombs and razing the densely populated Shitamachi area. Rather than relocating to the country for safety, residents stayed behind to defend their homes. Their efforts, however, were futile. Gusts of wind whipped the flames into an inferno, leaving in its wake a gruesome wasteland dotted with endless mounds of charred corpses.

Although the number of casualties exceeded that of the Great Kanto Earthquake of 1923, government reports carried by the radio and newspapers claimed the raid had only caused a small fire in the government department responsible for the imperial stables. That night, however, the crimson sky blazing over the northeastern part of the city had been visible even from Hanako's house in Omori, about ten kilometres away.

A few days later, a poet Hanako knew well came and told her the shocking truth. When he related that the cheerful, hardworking housewives belonging to the women's associations in those areas—women who had cared for the elderly and cooked for those who had lost their homes—had all perished, Hanako shut her eyes, overcome with anguish. Desperation tinged her friend's face, and he looked haggard and worn from wandering the blackened streets. "For years, they forced me to write things against my will," he said bitterly. "And now look at me. I'm too broke to send my wife and children to the countryside where they'd be safe. The rich all flee while the poor are left to die in the city, unable to escape this catastrophe."

Thereafter, newspapers began referring to the city as the "Tokyo war theatre," even though they were forbidden to criticize the war. The people were growing disillusioned with their leaders. Few now believed Japan would win. They simply longed for the war to end as soon as possible so they could sleep soundly again.

❀

Having graduated that spring from elementary school, which the government had renamed "national people's schools,"[2] Hanako's daughter, Midori, was now in middle school. The sight of her daughter dressed in patched *monpe* workpants filled Hanako with pity. Midori was only twelve years old. Had the world been at peace, she would have been enjoying her studies, losing herself in books, and cherishing whatever dreams and ideals sprang from her pure heart. Instead, her days were filled with mending threadbare clothes, making do without, and the constant fear of death.

As she sat sipping her tea, Hanako thought back to her own girlhood. Although strict rules had governed her life, her years in the dormitory, surrounded by foreign missionaries and immersed in their culture, had been rich and nurturing. Despite being poor, she had been able to create a beautiful inner world, composing poetry and reading literature.

Hanako's one comfort was the children's resilience, which they kept even in the midst of war. Her daughter, Midori, and her nieces and nephew who lived next door, remained uncowed by life's hardships, continuing to grow straight and true. Haruko and Kazuho, the daughter and son of Hanako's sister Umeko, and Michiko, the daughter of Hanako's brother-in-law Noboru, seemed tough enough to accept the harsh realities of wartime deprivation. They never complained, and the little joys they found in daily life brought smiles to their faces. Each time Hanako witnessed that spirit, it renewed her strength to go on.

Whenever gloom threatened to engulf her family, Hanako came to the rescue using a technique for escaping despair that she had picked up from the book she was translating: the imagination game. On days when rations were scarce and their meal was meagre, she would encourage everyone to conjure up a feast. After all, they could enjoy in their minds whatever delectable dishes they wanted. They would spend the dinner hour happily chatting about a favourite drink, describing beautiful tableware, and discussing different cooking methods. During these dark times, when each day seemed to bring more sad news, Hanako looked for ways to ease the wounded souls of her loved ones.

�*/🌸

At noon on April 13, 1945, news of President Franklin D. Roosevelt's death kindled hope in Japan that the war might soon end. But his successor, President Harry S. Truman, followed Roosevelt's lead. As if to proclaim his intentions, that very night air-raid sirens split the darkness that shrouded Tokyo.

Two nights later, a thunderous roar jolted Midori from her sleep. Air raids were so frequent now that she slept in her clothes. In the study, Hanako grabbed *Anne of Green Gables* and the Japanese manuscript she was working on and tied them up in a *furoshiki* cloth. Tucking this bundle firmly under one arm, she dashed to the bomb shelter in the yard with Midori, Keizo, and their maid, Fumi. Keizo took with him their ration book, as well as a beautiful leather-bound, gilded Bible and a hymnal, both printed by the company his father founded. He also clasped a jar of sugar he had managed to buy on the black market for Hanako, who loved sweets. Sugar was precious, and the jar was firmly sealed with wax.

The four of them hunkered in the dugout like animals in a den, listening intently to the noises outside as if their bodies were ears. Keizo's brow was beaded with sweat. Hanako worried about his high blood pressure as she gently dabbed his forehead with her sleeve. They heard shouts and the banging of buckets alerting people to a fire nearby. Cautiously, they emerged from their refuge.

Hanako's sister Umeko and her husband, Iwao, rushed over, gasping for breath. "Papa! Hanako!" Umeko called out. (Everyone in the family called Keizo "Papa," including his younger brother, Noboru, his nieces and nephew.) "It's too dangerous here," Umeko told them. "Iwao's going to stay and help the fire brigade, but the rest of us should get away!" Strapped firmly to Umeko's back was her six-year-old son, Kazuho, while beside her stood her daughter, Haruko, who was in grade six.

The family had already planned what to do if there was another large air raid: they would flee rather than stay to put out the flames. Tokyoites had learned a bitter lesson from the Great Tokyo Air Raid of March 10. Government-promoted bucket relays, diligently practiced during air-raid drills in every district, were effective in response to small air raids. But in a major raid, the opposite was true: staying behind to fight a fire multiplied the scale of the disaster. Hanako's neighbourhood association had therefore decided that if this came to pass, women, children, and the elderly should be evacuated. On this night, the night of April 15, over two hundred

B-29s appeared in the skies above Tokyo. In a massive three-hour blitz, they carpet bombed a broad swathe of the city from the districts of Shiba, Omori, and Urata to Kawasaki, Tsurumi, and Yokohama, devastating an area approximately ten kilometres long and three kilometres wide.

"Ume," Hanako said, "you go on ahead and take Midori with you." Recently, Keizo had been finding it hard to walk any distance because of his heart condition. Hanako would never think of leaving him behind, but she could not worry the others by telling them this.

"Listen carefully," said Keizo. "Head towards Ikegami Honmonji. If the temple's already full, go around to the field behind it. There should be a big air-raid shelter there."

"But what about you, Mother?" asked Midori, peering at her anxiously.

"Don't worry, Midori," Hanako said firmly. "We'll be fine. We can't leave right away, but we'll come later. Just be sure to stick with Umeko. Whatever you do, don't get separated."

Noboru's wife and daughter now joined them in the yard. Like Iwao, Noboru had gone to help the fire brigade. Bombs whistled through the air, then burst and scattered in a shower of flaming fragments. "Just like fireworks!" the children cried excitedly.

"Off you go," Hanako and Keizo urged them. "Hurry now."

🌢

The main street, Omote Sando, which led to the temple, as well as the street behind it, were jammed with evacuees. It was hard enough for the children to stick with Umeko in the jostling crowd, let alone make it to the temple grounds.

Ikegami Honmonji was the main temple of the Nichiren Buddhist sect and had been built at the end of the thirteenth century. It was the resting place of its founder, Nichiren, a Buddhist priest of the Kamakura period (1222–1282), as well as the wife of Ieyasu Tokugawa (1543–1616), the first Tokugawa[3] shogun, and the wife of Yoshimune Tokugawa (1684–1751), the eighth shogun. Also buried there were the seventeenth-century painter Tan'yu Kano and many famous kabuki actors. Midori and Haruko looked forward to the temple festival held every year on October 13 to commemorate Nichiren's passing. During the festival, the area was always packed with people and street stalls, but never had they seen it as crowded as this. Here and there, people had plonked themselves down by the side of the road. Some muttered prayers, while many of the elderly wished they were already dead and safely laid to rest. At that moment, a firebomb fell among the trees on the hill where the temple's cemetery lay. Apparently even being in the grave wasn't a guarantee of safety.

"It's no use," Umeko exclaimed. "We'd better go back and see if we can make it to the field behind the temple." Buffeted by the crowd, Midori and Haruko struggled after her.

🏵

Back at the Muraoka home, Hanako and Keizo looked down the deserted street. All the young men had been sent to war, leaving Tokyo with a ratio of twenty-eight women for every man. Once the neighbourhood women and children had hurried off to seek refuge, only the firefighters and the police remained behind.

On the other side of the railway tracks, a pillar of flame rose from a munitions factory, which was really just a collection of small, family-run workshops. The fire was more than four or five hundred metres away, but it looked much closer.

"Are you frightened?" Keizo asked.

"No." Hanako smiled, clutching her precious bundle to her chest.

"Me neither," said Keizo. "Not in the least."

Though it began as a brief, illicit affair, their relationship had been forged through surmounting repeated hardships. In the midst of this conflict, they might be killed at any moment, but come what may, Hanako had vowed never to part with Keizo for as long as she lived. There was also a job she had to finish: translating *Anne of Green Gables*. Not for the income, but as a testimony to her life.

The book had been a parting gift from Miss Shaw, a Canadian missionary who had returned home before the war. Hanako was convinced it was no mere coincidence that this book had come to her. Its protagonist, Anne, an unloved orphan, was eleven years old when a mix-up brought her to Matthew and his sister, Marilla. This mistake would change her fate. All her life, Anne had longed to find people she could call family and a place she could call home. The tale opens just as her dream begins to come true.

Like Anne, Hanako's fate had changed radically when she was in her tenth year. How different her life would have been if she had not been taken by her father to enroll in Toyo Eiwa Girls School[4], founded by Canadian missionaries. As the daughter of an impoverished tea merchant, Hanako would never have become a translator and, most likely, would never have met Keizo. It was the education she received from the Canadian missionaries and their spiritual influence that had shone a light upon her path. She could not help but see the will of God in the way this book, borne across the sea by a missionary from Canada to Japan, had become her companion through the ravages of war. She shifted the bundle in her arms and hugged it tighter.

Flames moved in on Keizo and Hanako from three directions. The only way left to flee was toward Omori Station. Silently, Hanako bid farewell to her books. While she loved her house dearly, as a writer, her books were her life. Books she had read as a girl, books from her years as a translator. More than half were English publications.

Suddenly, the attack ceased. Over three hours had passed since the air-raid sirens first sounded. A member of the fire brigade stopped when he saw them. "Mr. and Mrs. Muraoka, you didn't evacuate?" he asked.

"We were going to if it came to that," Hanako replied. Flames still smoldered on the other side of a narrow river that ran beside the street in front of their house. Many houses had burned, but the Muraoka property remained untouched.

"We lost most of the neighbourhood," the firefighter said. "We finally managed to stop the flames just up there. Fortunately there was no wind tonight. Still, you're pretty brave."

All the two of them could do now was wait. Hanako could not even focus on her work. Unable to quell her agitation, she kept stepping out into the yard and then back into the house again. Midori and the others finally returned at dawn. They were covered from head to toe in mud, even Kazuho, who was still strapped to Umeko's back. They had reached the air-raid shelter only to discover that it had been turned into an army storehouse. Still, they had been able to shelter there with the rest of the crowd.

"Auntie, did you stay here the whole time?" Michiko asked. "You didn't run away? You're amazing! How could you be so brave?"

"Well, everybody left without closing the doors, you see," said Hanako. "I couldn't let thieves come in, now could I? But don't worry, I locked everything up." Although she could have danced for joy to know her family was safe, she kept her voice calm and went into the kitchen to make some *onigiri* rice balls.

❈

It was not until 1952, seven years later (and about fifteen years after Miss Shaw had given Hanako the book), that Hanako's translation of Lucy Maud Montgomery's *Anne of Green Gables* was published in Japan as *Akage no An*, meaning "redheaded Anne."

Chapter 1

Early Life and Entering the Mission School: 1893–1903

Birth to 10 Years

Becoming a Scholarship Student

In the spring of 1903, nine-year-old Hanako trotted along beside her father, her hand in his, as they climbed the cherry-lined street of Toriizaka in Azabu. Unable to take her eyes from the trees overhead, she almost tripped several times. A clear blue sky peeped through the lace of unfurling blossoms, while gas lamps visible among the branches stood as reminders of Japan's rapid adoption of Western customs and technology a few decades earlier.

Rickshaws sped past Hanako bearing ladies garbed in kimono. Stately residences rose behind long red-brick walls that bounded each property. Here lived the *kazoku*[5], a privileged class just below the Imperial Family in rank. Numbered among the area's residents were the Kuni-no-miya family, which was the second oldest collateral branch of the Japanese Imperial Family, House of Peers member Kinyoshi Sanjo, Viscount Saneyoshi Yasuzumi, the politician Keisuke Otori[6], and the Yi family, which included the crown prince of Korea. For a poor commoner like Hanako, just to approach an area where such illustrious people resided was intimidating. It was within these affluent surroundings, however, that Toyo Eiwa Girls School had been established by Canadian missionaries nineteen years earlier.

Hanako's father came to a stop before the school gate. "This is it," he said, breaking his silence for the first time since they had reached the neighbourhood. "Here you can read all the books you want. But listen,

Hana: don't let the daughters of the peerage best you. Study hard and show them you're better than they are."

Being a Christian had given Hanako's father a connection with the school's founder, and he had worked hard to get his daughter transferred into the school's preparatory course. As a result, Hanako would be studying at the same institution as the daughters of the aristocracy and the wealthy—but only as a scholarship student. Scholarship students had to be Christian and were required to volunteer as Sunday school teachers for an orphanage in Azabu. Although their student fees were waived, they would be expelled immediately if they received low grades.

The school gate was at the top of a gentle slope covered in trefoil and planted with azalea and bush clover. At the bottom stood a four-storey wooden building that served as the school and dormitory. Bay windows graced the walls, their casements opened wide, and pansies bloomed in a flower bed in front of the entrance. Hanako could hear a piano being played somewhere. Students gazed out from between the white curtains, their hair in braids or coiled in a bun on top of their heads and adorned with a ribbon. Some students were playing tennis in the schoolyard wearing wide, pleated trousers called *hakama* over kimono, the long sleeves of which had been tied back with a *tasuki* sash.

Hanako and her father were met by the dorm matron, Miss Reiko Kamo, who wore a black, crested *haori* short coat over a kimono, and three foreign missionaries who wore long dresses with puffed sleeves. Hanako, who would live in the dormitory, had brought only her clothes wrapped in a *furoshiki* cloth and a wicker box that contained things she would need for studying, such as pencils and notebooks, as well as several books from Sazanami Iwaya's[7] world fairy tales series. The books were gifted from her father, and Hanako had read them so thoroughly she could recite them by heart. Her father slipped Hanako's bundle of belongings from his back and handed it to Miss Kamo, then turned to Hanako.

"From here on," he said, "this is your home."

"That's right," said Miss Kamo. "All people are equal before God." Her expression as she announced this principle was kind and magnanimous. "Social status makes no difference. The dorm students are like one big family."

"Can I go home and see Chiyo at festival time?" Hanako asked. Chiyo was her sister, who was four years her junior. Hanako's family sometimes went from their home in Minami Shinagawa to Shinagawa Shrine in Gotenyama, where the children played on the shrine grounds. Hanako looked forward to taking her little sister to the shrine fair every June during the large Tenno-sai festival.

"Of course," her father said. "But don't worry about us anymore, Hana. Just focus on your studies." He patted her head. Then, with a deep bow to the dorm matron and the missionaries into whose hands he had now entrusted his daughter's education, he turned and strode back up the hill.

Ippei, Hanako's Christian[8] Father

Hanako Muraoka's maiden name was Annaka and her first name was not "Hanako" but just plain "Hana." She was born on June 21, 1893, the eldest child of Ippei Annaka and his wife, Tetsu, in Kofu city, Yamanashi prefecture. Ippei, born in 1859, came from a family of humble tea merchants in Sunpu, a town that later became Shizuoka city. But by the time Hanako was born, Ippei had already become a zealous Christian and left home, relocating to Kofu, where he met his wife and moved in with her family.

In accordance with Ippei's wishes, Hanako was baptized at the age of two by Kotai Kobayashi, pastor of the Canadian Methodist Kofu Church and a founding member of Toyo Eiwa Girls School. Although Hanako had no way of knowing it at the time, she had taken the first step on a journey that would lead to a deep, lifelong connection with Canada and her translation of *Anne of Green Gables*. But how did her father, Ippei, end up joining the Canadian Methodist Church during Japan's tumultuous drive towards westernization in the late nineteenth century?

In 1867, Japan's last shogun, Yoshinobu Tokugawa (1837–1913), restored political power to the emperor and resigned from his position as ruler of the nation. However, he still retained substantial political influence, and forces seeking to consolidate power under the emperor staged a coup d'état the following year, establishing the new Meiji government with the emperor as its nominal head. Known as the Meiji Restoration, this marked the beginning of the Meiji period (1868–1912), a time of great change that saw the abolition of a class system dominated by the samurai class and dramatic reforms in such areas as taxation and education.

While Japan proceeded along the path of a modern, centralized nation, the former shogun, Yoshinobu, retired to Sunpu. Seeking to restore the Tokugawa family fortunes, Yoshinobu's former retainers who had followed him there promoted rapid modernization of the region, inviting teachers from other countries to educate the people in such subjects as medicine, military tactics, and foreign languages. These Westerners shared not only their expertise in different branches of learning, but also the teachings of the Bible, which formed their core values. To this region, where the soil had been thus readied to accept Western culture, came Reverend Davidson Macdonald. A medical doctor and Canadian Methodist missionary, he began sowing the seeds of Christianity after his arrival in 1874. Incidentally, although Macdonald was born in 1838 in Prince Edward County, Ontario, he had spent his early twenties on Prince Edward Island, the stage for *Anne of Green Gables*, and it was there that he had decided to become a pastor.

"All spiritual revolutions come from the dark side of the age. The circumstance in which Christianity was first established in Japan was no exception to this rule." These words are found in *Essays on the Modern Japanese Church* by Aizan Yamaji, a Methodist convert from the same period. As they suggest, Christianity offered an anchor for the shogun's former retainers and their families who, with the dissolution of Japan's feudal system, had been stripped not only of their former status and power but also of the cause they had believed in. People from other walks of life also began coming to the churches, including those moved by Macdonald's selfless service as an advisor to the Shizuoka Hospital and tea merchants who wanted to learn a foreign language to equip them for trade with other countries. Many who came converted to Christianity, and the faith spread.

Ippei Annaka, who loved literature to begin with, started visiting the Canadian Methodist Church[9] while peddling tea. He was soon so enamored with this new philosophy that it took priority over his family's tea business. Following the evangelists to the town of Kofu, he met Tetsu, the woman who would become his wife.

In Kofu, in addition to tea merchants, an increasing number of raw-silk merchants had become converts. That tea and raw silk headed the list of exports from Japan during the first half of the Meiji period was closely related to this connection between the merchants and Canadian missionaries. Many former retainers also lived in Kofu, which was once under the shogunate's direct control. One of these was Munizo Yuki, a survivor of the New Select Brigade (Shinsen-gumi), which was formed to protect the shogunate in 1863 but was defeated by the forces of the new Meiji government in 1869. Munizo's encounter with Canadian Methodists transformed him into an evangelist.

Over the first few decades of the Meiji period, Canadian Methodist missionaries established bases in Sunpu and Kofu, as well as in Azabu, Tokyo, and in each of these they founded a girls' school: Shizuoka Eiwa in Sunpu, Yamanashi Eiwa in Kofu, and Toyo Eiwa in Azabu. The level of girls' education in Japan at the time was poor, and women's social status was much lower than that of men. Required to subjugate their will completely to that of their male kin, women were not permitted to even voice their own wishes. When missionaries from overseas saw how Japanese women were forced to live in submission, they recognized the pressing need for women's education. In response, the Canadian Methodist Church headquarters in Toronto dispatched a group of female missionaries to Japan. Of course, this movement was not limited to Methodists. The establishment of mission schools by various denominations from the

West contributed significantly to the development of modern Japan, and particularly to women's and children's education.

Through his interaction with the missionaries and intelligentsia he met at the church, Ippei was baptized in this new culture. Recognizing Hanako's intelligence, he came to have almost excessive expectations for her, even though she was a girl. "Look at Kenji," he often said. "You must become smart like him."

Kenji, the eldest son of Reverend Kobayashi, the pastor of Kofu Church, was considered a child prodigy. When Hanako was four, he recited a poem he had composed at the church Christmas party. It began with the line "Mount Fuji garbed in white" and established the boy's reputation as a genius among the villagers. Thereafter, Ippei viewed Kenji as his daughter's rival.

Ippei was a free spirit, passionately pursuing his ideals, including his Christian faith, at the expense of his work. Completely unfettered by such social norms as "girls don't need an education," he was far too radical in his thinking to assume the role of a humble rural tea merchant. He often clashed with his in-laws' old-fashioned values, and quarrels were frequent. It was generally his wife, Tetsu, who suffered the consequences.

Although Tetsu attended church out of obedience to her husband, she was torn between these new ideas and the old customs with which she was familiar. Even as a child, Hanako sensed the strain within her home. While it was her father who fostered Hanako's appreciation for literature, it was because of him that she had to endure, from an early age, the oppressiveness of sharing space with people who had incompatible perspectives.

In an essay written at the age of sixty, the year after the Japanese edition of *Anne of Green Gables* was published, Hanako described her experience as follows:

> Later I learned that relationships within my family at the time were quite a snarled tangle. Dissecting my thoughts as a child, I think I

must have sensed this despite being so young, because I was always longing for a "peaceful life."[...]When I look back on my girlhood, I see myself as somehow set apart from those around me. I am not sure why. It was not that I fought with anyone or was antisocial. But I always seemed to be thinking of something different from my friends. Those days bring back memories that are both fond and sad.[10]

When Hanako was five, her father cast off the constraints of kinship and moved with his wife and children to Tokyo. They settled in the Minami Shinagawa area and set up a teashop to make a living. Minami Shinagawa was the site of numerous temples and still retained traces of its heyday as the first post station on the Tokaido, the highway that joined Edo to Kyoto during the Edo period when the Tokugawa shogunate ruled Japan (1603–1867). A sense of nostalgia for bygone days underlaid the cheerful vitality of their commercial working-class neighbourhood. Hanako's school, Jonan Elementary School, was located by the seashore, and she spent her free time playing on the sandy beach wrapped in the scent of the sea. She often declared to her schoolmates, "When I grow up, I'm going to build a house just for me. I'll live there on my own, keep it nice and clean, and spend all day reading books and writing."

At the age of seven, she was stricken with a high fever that lasted many days. She composed the following tanka verse from her sickbed:

Oblivious,
I spent my days believing
that I still had time,
though my foot was already
on the path that led towards death.

Upon reading this poem, her parents burst into tears, but fortunately Hanako recovered from her illness. On her first day back at school, she composed another tanka.

Returning to school,
a splendid sight greets my eyes.
Cherry trees in bloom,
white blossoms at their zenith,
glorious petals unfurled.

Hanako's deathbed poem had made her father proud, and for the rest of her childhood, Hanako derived great joy in composing tanka and haiku. Viewing the world through the lens of childish innocence, she effortlessly spun everything she saw into verse, whether it was the daily lives of people in central Tokyo or the changing seasons reflected in the sea, the sky, and the colours of flowers. Ippei's earnest desire to nurture the budding talent he witnessed in his child would pave the way for Hanako to surpass the class barriers her parents faced and pursue higher education.

The school and dormitory building of Toyo Eiwa Girls School in the early twentieth century, around the time Hanako attended the school.

❀

Another factor that aided Hanako's admission into Toyo Eiwa was a temporary decline in the fortunes of Japan's mission schools. Founded during the push towards westernization, these schools had initially attracted the wealthy, particularly the aristocracy. Their popularity gradually faded, however, with the subsequent rise in nationalism and the drive towards militarization, which culminated with the outbreak of the Russo-Japanese War in 1904, the year after Hanako entered Toyo Eiwa. Government restrictions on Christian schools cast a cloud over their prosperity, foreshadowing a time when their very existence would be threatened. In response, the schools had begun to return to their roots: the Christian spirit of humanitarian equality. It was within this historical context that Toyo Eiwa Girls School accepted Hanako as a transfer student.

Hanako's father, who had joined the socialist movement not long before Hanako was admitted, was particularly vocal in his support for equal education. Despite modernization, class disparity had grown, workers were subjected to cruel labour conditions, and the autocratic militarist government was a far cry from democracy. To address this reality, socialism in its initial stages raised the banner of an ideal society characterized by freedom, equality, and philanthropy, a cause that many Christians also supported.

The timeline below traces Ippei's footsteps as an early socialist.

1903 April 3 Arrested at a gathering for labourers

April 25 Gave a speech at a socialist rally

1904 January Joined the Society of Commoners[11] (Heiminsha) and participated in a socialist tea party

1906 June Joined the Japan Socialist Party[12] (Nihon Shakaito) as soon as it was formed. Donated 30 *sen*.

1907 February Became a party councilor and was later active in the Socialist Comrade Society (Shakaishugi Doshikai) and the Labour Promotion Society (Rodo Shoreikai).

But Ippei and his family sank ever deeper into poverty. Of his eight children, Hanako, Chiyo, Shozaburo, Kenjiro, Ume (later Umeko), Iso, Yuki, and Kunihisa, only Hanako, the eldest, would receive an education that matched his ideals. Except for Chiyo and Ume, all of Ippei's children left home, one by one, at a young age. Some were adopted by other families while others were taken on as apprentices[13] or domestic help. The genteel environment into which Hanako stepped at the age of ten was the gift of her father's dreams. But it was gained at a heavy price: the sacrifice paid by her siblings.

Befriended by a Sophisticated Senior

"Well then, let me show you around the school," Miss Kamo said after Hanako's father had left. Hanako followed her into the building. It seemed very quiet. There were still a few days before the new school year started and few students had returned to the dorms.

On the first floor was the assembly hall where morning worship was held. Rows of wooden chairs were set out on a red carpet. At the front of the room to one side was a mahogany organ, while in the centre was a stage with an altar. Miss Kamo led Hanako past eight classrooms, a staff room, the principal's room, and the dining room. Beyond this lay the lodgings of the Canadian teachers.

The second floor was mainly devoted to student dorm rooms. As they walked down the long corridor, Miss Kamo proudly pointed out the modern steam heating system installed along the wall. A wooden door opened, and a young teacher stepped out.

"Hello, Miss Kobayashi," said the dorm matron. "This is Hana Annaka, the scholarship student who was admitted today."

"How do you do. I'm Tomiko Kobayashi, from the English department. I'm in charge of teaching English writing to the new students, so I expect that we shall see each other in the classroom."

Hanako, however, did not respond. Forgetting to even bow in greeting, she stood stock-still, staring into the room the teacher had just exited. A library! Her father's collection was nothing compared to what she saw here. The room's magnificent wooden bookcases were packed with books. Hanako had taken the Japanese translation of John Milton's *Paradise Lost* from her father's shelf last year. Although it was too difficult for a nine-year-old, she had felt its worth even without understanding all the words and had basked in a strange sense of fulfillment. The joy she had experienced at the time surged through her at the memory.

"Can I read them all?" she asked.

"You should say, 'May I read them.' But yes, you may read them all," Miss Kamo said. "If you can, that is," she added with a chuckle. "Isn't that right, Miss Kobayashi?"

Reiko Kamo was a large, cheerful woman. Born to a samurai family that had lost everything during the Meiji Restoration, she had originally been employed at Toyo Eiwa to teach needlework. Impressed by her decorum, which came from a good upbringing, and her intelligence, which had been honed by suffering, the Canadian missionaries soon placed her in charge of the dormitory. She was a true mother to her charges, instructing them in every aspect of their daily life, from their demeanor and the language they used, to laundry and mending *tabi* socks. She also paid close attention to their diet and health.

Miss Kamo led Hanako up the stairs to the third floor. In addition to more dorm rooms, there was a music room where a student was playing the piano. It was from this room that Hanako had heard music as she passed through the school gate. Next they came to classrooms for needlework, cooking, and manners. This was Miss Kamo's territory, and she explained what went on in each room thoroughly.

On the fourth floor they came to a small, dimly lit room. "This is the prayer room," Miss Kamo said solemnly. "We call it the chapel. It was made for students to spend time alone in quiet prayer and to reflect on their sins. Because God's love is infinite."

Sin. Love. Hanako had often heard these words spoken by the preacher in the church and read them in Christian books and even in *Paradise Lost*. But although she was drawn to the beauty of the sounds, their meaning evaded her, and she hesitated to say them herself.

Miss Kamo guided Hanako to a dorm room on the second floor and left her there. Inside the door was a small vestibule to remove one's shoes followed by a sliding door of latticed screen covered with paper. The room itself was Japanese-style, raised one step above the vestibule and floored with thick *tatami* mats made of tightly woven straw. Hanako would share this space with four or five other students from different grades.

She had just begun to get settled when she heard a voice. "May I come in?"

"Yes," she answered.

A young woman slid back the paper-screened door and stepped into the room. "How do you do. I'm Chiyo Okuda," she said. Her voice was sweet and clear like a little bell. "The principal told me all about you. She asked me to offer you my assistance as there must be many things you wish to know. That's why I came."

The school offered three courses of study: preparatory, academic, and collegiate, which required two, five, and three years of study, respectively, to complete. There were about twenty students in each year for both the preparatory course and the academic course. Each year, six or seven graduates of the academic course would continue on to the collegiate course. Chiyo Okuda was in the fourth year of the academic course. Her grandfather, Keisuke Otori, lived in one of the large mansions that Hanako had passed on her way to the school. From the musical intonation of her speech, Hanako realized she must belong to the peerage that her father had told her about. This was the first time Hanako had seen an aristocrat up close.

Chiyo's hair was swept up in a soft, full bun and tied with a ribbon. She wore a long-sleeved, single-layered crepe kimono tucked into dark-purple *hakama* pants. To Hanako, Chiyo looked dazzlingly refined and even dashing. The girl had already launched into an explanation of various aspects of student life when suddenly she stopped and stared at Hanako's hair.

"One moment, please," she said. She took out a comb and, stepping behind Hanako, deftly redid her hair, tying it with her own ribbon. "To do up your hair without a ribbon is like wearing a kimono without a sash," Chiyo said. "That's what Miss Craig told us. There now. That's much better."

Eyes downcast, Hanako blushed, a mixture of shyness, joy, and anxiety churning inside her. Not knowing what to do, she felt she might burst into tears. Would she really be able to fit in, she wondered.

Chapter 2

Hanako Discovers British and American Literature: 1904–1907

Age 11 to 14

A Bumbling New Student

It took Hanako a long time to adjust to the strictly regimented dorm life and to the manners and customs of the high-born students. The first and most pressing issue was her spoken Japanese. Coming from a poorer class, Hanako lacked any training in the higher forms of polite speech, of which there were many, and she found herself being corrected whenever she opened her mouth to speak.

Meals, which were eaten together in the dining room, were another ordeal. Tuesday evenings when Western cuisine was served were the worst because they had to eat with a knife and fork. Hanako, who had never used cutlery before, was always nervous, making one mistake after another. Once she sent a piece of carrot flying across the table to land on the plate of a senior student. Seven or eight students shared a table with one of the missionaries, who gave them thorough instructions on table manners. For Hanako, however, these were even harder to master than the use of cutlery as she did not understand a word of the English spoken to her. It was enough to make her lose her appetite.

More than half of her seventeen classmates had already received three years of English education at the primary school affiliated with Toyo Eiwa. Some of them had even lived overseas or had one parent who was a Westerner. These students conversed animatedly with the missionaries in fluent English throughout the meal.

Although Hanako had always come first in her class, the culture at Toyo Eiwa was so different she felt like she was attending school in a foreign country. Unfamiliar with the alphabet, she froze when called upon in class to pronounce something in English, certain that the others must be laughing at her. Everyone was very kind, including Miss Kamo, the Japanese teachers, and the senior students who shared her room, but Hanako missed her family desperately, as well as her friends with whom she had played on the beach in Shinagawa.

Still, to go home was out of the question. She really wanted to study. And she wanted to live up to her father's expectations, too. English was the key. In order to stay, she would have to master the English language. Making up her mind, Hanako threw herself into her studies.

✿

One day, a senior student, who was one of Hanako's roommates, invited her to go buy some "dessert." Students were allowed to bring snacks, which they called "dessert," into their rooms, and it was something they all looked forward to. Together, the two girls passed through the school gate and out into the street. It was already dusk, and a man bearing a long pole with a flame on the tip was lighting the gas lamps one by one. Each time the gas caught the flame, it flared, lighting up the red-brick wall in front of the Sanjo manor. The girls walked down the hill to the Shogendo sweet shop located along Azabu Juban street. The shop's specialty was *kintsuba*, squares of sweet bean paste wrapped in a thin dough. Some of the squares were so large that Hanako laughed aloud at the sight. Her roommate bought a box of the largest size and Hanako carried the package. As they passed through the school gate and walked down the gentle slope, she heard the same tune being played on the piano as she had heard on the day her father brought her to the school.

"What song is that?" she asked.

"Träumerei."[14]

A pleasant breeze touched Hanako's face as she listened, enchanted by the tune. They had only been gone twenty minutes but she felt refreshed and cheered. When their roommates saw the package of sweets, they let out a shriek of delight that drew the students from the room next door. As they opened the box and gave everyone a piece, Hanako wondered if there could be anything more delectable than *kintsuba* shared with this laughing, chattering circle of friends.

Miss Blackmore: A Stern Principal

"Whatever you do, don't sniff during the worship service."

It was the first morning of the second term of Hanako's second year, just after the summer holidays, and the new school principal was the sole focus of her three older roommates' conversation.

"Don't sniff?" Hanako repeated, her eyes wide. "You mean like this?" She sniffed slightly.

"Yes, like that. Miss Boo detests that sound more than any other."

"Miss Boo?"

"The new principal. B as in Blackmore, so we call her Miss Boo."

Hanako giggled.

"It's no laughing matter, Hana dear. She was the principal four years ago, too, when we were underclass girls like you. One of our classmates sniffed when Miss Boo was talking, and she made her blow her nose so hard that it turned bright red. The poor girl cried for a long time."

"Is she really that scary?"

"The word scary doesn't do her justice. She's as massive as a rock and the incarnation of strictness. She's like a walking rule book. Once she caught me running in the hall, just a little mind you. But she told me in English, 'It seems you don't know how to walk down the corridor so let me teach you how it's done.' She made me walk up and down the hall for a full thirty minutes."

"Count yourself lucky," one of the others chimed in. "She made me do that for a whole hour."

"That's nothing," said the third girl. "When she saw me and my friends fooling around in the hall, she called us to her office and scolded us roundly. And that wasn't all. She made us write eighty times in English, 'I must not laugh or scamper in the corridor without good reason.'"

"Well, I had to write that a hundred times," the first girl said. "I already had enough homework to keep me awake half the night, so I ended up writing lines until morning."

"If you speak too quietly in her English class when she asks you a question," warned the second girl, "she'll send you outside, saying, 'You seem to have lost your voice. Go find it in the schoolyard.' One day she made me stay out there until the end of class. It was so cold I was sure it was going to snow. She fails almost all the students in her English conversation and grammar classes. I never dreamed she would be principal again. And why did it have to happen in the year we're to graduate? It's going to be a disaster. I just know it."

The girls chattered on, never running out of things to say. When the commencement bell rang, however, they picked up the muslin cushions they had made in Miss Kamo's sewing class and their wicker cases containing a Bible and a hymnal and lined up in the hallway looking so demure and proper they seemed like different people. On the first floor they filed into the assembly hall, from which organ music rang. The entire student body, which numbered about one hundred and eighty, gathered every morning in the assembly hall for a worship service from ten past eight to eight-thirty. Half of them were boarding students while the other half were day students who commuted from home.

A foreign woman stood silently on the stage. Hanako knew at a glance that this was Miss Blackmore, the woman her roommates had just been talking about. There were ten other female missionaries there, but this woman's solemn figure was by far the most imposing, proclaiming her the best suited to serve as the pillar of this school.

The service was conducted entirely in English. After they had sung hymns, recited prayers, and listened to the Bible reading, Miss Blackmore looked slowly around the room. "My girls!" she declared, and then proceeded to speak with great dignity. Miss Kobayashi, the teacher Hanako had met outside the library room on the day she first arrived at the school, was Miss Blackmore's newly appointed secretary, and she stood beside her now, translating everything the principal said into Japanese for the underclass girls, who were not yet used to English. The atmosphere in which the service that day was conducted was even quieter and more solemn than usual. And not a single girl sniffed.

❀

Miss Isabella Slade Blackmore was born in 1863 in Truro, Nova Scotia. In 1889, at the age of twenty-six, she came to Toyo Eiwa Girls School for the first time as a teacher and Methodist missionary. The year after she arrived in Japan, the Imperial Rescript on Education[15] was issued. Its

Isabella Slade Blackmore, the teacher who had the greatest influence on Hanako. Taken around 1910, when she was principal of Toyo Eiwa Girls School.

primary focus was the education of boys, and it aimed to instill patriotism and reinforce the imperial system of government. Christianity, which ran counter to the government's policy of fostering nationalism, was thereafter subjected to various restrictions. With the enactment of the Private School Ordinance[16] and the Ministry of Education Order No. 12[17] in 1899, government pressure on mission schools further intensified. Faced with such setbacks as the expulsion of foreign missionaries and the denial of

A group of missionaries posted to Toyo Eiwa Girls School from the Canadian Methodist Church headquarters in the late nineteenth century. The woman second from the left in the back row is Isabella Slade Blackmore when she was young.

official authorization for Christian-based educational institutions, many mission schools had no choice but to either eliminate Christianity from the curriculum or close. Mission schools for boys were particularly hard hit, suffering drastic decreases in enrollment because employment after graduation was dependent on one's educational background. Some schools managed to work around the ordinance by dropping religious instruction from the curriculum while building a chapel on a separate property where the students continued to worship. Toyo Eiwa School, which was built by Canadian Methodists for boys at the same time as the girls' school, was forced to make the bitter decision to abandon Christian education and become a university preparatory school. That school later became Azabu High School, which is still in operation today.

Miss Blackmore, who had been reappointed as the principal of the girls' school, however, refused to bow to the trend of the times. Instead, she focused strictly on English education, which was not subject to the regulations of the Ministry of Education, and continued to pursue the same Christian philosophy that had been practiced since the school's founding. Although this meant that the students would not receive publicly recognized qualifications upon graduation, Miss Blackmore never wavered in her conviction that the school imparted the skills and capacities needed in society.

✿

Classes in the morning were conducted in Japanese, while those in the afternoon were conducted in English, but greater weight inevitably was given to the latter because Canadian missionaries designed the curriculum. Japanese teachers taught the students Japanese language, Chinese classics, mathematics, science, Japanese history, Japanese geography, calligraphy, and needlework. In the afternoons, the missionaries, who taught in English, provided instruction in the Bible and the Bible reader, English grammar, English writing, English reading comprehension, English conversation, English literature, world history, and world geography. The first period in the afternoon was always Bible study, but the teachers made the classes more engaging by quoting non-Biblical works of literature, including in the lessons a variety of poets, such as Shakespeare.

Textbooks used for Japanese studies were virtually the same as those used in other Japanese girls' schools, but those used for English studies demonstrated the school's uniqueness. The textbooks for British history, world history, and world geography were all from Canada, the missionaries' homeland, and after 1909, the Ontario Readers series was used as the English-language primer. In addition, the missionaries taught music, knitting, dressmaking, cooking, and physical education. Most of the missionaries were highly educated women from eastern Canada, but there were also a few from England and the United States.

The missionaries revered and were greatly influenced by Queen Victoria, who had made sure that her daughters, despite being princesses, were trained in practical skills because even members of the royal family might one day have to live independently. The missionaries carried on this spirit, instructing the girls at Toyo Eiwa in skills that would allow them to survive in society and encouraging them to work hard. "Even if you do get married someday, it's better to have a skill just in case," they advised.

The Students' Literary Society

"Good day to you, Hana dear." Chiyo Okuda tapped Hanako lightly on the shoulder.

"Good day to you, Miss Chiyo," said Hanako. Of all the senior students, she loved this girl she had met on the very first day as if she were her older sister. Despite coming from a distinguished family, Chiyo was gracious and courteous to all, and never, ever snobbish. Nor did she ask about Hanako's background, instead tactfully advising her on her appearance whenever Hanako's humble origins showed. Right now, she gazed with satisfaction at Hanako, who was wearing a soft lime-green crepe kimono that Chiyo had given her. "I'm so glad that Miss Blackmore has come back," she said with a smile.

"But doesn't she scold you?" asked Hanako. "Haruko, Fumiko, and Nobuko all told me she's terrifying."

"I'm sure there's no one in this world who hasn't been scolded by Miss Blackmore," Chiyo said. "She even reprimanded the officials from the Ministry of Education. But that's just proof that she loves us dearly. No matter what people might say, everyone knows this is true. Although I suppose she has never scolded someone as exemplary as Miss Kobayashi."

Hanako nodded in agreement. She could not imagine Miss Kobayashi ever having run wild in her life.

"Miss Kobayashi has won Miss Blackmore's complete confidence," Chiyo continued, "and you know the principal is particularly exacting when it comes to English. Of course, you've already heard how wonderful Miss Kobayashi's translation is."

"Translation?"

"Converting English into Japanese. Miss Kobayashi's translation is superb."

Hanako recalled that Miss Killam, the previous principal, had also kept her secretary beside her to interpret for her, but Miss Kobayashi translated far more smoothly and concisely. "I wonder if I could…" Hanako murmured.

"What?"

"Oh, nothing." She had been about to say "translate like her" but swallowed the words. Deep inside, however, a kernel of rivalry had begun to sprout.

Oblivious to the ambition Hanako now nursed in her heart, Chiyo looked at her with shining eyes. "Hana dear," she said. "I've decided to ask Father to let me become a boarding student."

"You, Miss Chiyo?"

"Yes. Father wants to keep me at home so that I never lack for anything. But the school is so close, I can go home any time. I'm just so terribly jealous, you see. The foreign teachers love the dorm students more than the day students. They say they love us all the same, but it's only natural that their feelings for the dorm students would be stronger because they're together all the time. Besides, I'm dying to participate in the Literary Society. This is my last year in the academic course, and I'm determined to make the most of it."

Some of the day students from wealthy families found dorm life, despite its inconveniences, far more pleasant and satisfying than living in a grand manor where they were waited on by servants and driven to and from school every day in a rickshaw.

The Students' Literary Society to which Chiyo referred was an event held just for the dorm students on the last Friday of every month. They gave performances on the stage in the assembly hall, including choir and solo vocal concerts, piano, organ, and violin recitals, poetry readings, English plays, tableaux vivants, and dialogues. One month, Hanako and the other freshman students put on a candle procession. Wearing pleated *hakama* trousers over kimono with long, draping sleeves and each bearing a candle, they glided across the stage forming rows, crosses, and circles. As they moved, they sang:

> In this world of darkness,
> We must shine,
> You in your small corner,
> And I in mine.[18]

At the end, they turned to the audience and, one by one, recited a line from a poem. Hanako was in charge of reciting the last line: "Give us more light."

All the dorm students practiced hard during recesses and after school to prepare for their turn in the spotlight. The older students, who were given solo roles that showcased their individual talents, were the object of the younger students' admiration. The missionaries, who were usually quiet and reserved, instructed the students with such passion and expressiveness that Hanako had trouble believing they were the same people.

The missionaries gave their own performances as well, donning kimono and putting on adaptations of Japanese folktales such as "Peach Boy" (Momotaro) and "Little One-Inch" (Issunboshi) in halting Japanese. This always threw the dorm students into fits of laughter. At the insistence of the day students, who were regaled with accounts of each performance, the school held a Grand Literary Society Meeting twice a year, in May and November, put on by the entire student body. Inevitably, however, the dorm students, who had more experience, were always the stars of the show.

Learning Western Customs

Dorm students took turns helping the missionaries tidy their rooms and through this acquired such skills as bed-making, housekeeping, and mirror polishing. To Hanako, their rooms were a wonderland filled with elegant jars of lotion, talcum powder, beaded hair accessories, and pretty little plates. The missionaries also found chances to invite the girls individually to their rooms for English-style tea. Black tea was served along with sweets such as pound cake, chocolate pudding, and candied fruit that were almost unknown in Japan at that time.

If a student fell ill, the missionaries, who were well-versed in medicinal remedies and nursing, would put the patient to bed in their own room and care for her all night, administering homemade medicines and nutritious food and sponging her body with damp cloths. In the evenings, all the dorm students gathered in the principal's office for a worship service led by the students. The atmosphere was much more intimate than the morning worship service for the whole school.

By sharing daily life with the missionaries in this way, the dorm students learned Western ways of thought and customs and forged bonds of trust that transcended the line normally drawn between teacher and student. The girls also developed close, family-like bonds among themselves.

Dorm life was governed by a routine known as The Sixty Sentences. Composed by Miss Blackmore, they laid out in detail the daily actions of the students from waking in the morning to going to bed at night. The students recited them each morning, a custom that not only helped them to develop discipline in their daily habits but also to master the basics of the English language. At times, Miss Blackmore would ask the students to recite random sentences from the list as questions or negative statements, or to change the pronoun. This helped students who were not particularly good at English to improve.

The Sixty Sentences by Miss Blackmore

1. The rising bell rings at six o'clock.
2. I get up at once.
3. I take a sponge bath.
4. I brush my teeth.
5. I comb my hair.
6. I dress myself neatly.
7. I read my Bible.
8. I say my prayers.
9. I go downstairs.
10. I meet some of my class-mates.
11. We greet each other.
12. We go to the play-ground.
13. We play ball a little while.
14. The breakfast bell rings at seven o'clock.
15. We go to the dining-room.
16. We eat our breakfast.
17. I go back to my room.
18. I put my room in order.
19. I get my books ready for school.
20. I go to my class-room.
21. I study a little while.
22. The school bell rings at eight o'clock.
23. We all gather in the Assembly-Hall.
24. We have prayers.
25. The principal calls the roll.
26. We divide into our Japanese classes.
27. We begin our Japanese lessons.
28. We have a singing-lesson at ten o'clock.
29. We continue our Japanese lessons.
30. The noon bell rings at twelve o'clock.
31. I go to the wash-room.
32. I wash my hands.
33. I make my hair tidy.
34. The dinner bell rings at ten minutes past twelve.
35. We go to the dining-room again.
36. We eat our dinner.
37. I go back to my class-room.
38. School begins again at one o'clock.
39. We have a Bible lesson first.
40. We divide into our English classes.
41. We begin our English classes.
42. We have conversation at half past one.
43. School is out at three o'clock.
44. Some of the daily pupils go home at once.
45. Some of the girls sweep and dust the class-rooms.
46. We have a game of hide and seek.
47. The others play in the yard for an hour.
48. I go to the reading room.
49. I read the newspapers.
50. I write a letter to my home.
51. We have a supper at half past five.

52. We have evening prayers after supper.
53. We begin to study at quarter past six.
54. The little girls go to bed early.
55. The big girls go upstairs at nine o'clock.
56. We get ready for bed.
57. I say my prayers before getting into bed.
58. The last bell rings at half past nine.
59. One of the foreign teachers comes to our rooms to say "Good-night".
60. We all sleep quietly until the rising bell rings again.

The girls were just the right age to be interested in fashion. While tackling the mountain of tasks and subjects designed to help them develop their capacities for the future, they gazed wistfully at the clothes worn by the missionaries. The students would remark on the elegant dresses they saw different teachers wearing each day. They particularly admired those of the vice-principal, Margaret Craig. Miss Craig came from a well-to-do family in Montreal, Quebec, and had graduated with a degree from McGill University. In those days, it was extremely rare for women to earn a university degree, even in Canada. Miss Craig was one of Hanako's English teachers throughout her student years. Unlike Miss Blackmore, who was feared as the "law," Miss Craig was young, beautiful, and endowed with excellent fashion sense, winning her the students' adoration.

"Miss Craig is from one of the wealthiest families in Canada, you know."

"That explains it! But then why did she become a missionary and devote her life to God?"

"Just between you and me, I heard that when she was in university, she fell in love with a young gentleman, but difficulties between their two families made marriage impossible."

"Just like Romeo and Juliet."

"I know. In her despair, Miss Craig renounced the world and chose to dedicate her life to mission work."

"Poor Miss Craig! I bet she still loves him deep down."

"I heard that he's in Japan and that she accidentally bumped into him one day. Not only that, but they say he's happily married with a family."

"Goodness!"

Rumours like these spread quickly among the girls, regardless of whether there was any truth in them or not. Yet Miss Craig always stood up for the students, even when they misbehaved, mediating between them and the formidable Miss Blackmore.

Hanako Develops Her Talent

Although the school emphasized English-language education, it also trained dorm students in housework. On Saturdays and other holidays, they did laundry, cleaned their rooms, and sewed *tabi* socks under the supervision of Miss Kamo. If they did anything improper, she would invariably exclaim, "That's no behaviour for a young lady!" This phrase remained engraved in the girls' memories even after graduation.

Every first and third Friday after school, dorm students were allowed to leave the school grounds if they applied for permission and could even spend the night at home on condition that they returned by five-thirty on Saturday evening. Hanako would watch the other girls give Miss Kamo their permission slips and hurry off, vanishing one by one into the sunset. Then she would spend the evening quietly alone, book in hand. Although she could have gone home, she had done nothing worth reporting to her father yet, nor did she have enough money to pay for the train fare.

One afternoon in the early fall of 1906, Hanako went to the library. The beautifully crafted crystal doorknob felt cool to her touch as she opened the door. The library floor was covered in the same red carpet as the hall where worship services were held, and two large wooden desks, each with a set of wooden chairs, stood solidly in the centre of the room. Hanako slipped inside and closed the door behind her.

Most of the books on the shelves were in English. This was her refuge, the place where she felt most at ease. She came whenever she had a chance, whether between breakfast and the worship service in the morning, during the lunch break, or after school. More than playing piano or tennis, more than sewing or cooking, even more than talking with her friends, Hanako loved to read. As long as she had books, she knew no boredom.

Soon after entering the school, she had come to the library brimming with excitement and taken a book from one of the bookshelves. But when she opened it, the marks that streamed horizontally across the pages had looked more like patterns than words, leaving her puzzled. Even so, the bindings were of much finer quality than any Japanese books she had ever seen, and she sensed that a tantalizing world lay within the unfamiliar words and colourful illustrations.

The English-Japanese dictionary[19], which she considered an outstanding invention, had become her faithful ally. The rush of excitement when the meaning of an unknown word became clear; the ecstasy that pierced Hanako's heart when she discovered the perfect word from among many; the joy of stumbling upon a charming word while wandering off on a tangent: all these the dictionary offered. As such, it was the one treasure with which Hanako could not bear to part, not even for a moment. With its aid, she could slowly decipher the English language. Gradually the world of words from which she had been excluded opened its doors to her.

On this particular autumn day, she walked slowly through the empty library, gazing at the books before choosing. As she picked one from the shelf, she recalled a passage from Milton's *Paradise Lost*, which she had read in Japanese. "What in me is dark illumine, what is low raise and support." And, thought Hanako, when Eve stood before the forbidden fruit, didn't she say: "Here grows…this Fruit Divine…Of virtue to make wise…"?

🌼

Autumn deepened and the large beech tree in the schoolyard scattered beechnuts across the ground. Hanako continued to visit her library refuge while other girls vied with one another to gather the beechnuts, aided by the school custodian, who cleaned the grounds.

One morning in the spring of 1907, thirteen-year-old Hanako, who had just started her third year of the academic course, and her fifth year at the school, dressed quickly and dashed down the corridor towards the library as she often did. Just as she rounded the corner, however, she collided with something large and soft. Unfortunately, it was Miss Blackmore. Fixing Hanako with a fierce glare, the principal snapped, "Go to bed!" and pointed down the hall in the direction from which Hanako had just come. By now, Hanako had experienced this punishment, of which the senior students always warned the younger ones, many times. The dorm rooms had no beds, but Miss Blackmore's command really meant, "Go back to your room, close your eyes, and reflect on what you've done."

Hanako returned to her room. Her futon was still spread out on the floor; she crawled under the quilt and closed her eyes. However, she did not feel that this particular misdemeanor warranted much serious reflection. Normally, she would have dozed off, but today when she opened her eyes, they fell upon a book she had just started, and she rolled onto her stomach and began reading. The book that had caught her interest was *Uncle Tom's Cabin.*[20] Written by a woman named Harriet Beecher Stowe, it was said to have sparked the American Civil War, which led to the abolition of slavery. The fact that such irrational racism existed in a supposedly Christian country like America, coupled with the fact that a single book could have the power to change history, made a deep impression on Hanako's mind.

※

At the end of every month, the students were tested in each subject, and the results determined their seating order in the assembly hall and in the classroom. Who came first and last in each level was clear at a glance. At the end of term, the students gathered in the assembly hall where their grades were read aloud. While they had been taught that all people were equal in the eyes of God, regardless of their social rank, when it came to grades, marks were everything. English ability was evaluated with particular strictness, and a third of the class failed.

Hanako always gave priority to the subjects she liked, which meant that her performance was quite skewed. She preferred to learn in her own way and, when it came to her least favourite subjects, mathematics and science, she studied only enough to maintain a passing grade and no more.

Yutaro Ide, Hanako's math teacher, was concerned about her and tried many ways to help her understand how to think mathematically. One day he appeared in front of her where she sat reading an English book in the library. Handsome with clean-cut features, he was a very Japanese-style gentleman in his quiet, courteous manners. "A girl like you would probably study harder if you failed once," he ventured. "I'm sure your ability would greatly improve if you took more interest in your studies. What do you think? Would you like to repeat the year instead of moving on?"

"Oh no, sir!" Hanako exclaimed, jumping to her feet. "I would not like that at all!"

"I see," he said. "What a pity. But I suppose it can't be helped if you're so set against it. You've managed to scrape by with a pass so shall we leave it at that then?"

Although Hanako liked this teacher for his frankness, she simply had no desire to hone her mathematical sense. Still, thanks to her exceptional English ability, she was able to keep both her status as a scholarship student and her reputation in the school. When it came to English literature in particular, just reading the reader and whatever was assigned in class never satisfied her. She had to read every book she could find in the library, devouring *The Pilgrim's Progress*, *Robinson Crusoe*, *The Water Babies*, and *Little Women*, as well as the twenty-eight volumes of the *Elsie* books[21], an American children's literature series which took up the top shelf of one of the library's bookshelves. Whenever she found something particularly interesting, she would translate it and read it to the younger dorm students. For Hanako, stories were meant to be shared, and the passionate urge to tell them to others bubbled up like a spring from deep inside her.

Chapter 3

The Influence of Hanako's "Bosom Friend": 1908–1913
Age 15 to 20

Volunteering at the Orphanage

Hanako's passion for reading grew ever stronger. By the time she was fifteen and in her fourth year of the academic course, she had devoured all the eighteenth- and nineteenth-century literature in the library and plunged into romantic medieval literature. Reflecting on this period of her life, Hanako later described it as follows:

> Although the library offered nothing that could be called a novel written in Japanese, its collection of English literature was comprehensive. Books by much-extolled contemporary writers such as George Bernard Shaw, Oscar Wilde, Henrik Ibsen, and Maurice Maeterlinck may have been missing, but its shelves were packed with books to which a bit of age had only added luster: works by the like of Sir Walter Scott, Charles Dickens, William Makepeace Thackeray, and Charlotte Brontë, as well as those by many minor authors. The school drew up its own English curriculum, unrestricted by Ministry of Education ordinances, and so could devote more time to language learning than other schools. The academic level was thus quite high, which meant that any student with the desire to read could make rapid headway in English.
>
> Day in and day out, I spent every possible moment of my youth in a corner of the library absorbed in gothic romances set in the Middle Ages. I walked my own path, a young woman harboring in

her heart wild and beautiful dreams that belied the calm reflected on the surface; dreams which she shared with no one.[22]

Concerned by her overwhelming passion for literature, which far surpassed that of any other student, the missionaries kept a particularly sharp eye on Hanako. Students were forbidden to read the latest fiction, and naturally no copies of such books could be found in the school. Still, the missionaries worried that Hanako might somehow be exposed to popular literature, attempt to submit an article to a literary magazine, or worse, be influenced by progressive "modern ideas," which could attract the scrutiny of the police.

It was around this period that Hanako had the audacity to begin doubting Miss Kobayashi's interpreting skills, which were the awe of the entire student body. Miss Blackmore excelled at injecting a little humour into any topic, even when she scolded the students. But Hanako noticed that once Miss Blackmore's words passed through Miss Kobayashi's translation, not a trace of humour could be found. They became bland and curt, and merely relayed her points. Although she made no mistakes, Miss Kobayashi failed to convey the most crucial part: Miss Blackmore's humanity, the soul from which her words flowed. Hanako worried that the younger students would misunderstand the principal's true intentions, just as Hanako had once done.

Every morning during the worship service Hanako could not help wondering if Miss Kobayashi's approach was really as good as everyone seemed to think. But Miss Kobayashi, unaware of Hanako's critical thoughts, harboured great expectations for this bright young student. Whenever they met in the library, she would suggest another book for Hanako to read and frequently found reasons to call Hanako to the staff room to speak with her or to instruct her.

It was in this same year, 1908, that Canadian author Lucy Maud Montgomery's *Anne of Green Gables* was published by the L. C. Page & Co. in Boston, Massachusetts, quickly becoming a bestseller in North

America. As the Toyo Eiwa school's library did not carry new titles, Hanako's fateful encounter with the book would have to wait another thirty years. By curious coincidence, however, she spent her youth surrounded by Canadian women of the same generation as Montgomery and steeped in the same Canadian culture and education as Anne Shirley, the heroine of Montgomery's *Anne of Green Gables*. From Christianity to cooking, Hanako's experience at Toyo Eiwa would prove invaluable for translating the book.

※

Sunday was the Christian sabbath, a special day that dorm students were required to pass solemnly. In the morning, they attended Sunday school and the church service at Azabu Church (now Toriizaka Church), which was located right next to the school property. They did not have to wear their uniforms on Sunday, and some of the day students took this opportunity to wear their finest Western-style garments.

Once the day students had gone home, the dorm students gathered in their classrooms where they studied the Bible from one to two o'clock in the afternoon. This was followed by the Sunday Reading, during which they read an assigned passage from a Christian book. They were forbidden to read not only novels but also their textbooks on Sundays. Nor were they allowed to sing any tunes but hymns, and exercise such as walking or playing tennis was out of the question. At four o'clock in the afternoon, they gathered again for prayers; from five-thirty to six o'clock, they practiced English hymns under the instruction of the missionaries; and from seven o'clock, they had evening worship.

Before the morning worship service in Azabu Church, Hanako and the other scholarship students were required to teach Sunday school classes at the Nagasaka Orphanage run by Toyo Eiwa. This orphanage for girls was in Azabu Juban, just down the hill from the school, but the scenery there was completely different. The main street was lined with humble shops that did a bustling trade, while in the lanes behind the shops lay a shantytown of shoddy rowhouses where the poor lived.

There had been orphanages in Azabu Juban since 1894, but the Nagasaka Girls Orphanage was established by Miss Blackmore in 1903 when her students, who had witnessed two girls from impoverished families being sold, pleaded with her to help. It was not uncommon at the time for families to sell or indenture their children as apprentices or domestic help if they had too many mouths to feed, or if one or both parents fell ill or died. Both boys and girls could end up working twelve-hour days or longer, while for many girls an even worse fate of sexual exploitation awaited them in brothels. They had no chance to receive an education and were sent off without knowing the cruel fate in store for them.

Toyo Eiwa students founded the King's Daughters' Society (the "King" being God), and its members engaged in charitable works such as knitting socks for orphans and the poor and holding bazaars to raise money. Hanako put her love for books to good use by reading stories to the children.

"Akai kutsu" (Red Shoes), a popular Japanese children's song written by the renowned lyricist Ujo Noguchi in 1922, was based on the story of Kimi Sano, an orphan girl who lived in the Nagasaka Orphanage around the time Hanako was volunteering at the Sunday school. Sano was later adopted by a couple who were American Methodist missionaries. In the song, she accompanies her new family to America, but in reality, she contracted tuberculosis, making it impossible for her to travel, and her adoptive parents were forced to leave her once again in the care of the orphanage when they left the country. She passed away in 1911 at the age of nine.

As modernization progressed in Japan, the gap between rich and poor widened. This trend was aggravated by a recession that followed the end of the Russo-Japanese War in 1905, forcing an ever-increasing number of people into destitution and exacerbating existing social problems. The orphans were victims of these circumstances.

Unusual Transfer Students

Two years earlier, in 1906, a gentle, middle-aged woman named Aiko had moved into the room at the very end of the dormitory corridor on the second floor. Even the oldest students in the collegiate course were only twenty-one or twenty-two, so when this woman who looked old enough to be a teacher entered the classroom as a student, she was the focus of everyone's attention, and Hanako was no exception.

For some unfathomable reason, Aiko attended classes in many different grades instead of just one. Stranger still, Hanako noticed that Aiko's eyes seemed terribly swollen whenever she passed Aiko in the hall; so much so that Hanako worried the woman's already narrow eyes might become sealed shut.

The news soon circulated that Aiko was the wife of Roka Tokutomi[23], author of the bestselling novel *Hototogisu* (*The Cuckoo*).

"I heard she's here to study English while her husband is travelling in the West."

"Apparently he's on pilgrimage to Jerusalem, the Christian Holy Land."

"She said her husband's going to meet with Leo Tolstoy during his travels."

These and other rumours quickly spread through the school.

The Cuckoo was published in serial form in a newspaper in 1898, winning sweeping popularity as a novel and also as a play. Although the dorm students were strictly forbidden to read contemporary novels or to go to the theatre, Hanako and the other girls couldn't resist reading *The Cuckoo* when the teachers were not looking.

The story followed the life of Namiko, who, despite being cast off by her stepmother, manages to find happiness through marriage to Takeo Kawashima, a naval officer. Namiko's joy is short-lived, however, for Takeo soon leaves on a long voyage. During his absence, Namiko contracts tuberculosis and Takeo's mother sends her home, an act which essentially annuls their marriage. Upon his return, Takeo is furious to learn of his mother's cruelty but is forced to leave for the Russo-Japanese War before he can do anything about it. While he is gone, Namiko dies, pining for her husband.

The girls, who loved a good romance, wept for the ill-fated Namiko. Their sympathy was even greater when they learned that the novel was loosely based on the life of Nobuko Oyama, the eldest daughter of Japanese field marshal Iwao Oyama and the wife of Viscount Yataro Mishima.

Aiko Tokutomi quickly grew fond of Hanako. Although Hanako had not found the book very interesting, she was fascinated by the author's intelligent wife. When Hanako visited Aiko's room, she often found

September 8, 1936. Aiko Tokutomi, who spent three months in the Toyo Eiwa dormitory, and Hanako. They reunited for the first time in thirty years at the tenth anniversary of Roka Tokutomi's death.

Aiko writing letters to him. Sometimes Aiko would lie down, saying she had a headache, and Hanako would sit beside her and massage her head. She noticed that Aiko's eyes were swollen then too, but, ignorant of the nature of romantic relationships, she never realized that the cause was grief over separation from her husband. When Aiko left about three months later, Hanako missed her for quite a while.

Two years after Aiko moved out, another adult student came to live in the dorm: Akiko Yanagiwara[24], the daughter of Count Sakimitsu Yanagiwara and a geisha who became his mistress.[25] Akiko had been adopted by the Kitakoji family at the age of eight with the intention that she would marry their eldest son, Takeshi, when she turned fifteen. Her official engagement at fourteen cut short her education at Kazoku Girls School.

Although she bore her husband a child the year after they were wed, this marriage became unbearable, and she fled back home at the age of twenty. Aristocratic families valued appearances above all else, and it was considered a disgrace for a woman to leave her husband. Akiko, who found reading and writing poetry a refuge from her shame, asked her family for permission to return to school. This happened to be convenient for her half-brother, who had taken over the family after their father's death, and Akiko was accepted as a dorm student at Toyo Eiwa despite having dropped out of school in her teens. She used the same room that Aiko, the author's wife, had used on the west end of the second floor.

Akiko Yanagiwara (Byakuren), 1918. This portrait was made into a postcard. On the back is written "Miss Hanako Annaka September, Taisho 7"

Even among the students of Toyo Eiwa, Akiko's pedigree and beauty were exceptional. Attractive and slender-faced, she was the object of all the girls' fascination. Hanako's first conversation with her took place in the school garden, which was fragrant with white plum blossoms.

"How old are you?" asked Akiko.

"I'm sixteen," said Hanako.

For a moment, Akiko's face clouded as if she were feeling a mixture of pity and envy for the carefree nature of youth. Hanako and the other girls, who were being educated to preserve their innocence, had not been informed of the life Akiko had led before she came to the school. But Akiko had an elegant beauty unlike that of Hanako's ingenuous classmates. From the moment they first met, Hanako was captivated by this woman who had the mysterious air of a tragic heroine from a book.

As for Akiko, she looked upon Hanako, who was eight years her junior, as a free and happy little bird who could warble English poetry at will. Of all her worshippers, Hanako was the one Akiko most wanted beside her. With her command of the English language, Hanako could entice Akiko into the fresh new world of Western literature. Hanako in turn derived great joy from sharing with Akiko all that she had learned about Western history, geography, and culture through her linguistic ability.

"Ever since I met you, Miss Aki, studying seems much more fun and worthwhile," Hanako confided. "I'm not just studying for me anymore, but for both of us. And no one listens as enthusiastically as you to what I have to say."

"That's absolutely true, Hana dear. So please be my eyes and my ears. You have no idea how happy you've made me. Won't you read those English books and tell me what they say?"

"Never fear, Miss Aki. I shall study even harder for your sake."

Having no opportunity to speak with members of the opposite sex, Hanako's feelings for Akiko resembled the infatuation of first love. In spring they strolled beneath the cherry blossoms on the trees lining the street of Toriizaka, while in the fall they watched the gentle breeze ruffle the pink and white bush clover carpeting the school grounds. Hanako immersed herself in poetry compilations and novels picked randomly from the library and translated them one by one to read to Akiko.

As they spent time together, Akiko regained the lost years of her youth. Hanako had a spirit unlike that of any of Akiko's previous friends, and her vitality, which blazed forth unrestrained, rekindled the hope that had long grown cold in Akiko's heart.

✿

"Miss Aki, I've made a Japanese adaptation of Tennyson's *Idylls of the King*. Would you like to read it?" Hanako passed a black leather-bound notebook to Akiko.

"Tennyson?"

"Yes, he was a poet who served the royal family of England. This is a love story about Sir Lancelot and Lady Elaine, King Arthur and Queen Guinevere. Lancelot was betrothed to Elaine[26], but fell in love with the beautiful Guinevere, King Arthur's wife. When the pure-hearted Elaine found out, she was so overcome with grief that she died. While Guinevere won love, she had to live with this great sin for the rest of her life."

"This part here is beautiful," Akiko said after reading through Hanako's story. "'Alas, how cold are the laws that rule the world of men. They divide the burning flame of love which surely can never be two. The love of a maid is a glorious crown, while that of another man's wife is a thorny cross.' There aren't any expressions like that in Japanese literature."

"Yes, isn't it dramatic?" said Hanako. "I wonder what it's like to love someone so fiercely you'd turn your back on the whole world."

"Hana, you must come and stay overnight in my room this weekend. Please come. I'm longing to hear more. We can stay up and talk 'til morning."

That Friday, Hanako and Akiko could hardly wait until nighttime. After classes, students with family in Tokyo got their permission slips from the dorm matron and went home, leaving behind only the boarders from the country and the missionaries. At bedtime, Hanako took her pillow and went to Akiko's room where the two girls continued their conversation.

"Do you think that God would forgive even Queen Guinevere?" Akiko asked.

"God?"

"I was thinking of something Miss Blackmore told me," Akiko explained. "She said that if a sinner truly repents, God will forgive even the most grievous of sins."

Surrounded at the school by pure, innocent girls, Akiko sometimes felt defiled and torn by self-reproach. At such moments, she would go to the principal and pour out her pain. Jesus Christ, the Son of God, Miss Blackmore reassured her, had died on the cross to redeem the sins of everyone. If she believed in God and prayed as if she were His child, He would forgive her sins. Some days Akiko even considered getting baptized if it would mean she could be purified.

"I don't know," Hanako said frankly. Then she lowered her voice. "I'm actually not even sure if there really is a God."

"But you're a Christian, aren't you?" To Akiko, the sinless, spotless Hanako seemed the epitome of a child of God, and she was sure that Hanako's love of learning was a divine gift.

"My father had me baptized when I was a baby, so I was a Christian before I even knew what that meant. It wasn't by my own volition."

"Volition?"

"Yes. Of course, I don't mean that I don't believe in Christianity at all, but there are so many things in the Bible that I don't understand. Besides, although the teachers say we should fear God not man, I think the most beautiful love of all is one so strong it drives you to follow it through without fearing God or man, even if it means sacrificing someone else."

Hanako had yet to experience true love, but as a girl who spent every chance she could reading medieval romances in a corner of the library, her mind was filled with dreams of uninhibited love.

"You know, Miss Blackmore says that real love is the love of Enoch in Tennyson's *Enoch Arden*. It's in sacrificing what we want for the sake of others, for their happiness. The tears Enoch shed are genuine tears, she says, and those who can weep like that are fortunate. But that makes me sad. Is love really so cruel?"

Hanako was very dear to Akiko. Of anyone, Akiko believed that this girl just might be able to grasp happiness through her own volition. "Hana," she said, "tell me what you're reading now."

"Scott's *Kenilworth*. There's a scene where a husband, angered by his wife's betrayal, says 'I have made you the sharer of my bed and fortune.' I was so shocked, I turned the book face down, even though no one was in the library. Is that what marriage means? To share one's bed and fortune? What do you think, Miss Aki?"

Akiko's face clouded, but Hanako did not notice.

Studying Tanka Under Nobutsuna Sasaki

From the time she had moved back home as a divorcee, Akiko had sought solace in Japanese classical literature and in writing poetry, particularly thirty-one-syllable tanka. She continued to compose tanka in the dorm, and these she read to Hanako. Exposed to the spirit of Akiko's poetry, Hanako began to fear that she lacked sufficient knowledge of Japanese literature. With the Canadian missionaries in command of the school, education was naturally skewed towards English literature.

"I'd like to study more Japanese works," Hanako confided to Akiko. "Like you. But that's hard to do here."

"If that's your wish, let me introduce you to my tanka teacher, Nobutsuna Sasaki[27]," said Akiko.

"Do you really think Miss Blackmore would give me permission to study outside of school?" Hanako asked. She couldn't imagine the principal agreeing to let her study privately with a man.

"My teacher has close connections with the Imperial Household," Akiko assured her. "He's very distinguished so I'm sure Miss Blackmore will agree to it. I'll ask her myself."

Akiko's mediation worked. With Miss Blackmore's permission, Hanako went with Akiko and began studying under Nobutsuna Sasaki in Hongo Nishikata-machi.

※

An admirer of Norinaga Motoori (1730–1801), a prominent scholar of classical Japanese literature, Nobutsuna founded a tanka society called the Chikuhaku-kai, which produced not only many outstanding poets and authors, but leaders in other arts as well.

The first time they met, Nobutsuna smiled genially at Hanako. "Ichiyo was about your age when she started writing poetry," he said.

The author Ichiyo Higuchi[28] had started her writing career by studying at the Haginoya poetry school led by Utako Nakashima. Born in the same year, 1872, Ichiyo and Nobutsuna had occasionally participated in the same poetry recitals. Ichiyo had died at twenty-four, but during her brief life, she had managed to win high acclaim as a female fiction writer in modern Japan. Considering the state of Japanese girls' education and the male domination of Japan's literary circles, it was extraordinary that her short stories were published at all. Women who studied under male authors risked being made into mistresses, and it was rare for their works to receive recognition. Poetry was virtually the only literary path open to women.

Nobutsuna welcomed Hanako as his pupil but would not accept any tuition, proposing instead that she should teach his daughter English.

※

To be taken under Nobutsuna Sasaki's wing was recognized as a gateway to success for female writers, and now Hanako became his newest pupil. During meetings at the Sasaki home, she encountered many women endowed with outstanding talent, including Shigure Hasegawa[29], Miyoko Goto[30], and Takeko Kujo[31], a close friend of Akiko Yanagiwara. Hanako's association with other aspiring women writers would become a powerful stimulus for her own development.

Adding the suffix *ko*, meaning "child," to a girl's name was considered sophisticated and modern in those days, and it was around this time that Hana began calling herself Hanako instead of her birth name, which, to her, sounded old-fashioned and plebeian.

Every Tuesday after school, Hanako, bearing her most recent poems, accompanied Akiko to the Sasaki home where Nobutsuna advised his students on their writing and gave talks on such classics as *The Tale of Genji*, a classic Japanese novel by a noblewoman from the eleventh century, and the *Manyoshu*, an anthology of Japanese poetry compiled in the eighth century. Hanako was particularly enchanted by the fresh simplicity of the *Manyoshu*'s love poems.

Throwing herself into composing verses for Nobutsuna's review, Hanako declared that she would become a poet. Nobutsuna, however, already knew this was not the path Hanako should pursue. One day he handed her a copy of Hans Christian Andersen's autobiographical novel,

The Improvisatore[32], translated by Ogai Mori. "This is the quintessence of translated literature," Nobutsuna said. "You should read it."

Until then, Hanako had mostly read Western literature in the original English rather than Japanese translations. Although she had read Ruiko Kuroiwa's translations of *Les Misérables* and *The Count of Monte Cristo*, which were popular with the dorm students, Hanako had been too engaged in the stories themselves to pay attention to how the translator expressed the original in Japanese. Ogai Mori's translation of *The Improvisatore*, however, was different. Written in a slightly outdated and poetic style, it read like an ode rather than a novel. About ten years before, literary circles in Japan had shifted from using classical Japanese to a more colloquial style. Yet Nobutsuna, a poet himself, deliberately encouraged young Hanako to read a book that had been translated into classical Japanese. Reading Mori's translation was an eye-opening experience for Hanako. Intoxicated by the enchanting vocabulary and rhythm, she submerged herself in the beauty of the Japanese language.

Transported to Another World by Hiroko Katayama

Soon after Hanako began attending Nobutsuna's meetings, he introduced her to a poet well-versed in British and American literature. "Hanako," he said one day, "although you're extremely well read, you don't seem to have had much exposure to recent literature. There's a graduate of your school named Hiroko Katayama[33]. Let her instruct you." Hiroko Katayama was not only a leading poet of Nobutsuna's tanka society, but also a translator who introduced

Date unknown. A rare photo of Hiroko Katayama, who disliked having her photo taken.

the works of many Irish writers to Japanese readers under the pen name Mineko Matsumura.

Hiroko came to the dormitory to meet Hanako. It was her first visit to the school in many years, and she gazed up at the building in amazement. "My goodness!" she exclaimed. "How grand it has become." Although she was fifteen years Hanako's senior, her round face, fresh, neat appearance, and keen literary sensitivity made her seem younger than her years. Like Hanako, her English ability had been honed while living in the Toyo Eiwa dormitory with Canadian missionaries. Born the daughter of a diplomat, she had entered Toyo Eiwa Girls School in 1885 at the age of seven and graduated from the school in 1895. In 1899, at the age of twenty-one, she married Tejiro Katayama, who went on to become an executive of the Bank of Japan.

As Hiroko had left Hanako with an invitation to "come and see my books if you like," Hanako went to visit the Katayama residence. A few years earlier, Hiroko had sold her house in Nihonbashi in central Tokyo, which she had bought from Japanese author Natsume Soseki, and moved to Magome in Omori. At the time, Omori was on the outskirts of Tokyo, and its proximity to nature and slightly milder climate was better for her husband, who had a weak constitution.

Hiroko's husband recognized his wife's talent and supported her literary endeavors. Aware that society considered it beneath a man's dignity to make his wife work, Hiroko in turn treated him with the deference due a man of his social standing, refusing to accept any remuneration for her writing and outwardly maintaining the appearance of an upper-class lady dependent on her husband. She was also a gentle mother to their son and daughter.

Hanako was astonished by the Katayama family's wealthy, refined lifestyle, but what impressed her even more was Hiroko's study. She marvelled that the wife of this household had succeeded in carving out even such a modest space to serve as her fortress within the home. The bookshelves were lined with authors Hanako had never heard of such

as George Bernard Shaw, Oscar Wilde, Maurice Maeterlinck, John
Millington Synge, Baron Dunsany, and Lady Gregory.

Although Hanako had read practically every book in the school library,
that collection only offered titles deemed "safe" by the missionaries' strict
standards. Hanako now stood before a new door: one that would lead her,
with Hiroko as her guide, into the world of modern English literature.
The books on Hiroko's shelves would broaden Hanako's perspective and
take her down a path that transformed her from the dormitory's greatest
bookworm to a young woman striving for independence. Almost every
week, Hanako borrowed from those shelves a work of modern literature
to read in English. As she later wrote:

> Hiroko Katayama inducted me into the world of modern literature.
> And that world led me in my youth to a stillness far deeper than
> anything I had known before. But it was no longer the stillness
> of a dreamer, one derived from a mental idleness that avoided
> examining anything closely or confronting it head on. Rather it was
> a stillness that lauded deep uncertainty, rebellion and loneliness, a
> silence born from the lack of anyone to share the intensity of the
> flame burning fiercely within.[34]

※

Through Hiroko's collection, Hanako discovered a way of thinking that
went beyond moral judgments of good and evil to examine the essence of
human nature. One day, as Hanako sat reading in her usual corner of the
library, Miss Kobayashi peered over her shoulder. "What are you reading?"
she asked. The book in Hanako's hand was an English translation of
Maurice Maeterlinck's *Monna Vanna* from Hiroko's library. In the story,
Monna Vanna is ordered by her husband, Guido Colonna, to meet and
negotiate peace with the commander who has just defeated him. She obeys
out of her love for Guido, only to discover that the victor is a far better
person than her husband.

"Let me read it," Miss Kobayashi said in a way that brooked no refusal.

Hanako had been so moved by the story that she had scribbled notes in the margins, forgetting that the book belonged to Hiroko. Things like "those who have never known the finest can be content with second best, but should they meet the finest after years of such contentment, the result can lead to misery." Unable to erase her scribbles or tear out the pages, Hanako was mortified to have to hand the book over.

A few days later, Miss Kobayashi returned it with a strange look on her face. "You really shouldn't be reading books like that, Hana," she said. "I wonder if someone like you can ever find happiness. It makes me fear for your future."

The Rage of a Private Tutor

Christmas was a major event at the mission school dormitory. The dorm students rose before dawn and glided down the dark corridor bearing candles and singing Christmas carols. Stopping outside the door of each room, they sang. Dressed in just a white nightie, bare feet thrust into slippers, the missionaries opened their doors a crack.

"Merry Christmas," cried the students.

"Merry, Merry Christmas," came the reply.

The dorm students exchanged gifts. Hanako, who only had enough money to cover her fare home for the holidays, gave her friends modest presents of handmade book covers and Christmas cards with a poem she had translated from English into Japanese. She received her friends' tasteful gifts with a mixture of joy and sadness.

At the beginning of 1910, Miss Blackmore summoned Hanako to her office. Expecting the usual scolding, Hanako was so surprised by what the principal said that she had to repeat it. "A private tutor?"

"Yes. A politician named Teiichi Sugita[35] asked me to introduce someone who could tutor his daughter Yaeko in English. She goes to Toranomon Girls School, but is having a hard time with her English studies. You I can recommend with confidence, Hana. What do you think? Teaching will also be a good way for you to learn. Would you like to try it?"

"Oh yes, please." Hanako needed the income. Her family's finances were only getting worse. Her father had become so absorbed in the socialist movement that he neglected his work. While Hanako was home during the New Year's holiday, ominous-looking strangers had appeared on their doorstep, probably because her father had let the socialist newspaper, *Rodo Shimbun* (Labour News), use his address as the place of publication. Hanako's father's failure to support his family because of his involvement in political activities caused her mother endless worry. As the only one of her siblings able to go to school, Hanako had been agonizing over whether it was right for her to continue her studies.

From then on, every Saturday while the other dorm students played, she went to the Sugita residence in Hanezawa-cho, Shibuya. Once she began tutoring, she was asked by another family and then another. One of her new pupils was the youngest daughter of Viscount Yamao, who lived in a mansion beside the school. Sometimes the viscount would enter the room while they were studying. He always greeted Hanako pleasantly and thanked her for her work. The girl's mother was not the viscount's lawful wife but rather one of his hardworking servants. Whenever Hanako watched her student interact with her mother, she felt a lump stick in her throat. The mother was so pleased that her child had been granted the status of viscount's daughter that she did whatever the girl demanded.

At the end of each lesson, her student would walk Hanako to the front door. When they reached it, she would call out, "You there!" The elderly house steward would rush forward, his back bowed with age, to open the door, and the girl would smile sweetly at Hanako and bid her farewell. To Hanako, it seemed bizarre to stand in front of the door and call out for a servant instead of opening the door herself, yet her student behaved as if this were perfectly normal. As she hurried towards the gate, Hanako could not help grumbling in disgust. "Honestly! Nobles are the laziest people I've ever met!"

Her other student was the daughter of Mr. Huang, a Chinese merchant. Mr. Huang had sent his daughter to Toyo Eiwa just to learn English, but as she was unable to keep up academically, Hanako was asked to teach her privately as well. Whenever she visited their home, she was greeted by the girl's stepmother, a Japanese woman who, as Mr. Huang's second wife, had borne him a son. Joined by the unshakable bond of blood kin, the girl and her father would sometimes converse in Chinese, excluding the stepmother who could not follow the language. This woman, it seemed, bore many tribulations in her marriage for the sake of her son. Having no other outlet for her sorrow, she poured out her heart to Hanako, her step-daughter's tutor.

※

Through tutoring the daughters of these three households, Hanako was able to make enough to give some money to her mother. On the surface, the lives led by the families of the politician, the viscount, and the Chinese merchant all appeared magnificent, but even from the little Hanako had glimpsed, it was clear that their homes were unravelling at the seams and torn by complex relationships. Abject poverty rendered some children orphans while others lived in the lap of luxury, yet even women and children blessed with plenty looked unhappy.

The Family Register Act enacted in 1871 had allowed people to marry more freely, but it had also allowed men to register their mistresses as a relation in the second-degree equivalent to a wife, essentially legitimizing bigamy. Although the law was revised in 1898, its legacy continued, particularly in the upper classes, resulting in the emotional subjugation of women and children and long-lasting resentments and feuds among close kin. As she became aware of the contradictions and injustices within society, Hanako could not help feeling a helpless rage.

An Aspiring Author

Hanako entered the school's collegiate course in 1910 at the beginning of her seventh year in the dorm. By now, the dorm was like home, and she had become accustomed to advising younger students who were bewildered by the school's strict rules. At the Literary Society soirée that November, Hanako sonorously recited *The Revenge* by Tennyson in English. A little before that, she had attended an alumni gathering where she was reunited with old friends. Of this she later wrote in her journal:

October 12. What a pleasant autumn day it was, with yellow and white chrysanthemums blooming in profusion. The smiles on the dear, familiar faces of our "elder sisters" made the clear blue sky seem even brighter. The reunion commenced at ten in the morning with the choir singing joyous hymns that filled the parlor. As usual, Miss Yukino, our president, shared several reports, after which we resumed our cheerful chatter, sharing old tales. It seemed the well of memories that filled our hearts would never run dry. In the afternoon, the younger students performed a drill in the new gymnasium. Our hearts were already brimming with joy, and our eyes rejoiced to see the grace and beauty of the girls, their sleeves tied up with *tasuki* cords of red or white. From two o'clock, we were regaled by master storyteller Teisui. His tale of a faithful son who watched over his mother's grave at night in the pouring rain brought tears to our eyes. The evening wind felt chill, and at four o'clock we bid our dear sisters "Farewell," sending them off with prayers for their health and well-being. Left behind, an indescribable feeling rose inside me, and I could not help but pray yet again for their happiness.

The level of all the subjects taught in the English language in the collegiate course, including the new subjects of rhetoric and comparative religion, was even more demanding. When Miss Craig read the first passage of their English literature text, Hanako felt a jolt of recognition: Milton's *Paradise Lost*, which she had first discovered on her father's bookshelf at the age of ten and had read in Japanese, albeit without fully understanding the text.

What in me is dark illumine, what is low raise and support.

So those were the words I read! she thought. She felt a deep joy, as if she had been reunited with a childhood friend.

✿

In the same year, 1910, the Japanese government began cracking down in earnest on the socialist movement. In May, over a hundred socialists were arrested and charged with involvement in the High Treason Incident[36], an alleged plot by a handful of socialist-anarchists to assassinate the emperor. Hanako's father fled to Shizuoka to seek refuge with some relatives, sparing no thought for his children, not even his eldest son and heir, Shozaburo. Six years younger than Hanako, Shozaburo was apprenticed—whether into a specific trade or as menial labor, it is not known—but the family lost contact with him soon after, while Hanako's youngest sister and brother were adopted out, splitting the household apart. Whenever she thought of her family, Hanako was overcome with anguish, yet her feelings towards her father were complex.

"Here you can read all the books you want," he had told her in front of the gate on the day he had first brought her to the school. "But listen, Hana. Don't let the daughters of the peerage best you. Study hard and show them you're better than they are."

For Hanako, Toyo Eiwa was a paradise. She could read to her heart's content and laugh and sing with the other girls regardless of her birth or social status. But the day was coming when the friends with whom she was now studying would return home and marry the person their parents had chosen. Hanako had no home to which she could return. She would have to make a living, yet she did not want to stay on at the school and teach. For one thing, she was sure she could never be as serious and upright as Miss Kobayashi. Most scholarship students chose to dedicate their lives to Christianity, but for Hanako that path was even more inconceivable. There were times when she couldn't help questioning if there even was a God. What she really wanted was to make a living by her pen. To do that, she would have to carve out some kind of foothold, no matter how small, while she was still a student. But other than composing poetry and reading, she had no idea of how to pursue her ambition, and the anxious days passed by relentlessly.

While pursuing her studies, she continued her volunteer activities, and it was through these that she became involved in the *Fujin shinpo* (Women's News), a magazine published by the Japan Woman's Christian Temperance Union[37]. She started off editing but subsequently began contributing stories, poems, essays, and translations of fiction as well.

Formed in 1886, the Japan Woman's Christian Temperance Union was the first women's association established in Japan. The organization originated with the American temperance movement against the consumption of alcohol and tobacco, and was introduced to Japan by American female missionaries. In both Japan and America, drinking and smoking were compromising the health of many children, particularly of the poorer classes. When Hanako first became involved, the organization's president was Kajiko Yajima[38], who was also the first director of Joshi Gakuin, a mission school for girls, while the board was staffed by such well-known female Christian activists as Ochimi Kubushiro[39], Tsuneko Gauntlett[40], and Azuma Moriya[41]. The union lobbied for monogamy, the abolition of licensed prostitution[42], the prohibition of alcohol for minors[43], and the establishment of a Christian women's university. Later, the union also took up the cause of women's suffrage[44], retaining its focus on aiding women and children in crisis.

Many foreign missionary women who lived in Japan were involved in the Temperance Union's activities. Branches were established within every mission school for girls, and their students participated in collecting donations and signatures for union petitions as part of their extracurricular volunteer activities. At Toyo Eiwa, Miss Kobayashi, who was the epitome of temperance, served as the branch director. The union's magazine, *Women's News,* carried conference reports, articles on the temperance movement overseas, and essays by members of the board. The remaining pages, however, Hanako was free to fill as she wished, and she began directing into these her desire to write.

In Japanese literary circles, 1911 was the year that Raicho Hiratsuka[45] established the magazine *Seito* (Bluestocking), the first issue of which declared, "In the beginning, woman was the sun." This was also the year in which Henrik Ibsen's *A Doll's House* was performed in Japan, directed by Hogetsu Shimamura and starring Sumako Matsui[46]. The women's liberation movement, led by progressives who were dubbed "new women," flourished. "New women" (*atarashii onna*) was a term used in the early twentieth century for women who thought critically about their own experience. Seeking to break down outmoded conventions and formulate new values, these women attracted both the admiration of their contemporaries as well as their criticism.

Had Hanako been exposed to the burgeoning influence of those who sought to effect political change through the reformation of literature and the arts, she would likely have been swept up in that fervor. But within her sheltered "paradise," strictly guarded by Christian morality, she was divorced from the currents of social reform and the risks those entailed. Instead, she focused solely on her search for a way to independence.

Betrayal

In the early spring of 1911, a trembling Hanako sat facing Akiko in the little prayer room on the fourth floor of the dormitory. *What greater betrayal could there be than this*, she thought.

Just a few short days before, she had read in the newspaper that Akiko had previously been married. Her shock at the discovery was beyond words. But the source of her fury was the reason Akiko was in the news in the first place: Akiko had become engaged. At the age of just twenty-five years, she was about to sacrifice her youth to become the second wife of Denemon Ito, a man twenty-five years her senior, an upstart with no education who had made a fortune in coal mining. This marriage of convenience between a coal tycoon of humble origins and the daughter of a count who was related to the emperor caused a sensation, and made

Akiko the object of both public pity and curiosity.

"Aren't you ashamed to contract such a marriage?" Hanako demanded, her face pale.

"But I have no choice," Akiko protested. "I'm totally dependent on my elder brother and his wife. If I don't do as they say, it will only make trouble for everyone."

Hanako pressed on. "But Miss Aki, you don't love that man, do you?"

"Dear Hana, he has more money than he can possibly use. That means I can help serve children who are less fortunate," Akiko explained. "He's built a school in Fukuoka, and I hope to use what I learned here to teach the girls."

"That's just an excuse. How disgraceful!"

Akiko was torn with anguish, but Hanako, overwhelmed by her own pain, had little compassion to spare for the agony of her friend. Losing Akiko cut her to the core. Consumed with a rage for which there was no outlet, Hanako snapped, "To give him your hand and not your heart is a sin." This line came from a poem she had read, and with it, she declared their friendship over.

They had vowed to be friends for life, yet Akiko had been lying to her all this time. What then had been the meaning of all those days they had spent talking of love and literature?

How old are you?

I'm sixteen....

In the school garden where they had first spoken, Hanako wept alone. The white blossoms on the plum tree were blooming again, but their friendship had been cruelly blighted. Having lost her "bosom friend," Hanako was now truly lonely, even in the dorm.

❀

Akiko's wedding was the height of extravagance. Although no one from the school was invited to the ceremony, the teachers and her classmates were welcomed to a lavish reception held afterwards in a restaurant in

Shiba Park. Hanako refused to go. Akiko sent her a small, elegant silver box tied with a red braided cord as a wedding favour, but Hanako, without giving it a glance, shoved it deep into a drawer.

Graduation

In 1913, Hanako graduated from Toyo Eiwa's collegiate course. She was twenty years old. Representing her class at the graduation ceremony, she presented her graduation thesis, which was written in English and entitled "The Past, Present and Future of Japanese Women." She concluded with the words, "Our dream of a Christian women's university will surely one day be realized" and finished off with a line from Tennyson's poem "In Memoriam A. H. H.[47]" about how old systems change, giving place to the new.

Hanako was commended for choosing the unusual theme of Japanese women for her English thesis. Miss Blackmore, Miss Craig, and Miss Allen could not contain their joy. Miss Allen in particular, who had supervised Hanako's work, kept telling the guests that "Hanako wrote it on her own. She did it all by herself."

As Hanako listened to this, she was struck by her teacher's thoughtfulness. Miss Allen had strictly refrained from helping Hanako, except to point out mercilessly where she had gone wrong. Although it would have been faster for her to fix Hanako's mistakes, she had instead, with the utmost patience, rebuffed her and made her rewrite it herself. And she had done all this, Hanako now realized, so that Hanako could experience the joy of completing something on her own.

After the ceremony, all the students graduating from the fifth year of the academic course and the third year of the collegiate course, including Hanako, surrounded Miss Blackmore. One of the students said tearfully, "No matter how many decades may pass, I'm sure we'll never experience such joy as we did during our school days. The happiest time of our lives was the time we spent at this school." This made all the others cry as well.

Even at such an emotional moment, however, Miss Blackmore was still Miss Blackmore. In her usual austere manner, she fixed them with a stern gaze and said, "My girls! 'Grow old along with me! The best is yet to be.'" After quoting this line from Robert Browning's poem "Rabbi Ben Ezra," she continued,

> If you look back on your school life decades from now and sincerely feel that the time you spent here was the happiest, the most enjoyable time of your life, then I will have to say that this school has failed at education. Life is progress. Youth is a time of preparation. The best is not in the past but in the future. I want you to carry on with hope and ideals to the very end of this journey.

Afterwards, Hanako approached Miss Blackmore to thank her, but when she saw the warm smile lighting the principal's eyes, her heart was so full that she could not speak.

"Dear Hana, I am so proud of you. You are our pride and the pride of the whole school," Miss Blackmore said. She kissed Hanako's forehead repeatedly, then hugged her close. For some time, Hanako remained with her face buried in Miss Blackmore's soft bosom, unable to move.

Chapter 4

Books for Children and Adults Alike: 1914–1917

Age 21 to 24

Friendship Renewed

The train sped along the tracks in the bright sunshine, passing through fields covered in clover blossoms. It was the spring of 1914, and twenty-year-old Hanako sat gazing out the window of the swaying carriage on her way to Kofu. Hanako was born in Kofu, but her family had moved to Tokyo when she was just five, and she had few memories of her life in Yamanashi prefecture. She could not help feeling the hand of fate in her return as an English teacher. She stared absently out the window at the scenery, a book open on her lap.

After Hanako graduated from the collegiate course, Miss Blackmore had arranged for her to live at the dormitory for an extra year and teach the foreign missionaries Japanese. At the same time, she was also doing secretarial work for the Japan Woman's Christian Temperance Union while continuing her English literature studies. But Hanako, who was supporting not only herself but her family as well, needed a more reliable source of income. It so happened that Yamanashi Eiwa Girls School, a sister school of Toyo Eiwa, needed an English teacher who could also serve as the secretary for the Canadian principal. Hanako had decided to take the post.

So here she was, stepping by chance into the shoes of Miss Kobayashi. Would she end up teaching for the rest of her life too? Hanako contemplated her reflection in the window. Her long hair, which she used to keep swept up in a generous bun on top of her head, was now cut shorter and fastened in a more modest chignon. Her plump, rosy cheeks did little to convey the turmoil she felt inside.

It was not that she had given up on writing. She planned to cling to the little foothold she had created with her work at the Temperance Union's *Fujin shinpo* (Women's News) and the weekly journal *Fukuin shinpo*[48] (The Evangelical News). She also wanted to try writing fiction for the *Shojo gaho* (Illustrated Girls' Monthly), a literary magazine for teenagers to which Hiroko Katayama had introduced her.

But her family's situation weighed on her. At seventeen, Hanako's younger sister Chiyo had been sent to Hokkaido to become the wife of a farmer.[49] Despite being born in the same household, Hanako's and Chiyo's paths had diverged drastically. Hanako could not bear the thought of her poor sister eking out a living in some barren wilderness with a man she had never met until her wedding day. Chiyo, however, had accepted this fate without protest, and Hanako was not so selfish as to abandon her own duty as the eldest daughter to support the rest of the family, regardless of the burden.

Besides, Hanako told herself, as a writer she could never earn enough money in the beginning anyway. But as a teacher, she could make a living while continuing her studies and polishing her writing skills. It was the perfect arrangement. While thus accepting the reality forced upon her, she strove desperately to prevent her family obligations from sweeping away her dream.

That March, Hanako and her friends had pooled their resources to publish a small collection of poetry called *Sakuragai*, which included several of Hanako's tanka under the pen name Hinagiku (Daisy). Looking back on this period much later in her life, Hanako wrote:

I found the following verses in my old poem diary.

I thought to be a woman
was to be demure,
just like a doll.

If only I could die
while experiencing a joy
that wipes away
all trace
of self.

On an excessively quiet evening
at the end of spring,
I long for a breeze
to sweep my heart clean.

Judging by the words 'I thought to be a woman was to be demure, just like a doll,' I must no longer have thought so even then. They were penned on the eve of the Doll Festival, a reflection on my former belief that the only way of life permitted to women was to be reserved and modest, to endure with quiet patience. The poem expressed my rebellion against a feudalistic system symbolized by the dolls displayed at this festival for girls... As one who has been quite strong-willed ever since my teens, this poem was not about me personally so much as a criticism of what women in general, including myself, consider to be a woman's way of life.[50]

Tales of the opulent lifestyle that Akiko had led in Iizuka, Fukuoka, since her marriage to Denemon Ito had reached even Hanako's ears. Ito, who had made millions through his coal mine in Chikuho, lived on a two-acre estate in a mansion he had renovated for Akiko's comfort. She was called the "Queen of Chikushi" and allowed to while away the hours composing poetry.

But Akiko was weary of being relegated to the role of a doll adorning her husband's household. She was not even allowed to engage in philanthropic work. A life without purpose was vain and empty; no amount of wealth could change that. Forced to confront her own naïve idealism, Akiko poured all her pain into her poetry. A letter she sent to Hanako laid bare her feelings.

> People live in the present, the past or the future. An interesting philosophy, don't you think? I believe the present is the most important. For if the future means to live in heaven, then as the present is the nearer place, is that not where the 'self' is now?
>
> I like to use eyes as an example. Without eyes to see, there would be no colours or forms. So without the 'self,' there could be no parents, no friends, no country. In other words, without the 'self,' the nation would not exist.
>
> This is the faith of self-reliance. "I am my own Lord throughout heaven and earth."
>
> But from another perspective, we can say that although colours, light, and forms exist when there are eyes to see them, this does not mean that these things are non-existent without eyes. From this point of view, colours exist because they exist. As such, we can say that colours exist because there are eyes to see them and eyes exist because there are colours to be seen. If our parents exist because we exist, then we exist because of our parents.... There is neither non-existence nor existence.
>
> Do you understand what I am saying?
>
> April 16, Beppu
>
> At a desk in an inn. Beside me my husband and a Chinese man playing Go
>
> In a bright room lit by four electric lamps, outside the sound of a rushing stream, a night of falling blossoms

This letter dissolved the hard knot in Hanako's heart and provided the catalyst for resuming their friendship. Hanako confided to her journal the feelings that surged inside her.

The thought of you, Miss Aki, is so unbearably dear that I take out your many letters from bygone days and reread them randomly. Perhaps at this very moment, you too are sitting in your lonely room quietly taking out old mementos and thinking of me. If I can't suppress my longing thoughts of you, surely you must be feeling the same inexpressible yearning. Between two hearts that resonated and bonded as ours did, such a thing could happen. Or so I firmly believe. It is this belief that has enabled me to keep smiling come what may and will let me carry on doing so.

People make rules, but the heart of a woman is free. It is woman's prerogative to pour out her love. Even should the one who is the object of that love be reproved by manmade rules, those rules have nothing to do with the woman's feelings. No matter where one may go or what might happen, love remains.

Why then do we sometimes hate those we love?

If a person transgresses the rules by which people are sanctioned, society will declare that act a sin. Yet there is no sin in people's feelings. It is rules that create the sin. If a captive, drawn by the fragrance of a beautiful flower that blooms outside the king's cage, unwittingly escapes, the flower may hate the captive for having angered the king. Yet at the same time, she will harbor a tenderness and pine for the one who was so charmed by her beauty. The king has no right to censure the flower for missing the captive.

My heart is the heart of that flower. It is completely free. Though I know the rules made by men, I wish to keep this spirit of youthful freedom alive forever.

Today I wrote without thinking, not knowing what I said. Miss Aki, how does this letter find you?

When the cherries blossom,
you will come to me.
Would that I were a bird,
so that I could wait for spring
to sing with you.

Hanako felt she could understand Akiko better now that her own heart was troubled by a man: Renzo Sawada[51], whom she had met at a lecture at Azabu Church. Born in Tottori prefecture, he had started learning English from an American missionary at the age of twelve. In July, he would graduate from Tokyo Imperial University (now Tokyo University), after which he planned to take the exam for diplomats and consular officials and enter the Ministry of Foreign Affairs, following in the footsteps of his elder brother Setsuzo.

After running into each other at church several times, Hanako and Sawada had struck up a conversation about English literature and tanka poetry. Sawada gave Hanako poems he had written in beautiful calligraphy on rectangular strips of paper called *tanzaku*. He stopped by to see her with such excuses as "I happened to be passing by" or "I had some business near here." Hanako was aware that she was developing a fondness for him. Before she realized it, she had come to look forward to him dropping by unexpectedly.

Now, however, she would no longer be able to meet him so casually. Shouldering financial responsibility for her family, Hanako had taken up the teaching post in Kofu, while Sawada dreamed of joining the foreign service and setting out into the world.

All these thoughts passed through Hanako's mind as the train barrelled along the tracks, puffing smoke. Everything she had sought after—work, friendship, love—now shimmered around her like a heat haze. Although the future, including her dream of becoming a writer and her first romance, remained uncertain, the stirring of spring lightened the load on her heart and filled her with happiness. She was starting a new life. And no matter what might lie in store for her, her heart was free. It was simply not in her character to worry for long. Surely wonderful encounters and doors that would lead to the realization of her dream awaited her in this new arena.

As the train neared Kofu, it passed through Sasago Tunnel. When it emerged on the other side, Hanako and those sitting across from her burst out laughing. Their faces were black with soot, right to the insides of their nostrils.

Teaching English at Yamanashi Eiwa

Yamanashi Eiwa Girls School was situated at the foot of Mount Atago in Kofu. Nestled within this rich natural environment, the school drew students not just from Kofu city but also from neighbouring villages: daughters of wealthy merchants, farmers, and community leaders. Most students lived in the dorm, even the local village girls. Although they were a little less sophisticated than the girls in Tokyo, the atmosphere was no different from Hanako's alma mater.

The dorm matron, Miss Mikoda, had elegant, cosmopolitan features, unlike the plump Miss Kamo at Toyo Eiwa. The principal, Miss Robertson, was the heart of the school, brimming with enthusiasm and a sense of mission. More than ten missionary women worked at the school as well, and the rules and punishments for misdemeanours were almost exactly the same as those of Toyo Eiwa. The main difference was that Hanako was no longer one of the girls, but a teacher.

At the morning worship service, Hanako stood beside Miss Robertson and interpreted what she said into Japanese. The principal was large, in no way inferior in size to Miss Blackmore, so that Hanako looked like a little child when standing next to her. The attention of the entire student body, however, was riveted to this young teacher who had just arrived from Tokyo. From the beginning, the principal put Hanako in charge of the fifth-year students, who were pretty much the same height as Hanako. She was also tasked with teaching Sunday school. Later she recalled:

When I think that there are still people in this world for whom I have served as a teacher[52] in the literal sense of the word, I grow all hot and flustered inside. Kofu is the land of my birth, as well as the place where I spent my youth, so sometimes I still visit. But it alarms me to think that some of those who live there were once my former pupils, for however short a time.

Far from being a proper educator, I was just a brand-new girl-teacher fresh out of school. I was in charge of the fifth-year class of the academic course and felt intimidated by my students. We were more like friends, and often my authority carried no weight.[53]

Summer of that year marked the outbreak of the First World War[54]. Hanako first heard the news of Great Britain's declaration of war on Germany during the August school break, which she spent at Brookside Cottage, Miss Blackmore's summer villa in Karuizawa, a mountainous region near Nagano. Of her fellow teachers, Hanako had become particularly close to a Canadian missionary named Miss Alice Olivia Strothard, and she was staying with Miss Strothard and several other missionaries at the cottage.

The connection between Christian missionaries and Karuizawa began in 1888 when Alexander Croft Shaw, a Canadian missionary and member of the Anglican Church, visited the area and fell in love with its climate and natural scenery. As missionary work in Japan increased, the area became a place where foreign missionaries came to meet and spend the summer. Miss Blackmore opened her own cottage to missionaries and dorm students who could not go home for the summer holiday. This was where Hanako had spent every summer since entering Toyo Eiwa. Life in this exotic summer resort was centred in prayer.

In the summer of 1914, the war was all that the missionaries talked about. The view of those from countries on the Allied side, including England and Canada, was generally optimistic. Canada was a self-governing dominion of the British empire, and in an era when the nation that ruled the seas had the advantage, Great Britain boasted overwhelming naval supremacy. Everyone was confident the war would end quickly.

Hanako left Karuizawa early for Tokyo to meet Sawada, who was immersed in his studies for the foreign-service entrance exam. During breaks, the young couple went out for walks or tea. Sawada was preoccupied with Japan's evolving position in the world. Seeking to join the great powers, Japan was pursuing a policy of advancement into China and had seized Tsingtao (now Quingdao), which was the centre of German interests in China. This represented the perfect opportunity for Japanese diplomats to demonstrate Japan's prowess to Western powers. It was a pivotal moment when diplomats bore responsibility for the fate of the country. Hanako listened quietly as Sawada expounded passionately on this subject.

❀

Summer came to an end. On the day Hanako was to return to Kofu, Sawada suddenly appeared at the train station. Although he must have checked the train schedule in advance, he said as usual, "I just happened to have some business in the area, so I came to see you off." The sight of him filled Hanako with joy. She had been sure he would come. She smiled and waved until Sawada was out of sight, but when she sank back in her seat, swaying to the movement of the train, she was overcome with a sudden desolation.

Whenever Sawada came to see her, he always prefaced his appearance with the excuse that he was just passing by. Not once had he said outright that he had made a special effort to come and see her. What she longed for was a driving passion that made him rush to her side without a thought for what others might say; one that made him oblivious to censure and even to time.

After settling back into the Yamanashi Eiwa dormitory, she received the occasional package from Hiroko Katayama with new English books, as well as letters from Akiko and Sawada. In October of that year, Sawada sent her the happy news that he had passed his foreign service exam, and Hanako responded with a letter of congratulations.

Our Teacher Is a Writer

"Look! Our teacher Miss Annaka wrote this!"

"Goodness! You're right! But is this really our Miss Annaka?"

"Yes. I'm sure of it. After all, she's always writing whenever she's in her room."

"Is she a novelist?"

"She must be. Our teacher's a writer! That's why she's so good at telling stories. Maybe she'll become famous."

For the dorm students, this was big news. They were gathered around a copy of the *Illustrated Girls' Monthly*. One of them had discovered in the issue a story Hanako had submitted which was neither fairy tale nor "girls' fiction." They all read it, vying for a turn, then surrounded Hanako.

The *Illustrated Girls' Monthly* enjoyed healthy sales, but the author responsible for its popularity was Nobuko Yoshiya[55], not Hanako. Only twenty years old, three years younger than Hanako, Yoshiya had a solid following among adolescent girls. She had made a spectacular debut as a girls' fiction author with the publication of *Hana monogatari* (Flower Tales) in the *Illustrated Girls' Monthly*, and went on to publish a succession of serial novels.

The magazine was eagerly seeking another Nobuko Yoshiya, and Hanako was one of those they often asked for stories. The fact that she was a teacher at a mission school, a position much admired by the magazine's readership, was good advertising material, and, to the delight of her students, staff from the *Illustrated Girls' Monthly* came all the way to the school just to take her photograph. After this, Hanako always found posies on her desk, offerings left there by the girls.

Whether in the dormitory, during class, or at Sunday school, Hanako's students begged her for stories, to which she complied. Some of these girls later wrote about those happy times:

On Sundays we had to memorize the catechism. Miss Annaka was in charge. No one liked this subject, but we looked forward to it because she would always tell us an interesting story afterwards. Each time she would tell us a story for girls that she had made up herself. Whenever she said, "That's all for today," we would plead with her, "Tell us more! Tell us more!"
–Sadako Isobe (graduated 1921), from the Eiwa Alumni Newsletter

Miss Annaka! She was my Sunday school teacher and the teacher I remember with the most affection. I doubt there was any other who was as serious or as much fun as Miss Annaka. She never took a day off, even if she had a cold or a headache or if there was a raging storm outside. And she was never late either. I still remember her coming through the school gate clutching a bottle of medicine in her hand. The fact that our class had the best marks in our whole year was entirely thanks to Miss Annaka. I will always remember her with gratitude. She often said hilarious things with a perfectly straight face, which made them even funnier.
–Koko Kanazawa (graduated 1930), from *Ishizue no toki o ikite* (Founders of Yamanashi Eiwa: Our Living Mission)

On Saturdays, which were school holidays, Hanako was often invited to the home of one of her students. In some cases, a family would invite her to come and stay from Friday night onward. Once, Hanako visited the home of a family that ran a large grape orchard in Katsunuma, a town which was famous for its grapes, even in Yamanashi prefecture where vineyards abounded. Hanako joined the family in the vineyard beneath the autumn sky. They inspected bunches of grapes, the purple orbs of which were covered in a delicate white bloom. Cutting one bunch from the vine, Hanako and the family plucked off the grapes and popped them in their mouths then and there.

In the winter, Hanako would join large farm families around their hearths and share the local specialty, thick fat noodles called *hoto* cooked with miso and vegetables. The dish was ladled steaming hot from a big cauldron hanging over the coals. The students cringed at their mothers' rural dialect, their fathers' loud voices, and their grandparents' lack of sophistication, while simultaneously struggling to quell their own exuberance. But for Hanako, who had never experienced such family circles, these boisterous gatherings made her feel comfortable and at home.

As she got to know her students better through dorm life and storytelling and as her relationships with their families deepened, Hanako realized that even though adolescent girls longed for stories, there was very little for them to read other than girls' magazines. Compared to the West, Japan had failed to place importance on books such as those she had enjoyed in the library at Toyo Eiwa: books that could become a compass for a girl's mind as she matured into an adult. She had often heard the missionaries at Toyo Eiwa lamenting this fact, but only now, as a teacher herself, did she truly understand what they had meant.

※

Hanako sat across from the mother of a student in the dormitory drawing room.

"Miss Annaka, surely there's no need to ponder it so carefully."

"But—"

"It's a pretty good offer, don't you think?"

"Uhm, I—"

"You're getting on in years, and he's quite serious. How about just meeting him to see?"

Silence.

"Or do you have someone else you care for?"

"Thank you so much for your kindness, but I must refuse. I am terribly sorry."

Having finally convinced the mother to leave, Hanako heaved a sigh of relief. She could not count the number of times she had been approached with similar offers. One wanted to introduce her to the wealthiest man in the village, another to a graduate of the prestigious Waseda University who hated farming and wanted to enjoy literature, and yet another who knew someone who had made a fortune in America and sought an English-speaking bride to accompany him abroad. Hanako had received so many offers, she was tired of listening. These kind-hearted women simply could not bear to leave a young woman unmarried forever, and they seemed to have made it their mission to secure Hanako a good match because they kept bringing her new proposals. But no matter how wealthy the other party might be, Hanako could not contemplate a union that ignored the cues of her heart. She found the women's cavalier view of marriage so repulsive that it put her off marriage altogether.

Wondering if Miss Kobayashi had been subjected to the same trials, Hanako belatedly apologized in her heart for having been such an ungrateful student. Miss Kobayashi had stuck to her principles throughout.

Hanako's First Love Comes to an End

In the spring of 1916, Hanako received word from Sawada that he would be posted to France for several years. He had to see her before he left, he wrote. Barely able to contain her impatience, Hanako finally managed to finish her work for the school year and set off for Tokyo. On April 1, 1916, at four o'clock in the afternoon, she and Sawada met. Later, she recorded the poignancy of that evening as follows:

> Having reached Tokyo, she walked beside him through Sendagaya, which in those days was just empty fields. He was to attend a farewell party at six that evening and so was dressed formally in *haori* and *hakama*. Aware that they would be parted for years with no knowing how things would change during that time, they spoke earnestly, yet neither one shared any clear vision of the future. Indeed they were so well-mannered that even at this stage, he did not once touch upon what had caused him to delay his departure

to the very last minute, despite having to endure the speculative glances of his coworkers, while she never mentioned that she had made a supreme effort to get back to Tokyo that day just to spend one and a half hours walking through the fields with him.[56]

In the end, they spoke of nothing except their work, meeting and parting as they always had. After sending him off, Hanako could not bear to be alone. She contacted Azuma Moriya, a friend and her senior in age from the Japan Woman's Christian Temperance Union, and together they walked the streets of Ginza.

"You seem upset," said Moriya.

"Do I?" said Hanako. "It's just that I don't even know myself what to do."

Although she had no idea why Hanako had asked her to come, Moriya stayed and walked with her.

※

Several days later Hanako received a letter from Sawada. The bold script, penned in black ink, described his aspirations. The First World War had become long and protracted, with Allied forces now advancing, now retreating in Europe, the epicentre. Sawada had been posted to France, where the fiercest battle raged. As a diplomat, he bore a heavy responsibility. At the end of his letter, he wrote: It is not always May.

What does that mean, Hanako wondered. She repeated the words several times, then suddenly understanding dawned. May also meant the prime of one's life. He was telling her that the days of their youth were over. A few days later, Hanako received a beautiful postcard from London, where Sawada had stopped on his way to France.

Reading it, she felt a small pang in her chest, the lingering echoes of youth. She sent him a reply to be delivered before he reached his post. "Let us end this now. I hereby declare our relationship over. Farewell."

I will marry no one, she vowed to herself, *except a man who loves me single-mindedly and recklessly, one whom I can also love with complete abandon. The first condition shall be that we love each other and that we do so fearlessly. All other conditions are second to that.*

So she promised. Then she recited over and over, "It is not always May."

The Courageous Asako Hirooka

That summer, Miyoko Kobashi[57], a journalist Hanako had met at the Japan Woman's Christian Temperance Union, and Michiko Senbongi, a women's liberationist, introduced Hanako to Asako Hirooka.

Asako had helped found Japan Women's College[58], and although she was already in her mid-sixties when Hanako first met her, she was still vigorously promoting the education and development of women. She greeted Hanako with friendly ease, her generous figure exuding dignity. "Why don't you join our study group at my place in Ninooka?" she said. "We're inviting up-and-coming young women to study with us. You should come too."

Japan's involvement in the First World War had brought unprecedented prosperity to Japan. Karuizawa, which had been developed by foreign residents as a summer refuge, was turning into an ostentatious resort inundated with wealthy Japanese. Foreign residents who found this distasteful had begun building cottages and hotels in Ninooka, Gotemba, instead. The Hirooka villa was on a two-and-a-half-acre lot with a wide garden covered in a soft green lawn. Shapely Chinese mulberry trees planted by Asako's late husband, Shingoro, grew thickly in the centre of the garden. Designed as a mountain villa, the building's walls were sided with good quality cypress, and every room had a breathtaking view of Mount Fuji.

Asako was the daughter of Takamasu Mitsui, a member of the prosperous Mitsui family of textile merchants and money exchangers. Born in Kyoto in 1849, Asako was married at seventeen to Shingoro Hirooka, son of a wealthy family who ran Kajimaya, one of Osaka's largest merchant companies. Shingoro had no interest in the business, however, and spent all his time pursuing his many hobbies. Instead, the company became

Asako's passion. It was she who, at the age of twenty-eight, revived the faltering business's fortunes by branching out into the mining business. Slipping a pistol into her kimono sash for protection, she famously made her way to the mine in the pitch dark and admonished the unruly miners, winning their admiration for her courage.

She went on to display excellent business skills, running both the Kajima Bank and Amagasaki Boseki Ltd., a textile company, as well as establishing the Daido Life Insurance Company. After passing the reins to her son-in-law, she turned her attention to women's education. Having been denied an education by her own parents because she was a girl, expanding women's education became her second passion. Using her copious connections to obtain donations from leaders of Japan's business and political circles, Asako helped the scholar Jinzo Naruse[59] to establish Japan Women's College.

In her later years, Asako was hailed as a "heroine of the Meiji period." Yet despite her numerous business achievements and her contributions to founding the university, she never took any credit: as was typical of women born during that era, she did everything in her husband's name.

In her sixties, Asako became a Christian, deepening her friendship with Kajiko Yajima, president of the Japan Woman's Christian Temperance Union, as well as with other union members, and dedicating herself to training competent women who would go on to change society.

Hanako attended Asako's seminars two summers in a row. About twenty people, mainly graduates of Japan Women's College, gathered for the programs, which lasted a little over ten days. Members of the Temperance Union as well as some of Asako's friends and relatives also participated. At twenty-three, Hanako was the youngest. Lecturers at the first seminar included Toraji Makino, who later became president of Doshisha University, and Masumi Hino, professor of theology at Doshisha University. Participants listened to lectures on the Bible, comparative religion, and Indian philosophy, as well as a talk on women's issues in

America by Hide Inoue, a domestic science scholar and later the first woman president of Japan Women's College.

In an era when few women received higher education, participants of these seminars represented the finest selection of women with a strong social consciousness, even among graduates of Japan Women's College. Many progressive ideas were sparked by a debate on women's issues in Japan. Problems such as how to improve conditions in poor rural villages, the subservient state of women bound by the family system, and the importance of motherhood in society struck a deep chord with Hanako. But as she was more passionate than scientific by nature, and had been educated in a mission school that placed greater emphasis on the humanities, logical argument was not Hanako's forte. Although the discussions sparked many thoughts and emotions, she could not put her feelings into words fast enough to participate, and instead devoted herself to listening, following the lively debates intently.

Everyone who attended had witnessed first-hand the frustration of their mothers and other female kin and friends at being forced into subservience merely because they were women, and each had personally struggled against the curse of familial expectations. Their desire to learn and their sense of mission stemmed from painful experiences with systemic inequality and unjust customs.

There was one other participant who, like Hanako, was an enthusiastic listener: Fusae Ichikawa[60]. The same age as Hanako, Fusae went on to become a standard-bearer of women's suffrage in Japan, but it was at this seminar that the two first met. At the time, they were both unknown schoolteachers.

❁

Fusae Ichikawa was born into a farm family in Aichi prefecture in 1893. After graduating from upper primary school, she went to Tokyo and entered a mission school for girls. Neither the air of Tokyo nor Christianity suited her, however, and she quit after just three months, returning to her hometown to enter a public teachers' college for women, becoming a primary school teacher upon graduation. Fusae's mother was illiterate. Although Fusae's father was eager to have his children educated, he frequently beat his wife with a stick of firewood. From her early years, these beatings filled Fusae with a smoldering rage.

Fusae was deeply impressed by Asako Hirooka's essays, such as "The Need for Higher Education for Women," "Licensed Prostitution Represents Barbaric Thought," and "The Future of Japanese Women,"[61] which were published in Miyoko Kobashi's *Fujin shuho* (Women's Weekly). Fusae begged Miyoko to let her participate in the summer seminar over which Asako Hirooka presided. Asako looked upon the guileless Fusae with particular affection, impressed by the fact that she had retained her sincerity and zeal despite all the hardships she had endured.

1916. Asako Hirooka gave Hanako this portrait of herself when Hanako participated in the seminars at Asako's villa. It is inscribed with the words, *To my beloved Hanako Annaka, from Asako.*

Seminar participants shared the chores, including cooking and cleaning. In breaks between lectures and discussions, they took in the views of Mount Fuji, had lunch in the garden with Westerners staying nearby, and enjoyed each other's fellowship. During her free time, Hanako strolled on her own through the woods around Ninooka Shrine. The forest was much deeper than she had imagined, and the mist-laden air cooled her fevered brain after the discussions. The weather in the area was changeable, frequently altering the face of the landscape.

According to her journal, Hanako visited the woods often, sometimes even in the rain.

August 28 I wrote a letter in the woods.

August 30 Other than returning for meals, I spent the whole day in the woods. I stood still, letting the sound of running water seep deep into my breast.

August 31 It rained in the afternoon, and I could not go to the forest. In the evening, it cleared, and all of us walked through the woods after dinner.

September 1 Rain. Around ten o'clock, I took my umbrella and went shopping. I bought many boxes and stamp cases. On my return, instead of going straight to the house, I went into the woods. In the shelter of a large cedar beside the shrine gate, I stood a while and watched the falling rain. Then I walked deep into the woods to the water's edge and stayed there for a time. I thought about such things as the powerful emotions of powerful people. A truly great person is one so strong he is shaken but not ruled by the urgency of fierce emotions.

September 2 The rain kept falling, and I went shopping in a light drizzle. On my way home, the sky was clear. I walked through the forest wet with mist when a shaft of light dazzled me. The world is full of suffering. I want to smile at this transient happiness.

September 3 I went to the woods after lunch and stood at the water's edge, a spot I love.

On sunny days, the Westerners would take folding chairs into the woods and spend their time as they pleased. Hanako liked to take a book into the forest and curl up in her special spot beneath a tree. For her, quiet time engrossed in a book was bliss.

She was reading *A Girl of the Limberlost*[62] by American author Gene Stratton-Porter. The story was set in the Limberlost, an area in the state of Indiana that was covered in wetlands and old-growth forest far more extensive than the woods in Ninooka. The protagonist, Elnora, a high school student, lives on the edge of the Limberlost. As her mother neglects her and refuses to pay for further education, Elnora must save money for college by collecting unusual moths and plant specimens from the forest and selling them to the Bird Woman, a naturalist who lives in town. For Elnora, being in nature is her comfort and solace, filling the emptiness caused by lack of maternal love.

Gene Stratton-Porter was not only a writer but also a famous naturalist who particularly loved the region about which she wrote. In her works, she interweaves the lives of animals, plants, and even the smallest insects with the lives and feelings of the story's protagonists.

As Hanako read, tiny forest-dwelling insects crawled at her feet. Around her she could hear trees creaking and birds warbling. Immersed in nature, Hanako fell into the story of the girl whom the forest befriended and who worked to put herself through school, experiencing Elnora's joys and sorrows as if they were her own.

❀

At the end of an entertaining send-off party on the night before their return to Tokyo, everyone gathered around Asako Hirooka. For Hanako, who dreamed of pursuing a literary career, this inveterate businesswoman's approach to life was too different from her own for her to adopt Asako as a mentor. But Asako's stories of her eventful, independent life were more interesting than any lecture, and her words were imbued with a wisdom tempered by having endured great upheaval.

"I wasn't allowed to go to school," she told them. "Instead I got a living education by working in the business field." She spoke about how she had restored the fortunes of her husband's company, Kajimaya, resolved labour disputes at the Moji Mine, had been stabbed and almost killed by a rival merchant, and raised money to establish Japan Women's College.

She also praised her late husband, Shingoro, who had provided moral and emotional support throughout. Finally, she spoke passionately about entrusting the future of Japanese women to the next generation.

"I want you to use your education not just to raise your own status but to raise the status of every woman in Japan. Don't be concerned with *shoga*, the small self: Focus instead on what you should achieve in the wider world. I want you to find your *shinga*, true self. From here on, politics will be crucial. Unless we raise up female politicians active in governing this country, true emancipation for women can never be achieved. We must start by obtaining the right to choose our leaders, the right to vote, just as women in other countries have done. You must work together for the same goal." These words were greeted by enthusiastic applause.

This encounter with Asako Hirooka launched Fusae Ichikawa into the women's liberation and suffrage movements. Likewise, Hanako's two summers at Ninooka became a base point in her career as a writer. She resolved to focus on the true self rather than the small self. It was Asako who made Hanako realize that her pursuit of literature was not about personal gratification, but rather fulfilled Hanako's longing to contribute to society. As Hanako later wrote:

> You could say that the two summers I spent at Ninooka determined the course of my life to some extent.[...] I was disappointed with books for Japanese teenagers. This was no fault of theirs; there just wasn't anything suitable for them to read. The more Western books for young people I read, the more keenly aware I became of what could only be called a blind spot in the Japanese publishing world. It was in the forest of Ninooka that I first resolved to find a way to give young people in Japan the opportunity to read such books.[63]

Everyone, no matter who, must pass through childhood and adolescence to become an adult. We may aim for social equality, Hanako thought, but the state of the world will never improve as long as we fail to nurture the dreams and the emotional and mental health of young people until they are old enough to participate in politics. Even if we manage to establish a system that guarantees social equality, it will be useless unless the consciousness of each individual has been transformed and we have developed compassion for others.

Based on personal experience, Hanako was convinced that books had the power to nurture the minds of children and young women, whether rich or poor. She was determined to spread fresh, wholesome literature that could be enjoyed by children and adults alike in Japan.

Hanako's First Book Is Published

Winters in Kofu were freezing. But the teachers working at Yamanashi Eiwa did not light the wood stoves to heat their rooms. The First World War had dragged on far longer than anticipated, and desperate battles continued to rage in Europe. Four hundred thousand young Canadian soldiers had been sent to the Western Front and particularly northeastern France, joining the Allied Troops in the relentless trench wars against the Germans. Calling the conflict "our war," the missionaries lived frugally and prayed for the Canadian troops, united in spirit with the women protecting the home front.

Hanako joined the missionaries in their prayers, taught during the day, and spent the rest of her time working on translations in her room. As she wrote, spurred on by Asako's admonition that she should contribute to society, Hanako could see beyond the tip of her pen the faces of Japanese girls who were longing for good stories.

In December 1917, Hanako's first book, *Rohen* (Fireside), was published by the Christian Literature Society of Japan. The title encapsulated Hanako's image of her pupils' happy families as they gathered around the warm hearths in their farmhouses. In the preface, she condensed all that she was feeling and had experienced:

Just four years ago, while I was studying at my alma mater in Tokyo, an American saw me reading *Mother Carey's Chickens*[64]. "I think there are few books in Japan like this one that can be read and enjoyed by parents and children together," she told me. "Japan will need many books like this in the future."

The prayer that rose at that moment in this little heart of mine has never faded and still encourages me. Longing to become one of those who could offer such reading material to the families of my beloved country, I prayed that God would transform this weak vessel into a tool for this purpose. I also prayed that Japan would one day publish many fine books for families; books that could be read by parents and children together, without struggling over any of the content.

It was with that thought in mind that I chose the thirteen stories in this book, searching here and there and translating them (except for one I wrote myself). Perhaps some will complain that they are too ordinary. But I believe that "ordinary" is nothing to be ashamed of; rather, it is noble. I only regret that my own "ordinariness" is not sophisticated. Because I believe a refined "ordinariness" shares something in common with the extraordinary.

This will be my third winter in the mountainous region of Kai. Having collected in one volume what I have written during these last two years, I am ashamed at my own lack of skill. Yet the thought that even the jottings of this untrained writer are steps along the path to maturity made me long to compile and save them.

Oh, little book, my first ever to venture into the wide world! Those who take you in their hands will each have their own thoughts and feelings. What can this feeble voice of mine murmur in the hearts of those readers, each with different needs and ideas?

Still, this I will say boldly: Go, little book of mine! Go! May you become a fervent prayer that follows those courageous little ones whom I love wherever they may go as they spread their fragile wings and launch themselves into the limitless vault of the sky.

–October 1917, Hanako Annaka, in the school at the foot of Mount Atago

Chapter 5

Home of the Soul: 1918–1921

Age 25 to 28

Heir to the Fukuin Printing Company

Spring sunshine enveloped the Yamashita district of Yokohama. Once set aside as a settlement for foreigners, its wide, stone-paved streets were lined with Western-style buildings. Yet even here, the imposing three-storey red-brick office of the Fukuin Printing Company stood out. The building was flanked on one side by the company factory and on the other by its warehouse. Fukuin was the leading printing company in Yokohama, and its presses were powered by a thirteen-horsepower gas engine, a fifteen-horsepower electric motor, and a five-kilowatt generator. Since its establishment in 1898, it had served as the sole printer and binder of Japanese Bibles, hymnals, and Christian-related publications. From the beginning of the Taisho era (1912–1926), it had also printed Bibles and hymnals in English and languages used in China, Korea, Singapore, Siam, Malaya, the Philippines, and India. The books were shipped to their various destinations from Yokohama Port.

The company's founder was Heikichi Muraoka, and he was known to every Christian in Japan as Bible Muraoka. In 1919, twenty-two years after he had started the company, two of his six sons held key management positions, and business prospects were bright.

On this particular morning, Heikichi's third son, Keizo, arrived at the company to find the directors lined up at the entrance.

"Good morning, junior president," they said.

"Morning," said Keizo. "Where's Father?"

"The president has not yet arrived, sir. He should be here soon," answered Wakamiya, who had served as factory manager since the company's establishment. Keizo nodded and lined up alongside the others, his light beige suit a sharp contrast to their formal black attire. Every Monday morning at eight o'clock, the pastor of Yokohama Shiloh Church came to offer a thirty-minute worship service at the company. The entire staff, from the executives down to the workers, were required to attend, which was why the directors were wearing formal dress.

Not long after, a rickshaw appeared bearing Heikichi and Keizo's younger brother Hitoshi. Telling the directors to let him know when the pastor arrived, Heikichi strode past the staff towards his office. His two sons followed behind.

✿

Concealed beneath Heikichi's suit was an elaborate tattoo that covered his entire back, a remnant of his brief career as a yakuza gangster during his youth. By the time Keizo was born, Heikichi had long since left the underworld and become a devout Christian. Keizo once caught a glimpse of the magnificent tattoo on his father's back, but later could not remember what the image was.

Heikichi was born in Kozukue, Yokohama, in 1852. Influenced by his elder sister, he read William Martin's *Evidences of Christianity*, a primer on Christianity published in Qing-dynasty China, which played a significant role in the spread of Christianity in Japan during the early Meiji period. An encounter with people taught by James Curtis Hepburn, an American Presbyterian medical missionary, led to Heikichi being baptized by George William Knox, another Presbyterian missionary stationed in Yokohama. At the beginning of the Meiji period, Heikichi trained as a pressman at a French-language newspaper. In 1877, he went to Shanghai to work at the American Presbyterian Mission Press. There he learned European language typesetting and the latest printing technology. After he returned to Japan, Heikichi was hired as the plant manager at the Yokohama branch of the Oji Paper Company, where he was placed in charge of printing Bibles.

His penetrating gaze and courageous spirit won him the trust of foreign missionaries, enabling him to set up his own company in 1898.

The motto by which Heikichi lived was: Work is faith. Faith is work. He played a key role in helping James Curtis Hepburn and other American Presbyterian missionaries establish Sumiyoshi Church (later Shiloh Church) by acting as a guarantor and donating company profits. He went on to serve as a church elder, a most important post. Together with foreign missionaries, he invented original script typefaces, including one for the blind. His printing press was also equipped with a Korean (*hangul*) typeface, and the company had been printing three different Korean-language newsletters since 1914 for Korean residents of Japan: *Gaku no hikari* (Light of Learning), *Taishu jiho* (Popular Current News), and *Seinen chosen* (Youth Korea). As a Christian entrepreneur, Heikichi was also involved in a variety of groundbreaking ventures that indirectly supported the Korean independence movement and socialism. These activities entailed considerable personal risk and brought him under the surveillance of the government led by Prime Minister Takashi Hara. He did, however, charge higher-than-normal fees for such projects.

"I see you've got another new suit," Hitoshi said to his elder brother. "Nice colour."

"I know. I can't bear to wear black at anything but a funeral," said Keizo.

Heikichi, who had six sons and two daughters, had appointed his third son, Keizo, and his fifth son, Hitoshi, as his business heirs. Keizo had joined the printing company in 1907, at the age of twenty, after graduating from Yokohama Commercial High School, and had been helping his father with the business ever since. Hitoshi, who was born after his father's business had begun to prosper, had been sent to Meiji Gakuin, an American Presbyterian mission school which had its origins in an English school founded by Hepburn and his wife, Clara, in 1863. After graduation, he spent three years in London studying the latest printing technology before returning

November 1910. Keizo Muraoka (left), heir to Fukuin Printing Company, before he married Hanako, and his younger brother Hitoshi (right) before he left to study in England.

to Japan. The scholarly Keizo and his brother Hitoshi, who inherited Heikichi's business acumen, formed an inseparable pair destined to bear the company's future.

Heikichi's wife, who had been stricken with kidney disease, had passed away just eight days after Hitoshi left for London. She had been an even more devout Christian than her husband, supporting his work from behind the scenes. Having missed his mother's death brought Hitoshi even closer to his father and fuelled his appetite for business.

Heikichi's other children were Christians too. His eldest son, Jutta, was very bright but sickly. His second son, Shunji, whose dream was to become a Western-style tailor, had been adopted by a tailor named Matsuno, who needed an heir. It was Shunji who had made the suits Heikichi, Hitoshi, and Keizo were wearing. Heikichi's fourth son, Noboru, often rebelled against his strict, strong-willed father and resisted being bound by family ties, while Heikichi's sixth son, Kiyoshi, was still a student. Heikichi's eldest daughter, Yoshiko, had married Seichi Sano, son of a samurai family, while his youngest daughter, Yukiko, a devout Christian, had been adopted by the family of pastor Seigoro Minakami, who lived nearby, to raise her for future service to the church.

The Muraoka family included one other member: Haru[65], Keizo's cousin. Her father, who was Keizo's uncle on his mother's side, had run a pawn shop in Yokosuka, but when it went out of business, he had come for help to his brother-in-law Heikichi, who gave him a job at the printing company. Haru had already been put into domestic service, but Heikichi brought her home and treated her like his own daughter, sending her to Sumiyoshi Girls School, which had been established by people connected with Shiloh Church. Haru became particularly close to Yukiko, who visited often and attended the same school.

In 1904, the Kobe branch of Fukuin Printing Company was established, and Haru's father was transferred with his family to Kobe. Haru began working at the branch company too, binding books, and it was there that she met Toyohiko Kagawa[66], the pastor who conducted the company's Monday worship service. The two were married in 1913. When her husband went to study in the United States for three years, Haru came to live with the Muraokas in Yokohama and studied at the Kyoritsu Women's Junior College, a Christian school. Upon her husband's return, she joined him in Kobe where they moved into a slum district to help the poor and share the Gospel with them.

※

"How's Ginza? Everything going well?" Heikichi asked Keizo.

In 1914, Fukuin had established a branch in Ginza, and Keizo had been put in charge. The building was located right behind Kyobunkwan[67], a company founded by American Methodist missionaries to publish and sell Bibles and other Christian literature. "Things are going pretty well," Keizo replied. "We're getting a lot of work. And not just from Kyobunkwan, but also from the Salvation Army[68] and the Christian Literature Society in Tsukiji. Unfortunately, the union keeps going on strike. The other day I had to pull a cartload of Bibles and other books all the way to Tsukiji by myself to sell them."

The Russian Revolution of 1917 as well as the postwar economic boom had pushed prices up, making life harder for the masses. Strikes and riots to demand higher wages and shorter working hours had become frequent and widespread. Known in Japan as the Taisho democracy (1912–1926), this was an era in which workers pushed for better living and working conditions and, with growing stridence, protested against capitalists. Responding swiftly to the changing times, Heikichi had introduced an eight-hour workday in all his businesses.

❀

After the worship service, the starting bell rang, and all the employees headed off to their work stations. The printing presses rumbled to life with a loud clattering. Keizo's younger brother Hitoshi took off his suit and changed into his work clothes before rushing off to the plant.

Keizo, summoned by his father, returned to the president's office. Heikichi lowered himself into his large chair and folded his arms, frowning. "I met Sachi's father, Mr. Egawa, at church yesterday," he said.

Keizo stared at his feet, saying nothing.

"He was very apologetic," Heikichi went on. "He said he never dreamed that this would happen to his daughter and apologized for causing you so much trouble."

"No one's to blame," Keizo said. "She's sick. It can't be helped."

"When did you last see Yoshio?"

"About ten days ago. We had supper together at Jutta's house." Keizo had married Sachi Egawa in 1915. Like Keizo, she was a parishioner of Shiloh Church, and their fathers had business connections. Many people from both the church and the company had come to celebrate their wedding.

It was Heikichi's policy that his sons establish their own "home" and family when they married. This approach was highly unusual in the patriarchal society of that time. In the households of wealthy farmers, merchants and the upper classes, the head of the household controlled the fate of every family member. Those who were not his heirs stayed at home at least until they married, at which time the family head would support them to set up their own household. His appointed heir and family lived in the same house and obeyed him until he retired and bequeathed his authority to his heir. A mistress and any children fathered by the family head, as well as adopted relatives, might also be part of the household. The structure of the home and family were so different from Western society that Christian socialists at the turn of the twentieth century used the Japanese word *katei* to introduce the Western concept of a "home," in which the husband and wife were partners in a marriage and respected each other as equals, despite their different roles.

Following Heikichi's custom, Keizo and Sachi had established their own independent home. After the birth of their son, Yoshio, a year later, however, Sachi contracted tuberculosis and returned to her family home to convalesce. Keizo, who was busy running the newly established Ginza branch, sold their house, placed Yoshio in the care of his brother Jutta and his wife, and got a place for himself in Kanda.

"What are you going to do?" Heikichi continued. "Jutta says he'd be happy to adopt Yoshio, and I've received plenty of offers to introduce you to a new marriage partner."

It had been almost three years now since Keizo and Sachi had begun living apart, but they were still registered as married. In Japan, men held the reins in a marriage, and if the husband decided to divorce, the wife had no choice but to swallow her tears and accept it. A woman who was barren or fell ill was considered unfit to be a wife. Keizo, however, had been raised as a Christian since childhood. He could not bring himself to heartlessly discard Sachi just because she was sick.

"I don't feel like doing that right now," he said.

"I see." Heikichi gazed up at the ceiling. "I suppose not. After all, you had a child together." Although he worried about the social status of his son and heir, as a Christian, Heikichi likewise could not bring himself to ignore his conscience or abandon his principles.

Keizo found it painful to meet Sachi's parents and had stopped going to Shiloh Church. Instead, he attended the service at Fujimicho Church in Iidabashi.

"You'll need to think about Yoshio's education," Heikichi went on. "And it looks like Hitoshi will be getting engaged. Sorry that we're going ahead with it when your own situation is still unsettled."

"I know," Keizo said. "I just heard about it from Hitoshi. Please don't wait because of me. Hitoshi should live his own life, and Miss Nishimura is already like part of the family. There couldn't be anything better for both our families."

"If all goes well, we'll have the wedding by next year at the latest. Will you come to the church for it?"

"Of course I will. Regardless of my own situation, I wouldn't miss it."

Heikichi breathed a sigh of relief. "Here. Let me call you a cab," he said.

"No thanks. I'll walk to Yokohama station."

Heikichi nodded. "Still," he mused, "you really can't tell with people, can you?"

"What do you mean?"

"Sachi. She was so healthy." Keizo said nothing. "Haru got a bad eye infection in that slum in Kobe, you know," Heikichi continued. "She's gone blind in her right eye, yet she and Kagawa are still preaching the Gospel there. She's got grit. As for Tomoe, we'd better take good care of her because she's Mr. Nishimura's precious daughter."

"Tomoe's the type of girl who was born to be happy," Keizo reassured him. "And Hitoshi's madly in love with her."

❀

To reach the Ginza branch, Keizo took the train from Yokohama to Yurakucho. As he rode, he thought of Tomoe, Hitoshi's proposed bride. She was the second daughter of Shotaro Nishimura, one of the founders of the Sankyo Seiyaku, a pharmaceutical company, and a friend of Heikichi. The two men had worked hard together to establish Shiloh Church. Kind-natured and beautiful, Tomoe was a skilled pianist who drew the gaze of every young man at church. She and Hitoshi would make a good couple.

Keizo recalled how his brother's cheeks flushed with pleasure when he spoke of Tomoe. Hitoshi's marriage would not only halve his father's worries but lighten Keizo's load too. The church congregation loved to gossip, but with everyone's attention focused on the felicitous news of his younger brother's engagement, Keizo would finally be spared.

To Tokyo as an Editor

In March 1919, Hanako quit her job as a teacher at Yamanashi Eiwa Girls School and returned to Tokyo. Her book, *Rohen*, which had been published two years previously, had caught the eye of Masahisa Uemura[69], a pastor and prominent figure in the Japanese Christian world. "You should focus on Christian literature," he told her. While teaching, Hanako had translated Mildred Duff's *Where Moses Went to School*, and in 1918, Uemura asked Gunpei Yamamuro[70] of the Salvation Army if he could arrange to have it published. He had also contacted an editor at the Christian Literature Society of Japan in Tsukiji, which had resulted in their hiring Hanako.

The support and encouragement of someone like Uemura greatly cheered Hanako. She would soon be turning twenty-six. In early twentieth-century Japan, a woman who remained single beyond the age of twenty-two was considered past marriageable age, but Hanako's dream had finally been set in motion. Although the Tokyo to which she returned from her quiet life in the mountains would be the bustling outside world rather than the sheltered paradise of her alma mater, she had made up her mind to make the city her home.

Hanako's living quarters were located in a lodging house on the second floor of the Japan Woman's Christian Temperance Union Hall. Two live-in servants took care of meals and other household chores. On the ground floor was a dining hall, an office with a public pay phone, and a meeting hall. The latter was in frequent use for gatherings of Temperance Union members, such as Kajiko Yajima, Azuma Moriya, Ochimi Kubushiro, Tsuneko Gauntlett, Michiko Senbongi, and Miyoko Kobashi, as well as members of the Women's Press Club, including Yuriko Mochizuki[71] and Shigeri Yamataka[72].

In April 1911, the Yoshiwara[73] red-light district in Tokyo burned down. Seizing this opportunity, the Temperance Union, which had continued to advocate for the abolition of licensed prostitution, launched a campaign to prevent the district's reconstruction. They failed, however, to gain enough support to achieve this cherished goal. Girls from poor families were still being sold to brothels, where they were forced to service multiple customers a night or subjected to hard labour. The meagre income they made was swallowed up by loan payments. Not only were they trapped within a world of suffering, they lived in fear of being cast away like living rubbish should they fall sick.

The failure to prevent the reconstruction of Yoshiwara reinforced the bonds among women working to eradicate licensed prostitution, including members of the Temperance Union and the Salvation Army, as well as female journalists. They had been made keenly aware that as long as men made all the laws and women had no voice in decision-making, the system would remain in place and the earnest appeals of women throughout the country would be easily squashed. Women's suffrage, and through it legal reform, became their rallying cry.

Whenever Hanako participated in these gatherings, she was reminded of the words of Asako Hirooka: "From here on, politics will be crucial. Unless we raise up female politicians active in governing this country, true emancipation for women can never be achieved. We must start by obtaining the right to choose our leaders, the right to vote, just as women in other countries have done. You must work together for the same goal."

Asako Hirooka's life had come to a close at the age of sixty-nine on January 14, 1919, the same year Hanako returned to Tokyo. Fusae Ichikawa, with whom Hanako had spent a summer at Ninooka, took the above words as Asako's dying wish and, together with Raicho Hiratsuka, arose to lead the women's emancipation movement.

A Fateful Encounter

Hanako commuted by streetcar from her lodgings to her job at the Christian Literature Society in Tsukiji Akashi-cho. Established in 1913 through the joint investment of missionaries from different Protestant denominations, the society was an ecumenical publishing company dedicated to producing Christian literature. Located within Tokyo's former foreign settlement, which was known as the Occident of Tokyo, the company stood on a site with a splendid view of the placid Sumida River, which flowed right in front of the property. The office building itself was a modest two-storey brick building with a tower that looked like a dwarf's cap. White roses had been trained into an arch over the gate and the green ivy growing up the walls presented a striking contrast to the red brick. Hooded gulls occasionally stopped by to rest their wings.

Tsukiji was originally a cradle of scholarship. It was here that Keio Gijuku University had begun in the mid-nineteenth century, developing out of an institute for Dutch studies[74] started by Yukichi Fukuzawa, an influential educator and advocate of Western learning. After the Meiji Restoration, Tsukiji became a designated foreign settlement within the bounds of which foreigners were permitted to live and work. Many mission schools that are still well-respected educational institutions today were founded there. Although quite a few of these relocated to other areas when the foreign settlement system ended in 1899, Rikkyo Gakuin and St. Margaret's School remained and were located very near the Christian Literature Society, where Hanako worked.

Hanako's English ability was an asset for the publishing firm. English documents, such as textbooks for different mission schools and Sunday school stories, piled up on her desk awaiting translation. Tenma Nobechi[75], editor of the weekly journal *Fukuin shinpo* (The Evangelical News), had asked her to contribute short story translations for a new children's magazine called *Shokoshi* (Little Children of Light).

The Christian community in Japan was very small, and Hanako's first day at work had culminated in a crushing blow. "Oh, I've heard all about you," someone crowed. "I hear you were a splendid *scholarship* student." The person who had loudly proclaimed Hanako's status in front of her coworkers was Mrs. Matsuki, the relative of a famous pastor who had deep ties with Hanako's alma mater. Mrs. Matsuki took great pride in her samurai heritage, and thereafter it seemed to Hanako that she took every opportunity she could find to express contempt for Hanako's origins.

❀

One windy spring afternoon, Hanako was in the editing department working on a rush translation, when a shrill voice penetrated her thoughts.

"You know, Miss Annaka, I am quite well acquainted with Renzo Sawada's elder brother, Setsuzo. He works in the foreign service just like Renzo."

Pen still in hand, Hanako froze. The voice belonged to Mrs. Matsuki, who had brought some work over to Hanako's desk and was now dallying beside her. With an innocent smile on her face, she continued, "I hear Setsuzo's younger sister is betrothed to a son of the Kajima family. As for Renzo, apparently he's getting engaged to a daughter of the Mitsubishi family. You can have no idea how worried Setsuzo was when it was rumoured that Renzo had a crush on you. I mean really, they are distant kin of the Mitsubishi family themselves you know."

So, Hanako fumed, *even some Christians are capable of this kind of cruelty. They do good works on the one hand, while on the other striking people to the heart with their vicious words. Filled with petty vanity and prejudice, they look down on others, forgetting that the Bible teaches all are equal before God. In the end, she's just trying to tell me that I wasn't good enough for Renzo; that we could never have gotten married anyway. Well, so what?*

Hanako could not raise her head. Her lips were trembling and the book in front of her was just a blur. She kept her eyes on its pages, trying desperately to rally her feelings—feelings which she later expressed in a poem lamenting life's tempests from which "paradise" had once sheltered her.

Cherry blossoms bloom,

then fall,

petals trampled underfoot,

longing all the while

for the days when they were still in the bud.

At that moment, the door burst open and someone strode into the office.

"Good day, everyone!"

Hanako raised her face blankly. Before her stood an exotic-looking gentleman with big dark eyes dressed in a fashionable pale beige suit. It was April 8, 1919, the day that Hanako and Keizo Muraoka first met.

An Illicit Love Affair

In June 1919, Hanako visited Toyo Eiwa Girls School with Chiyo, whom she had not seen for some time. Chiyo, who had been like an older sister to Hanako in the dorm, had since married, and was no longer Chiyo Okuda, but Chiyo Shiobara. Miss Blackmore had taken ill just before she was to return to Canada, and Chiyo had asked Hanako to help her tidy Miss Blackmore's room while the principal recuperated in hospital.

Hanako gave Chiyo a copy of her newly published translation of *Where Moses Went to School*. "My goodness, Hana," Chiyo exclaimed, looking at the inscription. "The book you translated was printed by Fukuin."

"Yes. Mr. Keizo Muraoka from Fukuin read the manuscript before we met and remembered my name. He said he found it so fascinating that he forgot about his work. He praised the translation profusely, but I told him it was just because the original is so good."

"This Keizo Muraoka, which son is he?" Chiyo asked. "My husband knows Bible Muraoka very well." Chiyo's husband, Matasaku Shiobara, was one of the founders of the Sankyo Seiyaku, a pharmaceutical company established in 1899 in the Bentendori area of downtown Yokohama by the joint investment of three men: Chiyo's husband, Matasaku Shiobara; Genjiro Fukui; and Shotaro Nishimura. The latter was Heikichi Muraoka's friend, whose daughter was engaged to Heikichi's son Hitoshi. Chiyo's husband knew Heikichi very well, as they were both entrepreneurs in Yokohama.

"The older son," Hanako said in a small voice. "The one in charge of the Ginza branch."

"Oh, right, that one. The poor man. I heard that his wife got sick just when they were rejoicing over the birth of their little son and heir."

Hanako fell silent. Having been brought together by *Where Moses Went to School*, she and Keizo had fallen passionately in love, and she had been hoping to confide in Chiyo the painful emotions that filled her breast. But the social circles within which they moved were just too small.

"Hana dear, is something troubling you?"

"What? Oh, I'm sorry. It's nothing."

"You looked so sad just now."

"No, really, it's nothing. It's just that one woman at the company is a bit mean sometimes, and I find that hard," Hanako said, diverting her friend's attention.

"Someone mean?"

"Mrs. Matsuki. She's says lots of things about me. That I come from a poor family, that my father was caught by the police because he's a socialist. What's worse is that she says these things in front of my coworkers."

"I see. Yes, that's the kind of person she is. Even Reverend Matsuki is like that sometimes. I suppose it's just the way of their family. Don't forget that I'm behind you one hundred percent, Hana. I think you're truly admirable. You carved your own path to the future even while supporting your family. Don't pay any attention to the spiteful things Mrs. Matsuki says. You should forge ahead with pride."

How shocked Chiyo would be if she knew that Hanako was having an affair. Chiyo, who now wore her hair in a demure oval-shaped chignon that marked her as a married woman. She would be even more shocked to learn that Hanako's lover was Keizo, son of the Muraoka family whom Chiyo's husband knew so well. Hanako didn't want to burden her kind and gentle friend with worry. The only person in whom she could confide her love was Azuma Moriya at the Temperance Union. If only Miss Aki were here! Hanako felt sure that Akiko would understand her feelings.

Where Moses Went to School, the book that had brought Hanako and Keizo together, was published on May 25, 1919, by the Salvation Army press. Both their names were written in the inscription with the publisher's name sandwiched between.

Translator: Hanako Annaka
Publisher: Gunpei Yamamuro
Printer: Keizo Muraoka

In her own copy, Hanako had written beside these words: *May 25, Taisho 8 (1919) To be commemorated as the day I found the home of my soul. —* *Hanako*

This was the day that Keizo had first held her in his arms and kissed her.

🌼

Strong emotions surge and collide within the pages of the seventy or more love letters that Hanako and Keizo exchanged over the space of six months, beginning in April of that year: a passionate yearning to realize this "love that was fate," coupled with doubts about whether such a love could justify hurting others. Keizo fervently wished to separate from his ailing wife and wed Hanako, while Hanako was torn between love for him and her guilt at their illicit affair. Four letters they exchanged at the time reveal their feelings.

June 20 [A letter from Hanako to Keizo]
I wonder how your day was. Last night, you talked about so many things. How happy I was to listen. When I hear what you are thinking, all the dreams you hope to achieve, I think how foolish I am—I who could never even hope to keep up with you.

I shall become a young woman who no longer frets about such things. Knowing that you love me, and how very much I love you, I can believe that our love will solve everything. This thought makes me smile. Do you remember what I told you last night? That I would be content just to live near my parents? That wasn't the truth. In fact, more than anyone else it is you I would rather be with, wherever you are.

Miss Moriya said, "You're so fortunate to be loved, especially by someone like Mr. Muraoka." I agree. Yet I find it exceedingly strange that you should show me such kindness. Why would you? To such a plain young woman? I will strive to become worthy of you, so please forgive my shortcomings. I am yours.

The woman who lives in the room next to mine received lilies of the valley from Hokkaido and gave some to me. They sit here on my desk, surrounding me with their sweet fragrance. Each time I look at them, I want to give them to you. But if you took home flowers, people might think it strange, and so I hesitate.

How I long to see you; to walk by your side beneath the shade of the willows in Ginza and speak of the beauty of this city at night.

Good day to you. And good night.

August 12
To Mr. Keizo,

On this lonely night at such a time, how it would lift my spirits to receive a phone call from you. I miss you.

Stop thinking, I tell myself, but thoughts still run through my mind. When we're together talking, I never think bad thoughts; I can believe that everything will be all right. But alone like this, I can't help remembering past sufferings, worrying about the present, fretting about the future, and I wonder if, just as I feared, it might have been better that we had never met after all.

I have suffered; suffered and survived, though that suffering cannot compare to what many others have experienced. In fact, there is really only one hardship I bear.... For me, my family has always been a burden. To shoulder that burden, I gave up my dream of carrying on with my studies. In retrospect, perhaps it would not have been so hard to continue. After all, I like studying. But as a girl of just twenty, to balance my studies with family responsibility seemed too heavy a load. So I abandoned my hopes and my plans and chose the road of filial duty. And now I find myself wondering if I should also abandon my happiness to fulfill my duty as a daughter.

On desolate nights, in the dim light when no one is there to see, I let my tears flow unchecked, then put on a smile whenever I am with others. But since we met, I have learned to cry in front of you. That is how much you have come to rule my mind and heart.

I believed I wasn't the type to fall in love with a man. I prided myself on my strong resolve. But now that I know my own weakness, the joy of being loved almost overwhelms me. As long as this memory lasts, I can face any fate, no matter how tragic, without losing my mind.

I did not love you because I expected to become your wife. I loved you regardless of whether we wed, regardless of the mundane affairs of life. As such, I will not [...] my fate. I am happy. So when you think about me, judge objectively. Then decide as you wish.

I do not want to become a burden on you; you who are my most precious. I wish to keep you in the bright, free world.

Let us talk about this again. I think, however, it's best for me not to go out this Sunday. I have been out so much, I worry what others may think. If you come to the morning service, I will at least see your face, although that may be painful for me. Let us meet again another day. No matter what happens, I am always your Hanako, am I not?

I'm tired now, and my head aches. —Good night.

Hanako

August 17

To Miss Hanako,

I knew that there would be no letters, yet their absence leaves me feeling somehow disappointed. The woman I have been seeing almost daily for the last twenty days or more is off to Kofu.

Loneliness fills my heart. In the dim light of dusk, I gaze in the direction of Kofu and wish happiness to the one I hold most dear. I fret that she may be careless and catch a cold, and I wonder if she packed a lined *haori* coat for the mountains of Kofu, which are so much cooler than Tokyo.

Don't drink the water. It might ruin your digestion and give you diarrhea come autumn. Remember to take care in all things. Today was a lonely day with no letters…

Today I went to Maruzen. I saw two or three books that I would like, but did not buy them. Instead I enjoyed looking at the shelves stacked with rows of books, just like young women enjoy looking at all the wares displayed in kimono or accessory shops. I imagined reading a book together, pausing to talk when we tired of it, then let my thoughts roam to all the other things we would do when we tired of talking, and a vision of our new life as a family rose in my mind. What a beautiful daydream.

Watching young housewives, their hair secured in the oval bun of a married woman, I wanted to dance with the knowledge that I will soon transform the one I love in that way. Hana dear, always young and beautiful, lustrous and shining, you are the life of […] both body and spirit.

Tomorrow, I will meet with Mr. Fukunaga and consult him about the problem of the family register (we just need to have our marriage recorded in it). I will make sure everything is resolved by the time you return from Kofu. Then you will no longer be a flower in the shade. As long as your mind is at ease, then I am happy.

You must be tired from the train journey. You should go to bed early and rest.

For some reason, I seem to be tired too, so I plan to go to bed early as well. I will write again tomorrow.

Goodbye.

xxxxxx from Keizo

September 25.

To my dearest wife

I just finished supper after coming back from the company. There was a letter, so I ate my supper in a state of bliss. Today I am trying to keep my happiness from showing. This morning on my way to the office, I stopped by Sendagaya and told Miss Moriya that I have settled the issue with the family register. That made her very happy. I told her she should consult you about what to do from here, so I expect she will be in touch.

The time when we can finally be together, free from worry, is drawing near. Rejoice. We only need to bear this hardship a little longer. This is the suffering that comes before achieving success. Nature bestows no gifts without suffering. Hold onto hope through the difficulties and nurture your health so that you stay well.

When you come to me, I will pamper you so thoroughly that you'll soon forget these trials. Cheer up. You must not fret. You need to rest your nerves a little. What joy we will feel when we are married.

I was thinking of dropping by the Christian Literature Society today, just for a moment, but the weather was bad and a bit too cool, so I decided against it. Still, I wanted to see your face.

I gave you quite a surprise the other night it seems. I would not have gone if I had known how much it would startle you or that it would cause the kind of trouble you described in today's letter. But I wanted to make sure you knew that the procedures for the family register are done. When we met like that, I felt a little awkward too. Still, when I saw you, I was reluctant to go home right away. You are so adorable that I cannot resist kissing you. A parting kiss. You must have thought me quite a nuisance.

Still, it is human nature to long to meet when one knows one should not. Even when our fingers brush ever so slightly, I can feel my heart pounding so fast the blood surges through my body.

It comes down to this. You and I were not made to be apart. Since the beginning of Creation, we were destined to be one. Even when tired from fretting about what the future may bring, we should never, not even for a moment, imagine that our union was not meant to be. Life is the realm of hope. And to [...] is to have hope that it can soon be realized. You must not be faint of heart. When I hear how you feel, I want to call you to my side, and when you want to cry, I long to hold you in my arms. I am quite confident that I could turn your tears of pain into tears of joy.

On an evening so chill that I long for a charcoal brazier, the autumn night seems somehow lonely. I have missed you so; if we were together now, I would kiss you.

I will stop here because today I am a little tired.

Sept 25, 1919

xxxxxxxxxx Keizo

On October 24, six months and sixteen days after they first met, and just five months after they first kissed, Keizo and Hanako were married in Tsukiji Church in a ceremony presided over by the Reverend Naokatsu Kubushiro. Hanako described the moment as follows:

> "Do you take this woman to be your wife, to love her as long as you both shall live?" That's what Reverend Naokatsu asked Keizo, or words to that effect.
>
> Whether bride or groom, most people are barely audible when they respond to this question. Keizo, however, startled not only me but the pastor as well by announcing in a booming voice, "I do!"[76]

After the ceremony, the newlyweds and wedding guests gathered for a joyful lunch at Tsukiji Seiyoken, the first restaurant to serve Western cuisine in Japan, before sending the couple off from Shinbashi Station to their honeymoon in Hakone.

Not long after, Hanako received the following letter from her dear friend Akiko Ito.

> To my dear Hana
>
> How disappointed I was when my letter to you, which I sent off with considerable trouble, came back. You sound busy, but happy too, and that makes me happier than anything.
>
> My feelings for you will never change. If you thought something was odd, it must be because you are odd. Wasn't

there a time when you responded to my letters only after a very long delay or worse, not at all? Yet that did not change how I thought of you. Although you've found someone better than anyone else in the world, I am certain this won't change the bond between us as women.

My heart is filled with joy for you. As your "older sister," I am sending you a black crepe *haori*, as well as the best *maru-obi* I can afford. I am a little worried about what your husband may think, but hope you can explain.

Evening of the 25th
from Akiko

Hanako and Keizo compiled the seventy letters they had exchanged until their wedding and placed them safely in a box. They lived in a rented house for a few months, after which they purchased a home in Araijuku, Omori. One reason they chose the location was because it was near Hiroko Katayama, Hanako's revered friend and mentor. It was Hiroko, as well as Azuma Moriya, who had convinced Hanako that marrying Keizo was the right thing to do: that and the fact that Keizo's wife's parents had asked Keizo to annul his marriage to their ailing daughter.

Sometimes Hanako would visit Fukuin Printing Company in Yokohama on an errand for Keizo. Whenever she did, Keizo's father, Heikichi, would exclaim, "Oh! My dear!" and envelop her in a big hug. Once her errand was done, he would tell her to wait at the house in Otamachi, then call a rickshaw, warning the driver that he had better treat this customer with extra special care because she was his "precious daughter-in-law."

Hanako and Keizo were drunk with happiness. Their wedded bliss was so complete they forgot that in the shadow of their joy lay the sorrow of a woman and a little boy from Keizo's previous life. The year after their wedding, Hanako, who had continued working industriously, felt a change occur inside her: her body had started preparing for motherhood.

Hanako, who, at twenty-seven, still saw herself as an immature young woman, was to be a mother! In her journal, she recorded the anxiety she felt about the fast-approaching birth and the profound emotions this new experience generated.

September 7, Taisho Year 9 [1920]
As the due date nears, I feel helpless and afraid. My heart will not be still.

The day I will be tested approaches. Oh, maternal instinct concealed within, help me to bear this bravely.

To welcome to the world
this darling child of ours,
I sew clothes
with which to dress
our healthy baby.

September 13, at five-forty-five in the morning, a boy is born. When I hear his first lusty cry, tears of joy and affection fall unchecked.

You,
who have chosen
to come into this world
through this silly fool,
gaze at me as your one and only mother.

Our house overflows
with the happiness that fills me
whenever someone calls me "Mother.[77]"

Hanako and Keizo wept and offered prayers of gratitude for the birth of their son, whose cries rent the early morning air. They named him Michio.

He grew strong and healthy. After tiring himself out with crying, he would sleep peacefully beside Hanako as she sat working on translations. At times, she felt like kneeling in reverence before him, awed by the gift of this child.

When he reached the age of two, Michio began throwing tantrums, making life difficult for their maid, Hide (pronounced Hee-deh), who was only sixteen and had moved to Tokyo from the country.

Every night, Hanako prayed with her son, "Dear God in heaven, today Michio said mean and silly things, making trouble for dear Hide. Please forgive him. He has become a little naughty these days. Please help him to be a good boy tomorrow and guard him in his sleep tonight. Amen."

"Sorry, Hide. Amen," Michio prayed solemnly.

Then Hanako would lie down beside him and gaze at his face as she told him bedtime stories. As Japan had few picture books for mothers to read to children who had not yet learned their letters, Hanako made up her own nursery tales.

The Byakuren Incident

On October 23, 1921, Hanako stared in shock at the newspaper. The headline proclaimed the scandalous news that Akiko, who was now a celebrated writer known by her pen name Byakuren, had eloped with a socialist named Ryusuke Miyazaki[78]. Not only that, she had posted a notice in the *Osaka Asahi Shimbun* newspaper declaring that she was terminating her marriage to Denemon, to whom she had been married for ten years. On October 25, the *Osaka Mainichi Shimbun* carried a statement from Denemon contesting Akiko's declaration.

This matter became known as the Byakuren Incident, thrusting Akiko into the limelight as an object of both censure and curiosity. Everyone speculated about whether she would be charged with adultery and what her dishonoured husband would do.

Although aware of Akiko's anguish when she had been pressured to wed Denemon, Hanako had been too naïve and immature at the time to forgive her friend for going through with the marriage. Having fallen in love with

Keizo, however, Hanako could now understand the tragic fate Akiko's lineage had caused. The self-righteous clamouring of society infuriated her. Miss Aki was not a doll. She was a living woman who felt both joy and pain. As she thought of her friend, Hanako suddenly recalled the letter Akiko had sent her the previous month. Hastily, she pulled it out and ran her eyes over the words.

September 2, 1921 In Kyoto   Akiko Ito
To Hana dear,

I have been happily rereading letters received from you in days gone by. Whether you send me news or not, I am sure that when we meet again, we will still share the same sentiments. Though these heartfelt letters of yours were written years ago, I clearly remember that dear, familiar time as if it were just yesterday. Hana dear, it makes me so happy to know that you are living as you choose.

With age, we begin to think about so much more. You could say that we are better able to recognize a wind that will bring good fortune. When we meet again in the fall, I must find out what you think.

After we parted at school, I too came close to the brink of death. I tried giving up and bewailing my plight, but I have since realized that giving up is never the correct moral choice. Rather, I believe that to keep hoping until the very end is an act of true courage.... You said that you were writing to me "not as Miss Byakuren." That name, to which even I am not accustomed, has been a real nuisance. It is high time everyone forgot it.

Remember how you used to tell me Western stories as we wandered among the bush clover in the schoolyard? What fond memories those are.

from Akiko

Letter still in hand, Hanako's fingers began to tremble. Akiko had already made her choice when she wrote this. Although worried for her friend, Akiko's courage thundered in Hanako's heart.

Ryusuke Miyazaki, Akiko's lover, was the son of Toten Miyazaki, a philosopher who had supported the Chinese republican revolution of 1911 and helped Sun Yat-sen, the provisional president of the republic, during his exile to Japan. Toten's elder brother, Hachiro, was the leader of the Freedom and People's Rights Movement that supported the Satsuma Rebellion of 1877 led by Takamori Saigo against the Meiji government. Hachiro was shot and killed in battle, but Toten and his two younger brothers, influenced by his example, had all become political activists too. Toten's son Ryusuke had inherited the Miyazaki family's rebel spirit.

Placing her whole trust in Ryusuke, Akiko eloped, an act that sent shock waves through society and forced her elder brother to resign from his post in the national government. Akiko, however, had taken her first steps towards independence, and she remained dignified throughout, undeterred by the winds of opposition. The following letters she sent to Hanako after she escaped from her marriage to Denemon convey her determination and the bracing joy she was experiencing for the first time in her life.

> October 25 Three days after running away. From Akiko to Hanako
>
> How happy your letter made me!
>
> In such matters, siblings and family are useless.
>
> There is nothing more welcome than a friend who truly knows my heart.
>
> I am in exceedingly good health and spirits; safe and carefree.
>
> When things settle down a little, I would love to see you again.

November 6   From Akiko to Hanako

I read your kind letter many times with joy. You and I once talked about how we would live together in the future, friends forever. I wrote about that in my dedication "To H" for my new novel, which will be published in the January issue....

Mr. Yamamoto also knows. But we won't announce it yet because there is still such an uproar. So if you are planning to write to me, I will make sure that if you address it to Ryusuke Miyazaki from Muraoka, it will be delivered to my hands alone and not fall into those of any other. Please do not write "Akiko" on the envelope.

We have rented a house in the neighbourhood and will likely hand over this house to him tomorrow or the day after. Once we have moved and things are a bit quieter, I look forward to visiting you in Omori. I will let you know before I come. I will write in more detail later.

December 17   From Akiko to Hanako

The other day I was truly happy that you came so far to see me. It is at times like these that I realize how precious friendship is. A true friend never changes, no matter what. This thought fills me with gratitude.

It appears that Mr. Tetsu has come to Tokyo, and Mr. Yamamoto will also come back tomorrow, so everything is moving ahead.

You may rest easy as I am fine. Life is good, and I am looking forward to a bright future.

Please give my regards to Mrs. Katayama.

Hanako's letters to Akiko, in which she promises not to reveal the contents of their correspondence even to her husband, are full of sympathy.

December ? From Hanako to Akiko

As you know, I long to see you. Still, I am very relieved. Even just to have successfully removed your name from the family register and to have been accepted by the Miyazaki family is wonderful news.

As for me, Miss Aki, I don't care what people may say about what you did, whether good or bad. Even if it was bad, what's done is done. As long as it is settled that you and I are eternal friends who will never part, then that is […] for me. I would pray for your future happiness even at the risk of my life. I beg you to be happy and fully enjoy the pleasure of a home. And please, please do not give up writing.

In a normal household, it's extremely difficult to pursue any path other than that of a housewife, to balance any other work with that of the household chores and supporting one's family. Yet still, I beg you, don't give up your art....

Please take good care of your health and give my regards to Mr. Miyazaki. I am sure that we will meet somehow or other. There is no other way to convey all that is on our minds than to meet and talk.

December 14 From Hanako to Akiko

I just read your letter. I waited a long time on the twelfth and the thirteenth. But I also guessed you must have been tired from going out, which you are not used to. Or that you had run into various difficulties such as being waylaid by reporters.

Please do come and visit soon. If you come as far as Omori by train, head in the direction of Sanno and Ikegami. It's about a twenty-minute walk.

Go as far as the bridge called Dedobashi and turn right. The house at the end of the street is the Kato house. Go left at the Katos. Three houses down is our house. You will know it by the nameplate.

I will not say anything of your movements here, but don't worry. Everything will be all right. You need not fear that the newspaper reporters will find out. I have not even told my husband about these things. Friends, I believe, are joined by a special bond and share sacred secrets.

December 31 From Hanako to Akiko

I am worried about you because I have not received any letters.

How are you doing? Please tell me what has been happening in your life. No matter what happens, no matter what the circumstances, you and I are always "Miss Aki" and "Hana dear," and I want to follow wherever you may go.

I have not seen your name in the news for a while. But yesterday something happened that bothered me a little. However, I will stop here for now as I am busy preparing for New Year's Eve. I am praying with all my heart that this will be the year you seize true happiness.

Let us meet during the New Year holidays for sure.

Also, I did not know where to send your New Year's card so I addressed it to Mr. Miyazaki. Please give him my regards.

I will keep whatever you should tell me safely locked away in my breast, telling no one else. So please do let me know how things are.

These two friends were reunited in December 1921, ten years after they had parted at Toyo Eiwa Girls School in the spring of 1911 when Hanako had been seventeen and Akiko twenty-five. Hanako had never seen Akiko looking so happy and radiant. Now with child, she had been transformed from someone resigned to her fate and shrouded in sorrow to a vibrant woman exuding strong determination.

Chapter 6

Overcoming Sorrow: 1922–1927

Age 29 to 34

The Great Kanto Earthquake

The Fukuin Printing Company celebrated its twenty-fifth anniversary in 1922. On a sunny afternoon in May, the company held a gala at the Yokohama Grand Hotel. The celebration was attended by many guests, including local businessmen dressed in tuxedos and bowler hats, representatives of the publishing industry, pastors, and foreign missionaries. To mark the occasion, Fukuin changed from a limited partnership to a joint-stock company, and Heikichi passed on the mantle of company director and manager to his son Keizo.

Shortly after, on May 20, Heikichi died peacefully, as though relieved to have laid down his burden. He was seventy years old. The next morning, a large headline in Yokohama's business newspaper declared: HEIKICHI MURAOKA, PRINTING INDUSTRY PIONEER, DIES.

Keizo's cousin Haru rushed from Kobe to Yokohama with her husband, Reverend Toyohiko Kagawa, who conducted Heikichi's funeral ceremony at Shiloh Church. All those who had so recently attended the anniversary celebration came to honour Heikichi and his achievements.

As the choir sang hymns to send Heikichi's soul on its way to heaven, Hanako recalled how Heikichi used to exclaim "My dear!" and envelop her in a big hug whenever he saw her. He had been overjoyed that his daughter-in-law was also involved in the Christian publishing industry and had wholeheartedly welcomed her, along with her dream of pursuing literature, into the Muraoka family.

Beside Hanako sat Tomoe, Hitoshi's wife, whose face was buried in her handkerchief. About ten days before Heikichi's passing, Tomoe had given birth to a son, Hajime, and Hitoshi had brought the newborn to his father's bedside. Heikichi had passed away with a peaceful expression on his face, surrounded by his sons and their families. "It's a comfort to me that Hajime was born in time to meet my dear father-in-law before he died," Tomoe said tearfully.

"It must have been a comfort to him to know that Hajime was born safely," Hanako said. "He looked so happy. I'm sure he'll be watching over both our boys from heaven." Hanako showered Tomoe with concern, knowing that she had not yet fully recovered from giving birth. Michio, who would turn two that year, slept soundly through the long funeral service in the arms of Hanako's maid, Hide.

Keizo was now the senior managing director of Fukuin and Hitoshi was the managing director. They had lost their father, who had been a stalwart pillar to them, but they proclaimed to those assembled that they would carry on his wishes and work together for the further development of the company.

Keizo's black suit accentuated his strong features and gave him a dignity befitting the heavy role he would now have to bear. Eyes wet with tears, Hanako stood to one side watching Keizo address the guests. *What a fine man*, she thought. Her heart swelled with pride in her beloved and with the yearning to become a wife worthy of him.

Hitoshi admired his older brother Keizo, as well as the woman he had chosen as his bride, and often came to visit. He was a lovable character, full of compassion and energy. "In England," he told Hanako, "books are like works of art. It's my goal to produce ones as beautiful as those in England. We'll publish all your books, too." He would talk for hours with Hanako and Keizo about magnificent cloth and leather book bindings, the latest printing technology used in the British and American publishing industries, and their shared dreams for the company's future.

September 1, 1923, was a hot, blustery day overcast with an angry sky. Keizo left home early to go to the Ginza office. Japan was still recovering from an economic slump, and the company had had to lay off some of its factory workers, who were now demanding an allowance. Swamped with paperwork and meetings to handle these litigations, Keizo had left the Yokohama plant in the hands of Hitoshi and the veteran Wakamiya.

After seeing Keizo off, Hanako quickly set to work on the household chores. The sun rose higher, chasing away the dark clouds but intensifying the sweltering heat. In the afternoon, Hanako would work on manuscripts for the children's magazine *Little Children of Light* and *Fujin shinpo* (Women's News), as well as a translation for the publisher Kyobunkwan. When Hanako finished the chores, Michio, who would soon be three, crawled into her lap.

"Mommy, tell me a story," he begged. He had begun to pester Hanako for stories recently, and she smiled as she wiped the sweat from his forehead with her hand.

"All right, Michio," she said. "But just one, because it's almost lunchtime." She sat him down where the breeze flowed on the *engawa*, a narrow wooden deck sheltered by the eaves, and knelt across from him. "Now, let me see," she began. "Well, when I was doing the laundry just now. Yes, that's it. Just as I was washing your clothes, a clump of tiny bubbles rose up and fell to the ground. When I looked down, I saw a frog sitting there."

"A frog?"

"Yes, a green frog with great big eyes. It looked very surprised. 'I'm so sorry!' I said, but it hurried away, hopping and bowing."

Michio chortled. "Poor little froggy."

Hanako rose to go and make lunch. At that moment, the earth beneath her jolted upwards with a terrible roar, then undulated wildly from side to side. The dish cupboard fell over with a crash, and Michio clung to Hanako, wailing with terror. Grabbing him close, Hanako jumped barefoot into the yard, crying out to their maid, "Quick, Hide! Earthquake! Into the yard!"

At 11:58 A.M., an earthquake with a magnitude of 7.9 centred in Sagami Bay struck the Kanto region, particularly Tokyo and Kanagawa.

The aftershocks continued for a long while, and each time the earth rumbled and shook anew, Hide screamed hysterically.

"Calm down, Hide dear. Please," Hanako chided her maid, while at the same time trying to soothe Michio. Glancing up at the sky, she saw an ominous thunderhead rising, far larger than any she had ever seen before.

Losing Loved Ones

Keizo ran into the street. The entire Ginza area was in an uproar. Most of the buildings facing the main street appeared unharmed, but the streets behind had suffered heavy damage. People shouted for help as they tried to extract victims trapped under the rubble, and flames were beginning to sprout up here and there. Some people stared about in shock, looking dazed and frightened, while others seemed to be almost enjoying the excitement of the sudden calamity. Keizo decided to wait with his employees and the staff from Kyobunkwan until the aftershocks subsided.

"Mr. Muraoka!" A man caught sight of Keizo and wove his way through the crowd towards him. He had escaped to Ginza from the Tsukiji district. "The damage there is terrible," he said, his face taut. "All the roof tiles slid off the Rikkyo University dormitory. The Christian Literature Society, the Tsukiji Catholic Church, and many other buildings are barely standing. On my way here, I saw homes flattened, with the second storey now the first. Fires are breaking out too. It's very dangerous, so don't go back inside the building."

Transportation had been brought to a standstill, and electricity and telephone services were down. During the long walk home, Keizo saw huge columns of fire rising from multiple directions, and black smoke belched into the darkening sky. With each hour, the number of people wandering the streets increased, either burned out of their homes or searching for missing family members. Keizo walked non-stop. Drenched with sweat, he finally reached his home in Omori at nine o'clock that night. Hanako was waiting for him. Fortunately, their house remained intact, but there was still a risk that it might collapse in an aftershock, so they spent an anxious night camping in a nearby field along with other families from the neighbourhood. Straw mats were spread on the ground, above which mosquito nets were hung for the children to sleep under.

Although the Muraokas did not know it at the time, a fire had broken out at about two o'clock the same afternoon in a geisha house in the southern part of the Ginza district. The flames spread west and south, burning everything from Sukiya Bridge to Kobikicho. The conflagration merged with a fire that had started to the west of Ginza at the Tokyo Dento Electric Company, and, by a little past four in the afternoon, the central Ginza area was reduced to ashes. Meanwhile, a fire that had started north of Ginza at Honmachi jumped the Kyobashi Bridge when the wind changed direction, and spread north to south through the centre of Ginza.

In addition, flames whipped up by the westerly wind spread from Uchisaiwaicho to Maruyacho in south Ginza, consuming the few buildings that had survived the earlier fire. While Keizo had been walking home, all of the buildings in Ginza that had withstood the ruinous earthquake were destroyed by fire.

That night, a fire that started in Hongan-ji Temple spread through the district of Tsukiji. The only structures left standing after it had burned itself out were St. Luke's Memorial Hall in Teppozu and a telephone box that stood at the foot of Karuko Bridge. Countless charred corpses bobbed in the waters of the Sumida River.

On the morning of September 3, the Muraoka family stopped camping outdoors and moved back into their house. Keizo left early the same morning to find out what had happened to the Fukuin Printing Company in Yokohama. Transportation, electricity, and phone services had all been severed, and no newspapers were being delivered because the offices of every newspaper company had been razed. The only way Keizo could get reliable information was to walk the fifteen kilometres to Yokohama and see for himself. With water drawn from a neighbour's well, Hanako had cooked some rice to make *onigiri* rice balls for Keizo's journey.

When Keizo reached Yokohama, a pall of grey smoke still obscured the sky. The beautiful, exotic town where he had grown up lay in ruins buried beneath a thick coat of ash. Everywhere he went, the scenes unfolding endlessly before his eyes seemed straight from Buddhist scrolls depicting hell: firefighters silently collecting corpses; dazed families wandering in search of their loved ones; scraps of paper bearing messages fluttering on collapsed homes. Scavengers dug diligently through the rubble where a jeweller's and a watch shop had stood.

No trace was left of the Grand Hotel where, just the year before, they had celebrated the company's twenty-fifth anniversary. Nor was there anything left of Shiloh Church. The red-brick office building of Fukuin Printing Company should have been visible in the distance, but instead there was just a mound of blackened debris. The heat still smouldered in the ground beneath Keizo's feet where he stood, unable to move.

Keizo did not return home for four days. During that time, Hanako had managed to get a hold of a news bulletin printed by a newspaper company. The damage from the earthquake was even greater than she had imagined. Located on the outskirts of Tokyo where the land was still rural, Omori had escaped most of the fires, but rumours fanning fear and uncertainty had spread rapidly even to her area: rumours that Korean residents were poisoning people's wells or banding together to attack and commit arson.

Citizens spontaneously formed vigilante gangs, hunting down Koreans whom they beat and killed, as well as some Chinese by mistake. Instead of intervening, some soldiers joined civilians in the violence, and, within the space of a week, between three thousand and six thousand Koreans were massacred. The police seized this chance to crack down on and eliminate socialists, declaring martial law, and soldiers and police officers patrolled the city.

Keizo finally made it home on the night of September 7. Hanako's relief at his return was short lived. One look at his face told her that some terrible tragedy had occurred. He looked so haggard that he seemed to be a different person from the man he had been just a week before.

"There's nothing left of Fukuin," he told her. "Seventy workers were trapped beneath the building. They burned along with the Bibles." His voice shook with helpless rage as much as with grief.

"No! And Hitoshi? What about Hitoshi?"

Keizo shook his head. "I couldn't find him. All I found in the rubble was his watch chain. I took it to Tomoe. I think there's no hope."

Hitoshi. Always so alive and vibrant. Gone. The thought of Tomoe left behind with their son, Hajime, who was only one year old, broke Hanako's heart.

"I need to lie down for a while," Keizo said. Hanako put some water on to boil and hastily laid out his futon, then sponged his body clean. Keizo collapsed onto the bedding and closed his eyes. After a while, eyes still closed, he whispered, "The Minakami house burned to the ground too. They all died."

Hanako stared at him speechless.

Yukiko, Keizo's younger sister, had been adopted into the household of pastor Seigoro Minakami. So had the seven-year-old Yoshio, Michio's older brother, Keizo's son with his previous wife. When Keizo married Hanako, his brother Jutta had adopted Yoshio, but Jutta, who had a delicate constitution, had fallen ill, and just a few short months before, Reverend Minakami had welcomed Yoshio into the Minakami family.

Once she regained her voice, Hanako cried, "Keizo! Keizo?" but he was fast asleep. The death of Yoshio, who had spent so little time with his birth parents, lay heavily on the hearts of Keizo and Hanako.

Supporting the Family

From then on, heaven seemed to turn its back on Keizo. He was betrayed by a company director who had worked for the firm since Heikichi's time. In the midst of the chaos caused by the disaster, while Keizo was preoccupied with rebuilding the company, the director absconded with the official company seal and important documents with which he had been entrusted. Worse, he cancelled all of Fukuin's contracts to print Bibles and hymnals for the American Bible Society, the British and Foreign Bible Society, and the Scottish Bible Society.

Keizo had always been more of a scholar than a businessman. Now that he had lost both his father, who had built the company from scratch, and his brother Hitoshi, who had inherited his father's business acumen, Keizo was an easy mark. The site on which the company had stood in Yokohama passed into other hands. Although the electric street lights in Ginza were lit again by the end of the year and notable shops such as the watchmakers K. Hattori & Co., Kimuraya bakery, Itoya stationary store, and the Mitsukoshi department store reopened in newly built premises, Fukuin's Ginza branch was never resurrected.

Having lost so much in so little time, Keizo was exhausted both physically and emotionally. The deaths of many close kin and employees, the betrayal by a man he had trusted, the collapse of the business he had inherited from his father—all of these misfortunes tormented him. And, although he never spoke of it, Hanako knew he was also wracked with guilt over Yoshio's death.

Each night, Hanako lay beside Keizo, listening to him moan in his sleep. As she listened, she thought, "I can't lose him. I simply cannot live without his love. I must protect him and our family no matter what."

It was Keizo who, through his unstinting love, had saved Hanako from loneliness and suffering. Now it was her turn to devote herself to him. They had vowed before God to love and support one another in sickness and in health for as long as they should live. That is what marriage meant. If she took on more work, they could survive somehow. She simply had to keep Keizo's health from declining any further. She could not let death break their bond and take him from her.

When Keizo told her he would look for a job to support the family, she stopped him. "You just focus on restarting the printing business," she said firmly. "I'll make sure we have enough money to put food on the table."

She could not bear to see Keizo, her dignified husband on whom she had gazed with such pride at his father's funeral, suffer the hardship of working for someone else in an unfamiliar job. She longed to give him a chance to rebuild the printing business and create a place where he could use his knowledge and experience.

"I'm so sorry, Hanako," Keizo said. "I know this will be hard on you, but I thank you. I'll try to rebuild the company by the time I'm forty. Until then, please take care of us."

Hanako was now thirty; Keizo, thirty-six.

❀

Once again, Hanako worked to support her family. She had enjoyed the status of the "company president's wife" for less than a year and a half, but this change did not bother her. After all, she had been working since she was sixteen. This time she was responsible not only for her family of birth, but also for the family she and Keizo had established. Now, however, she had Keizo, which made the load seem far lighter than when she had supported her family all on her own.

Her greatest asset for earning money was her English ability. In addition, she began writing down the tales that she told Michio and turning them into children's stories. While contributing translated fiction monthly to the *Women's News* published by the Temperance Union, Hanako continued to translate children's stories. In November 1924, her collection of nursery tale translations was published as *Shima no musume* (Island Daughter) by Aozorasha.

The offices of the Christian Literature Society of Japan where Hanako used to work had been reduced to ashes by the earthquake, and the organization merged with the Kyobunkwan bookstore and publisher in Ginza while retaining its English name. When the Society reopened within the new premises of Kyobunkwan on Ginza's main street in 1926, Hanako began commuting there to work where she assisted with the publication of numerous books and was also engaged in editing the children's magazine *Little Children of Light*, which had been restarted by editor Tenma Nobechi.

About a year after the earthquake, Keizo and Hanako had begun slowly regaining their former vitality, and in 1926 they launched their own publishing and printing firm called Seiransha Shobo. The greeting they distributed to commemorate its establishment was a declaration of intent, clearly expressing their aspiration to publish books for women and children. It read as follows:

The Aims of Seiransha Shobo
In founding Seiransha Shobo, our sole aim is to benefit women and children.

A distinguishing feature of our company is the provision of good books at a low price.

For this reason, we will not waste money on ostentatious advertising.

Instead, we will strive to develop our business through the support of each individual customer.

If you wish to support our endeavors, please send us your name and address.

Whenever a new book is published, we will notify all our supporters of the details, including the title, author, and price, for their convenience.

Seiransha Shobo   613 Nishinuma Araijuku, Omori, Outer Tokyo
Telephone: Omori 870

To establish the company, Hanako and Keizo borrowed capital from their friends: four thousand yen from Hiroko Katayama and one thousand yen from Azuma Moriya.

At the time, it cost an exorbitant sum to purchase a phone number, but they obtained the number Omori 870 very cheaply from Masujiro Honda, the translator of *Black Beauty*. Hiroko Katayama had contacted Hanako one day and said, "Mr. Masujiro Honda is moving overseas and

1922. Hanako during the happiest period of her life, when her husband's business was going well and their son, Michio, was a healthy boy of two.

will be closing up his home in Omori. He told me he wants to give his phone to someone who's trying to make a new start after the earthquake. He said if he wanted to make money, he could sell it for a high price, but he'd rather know his phone is being used for a purpose that will make him happy to think about in the future. Hana dear, I think you're the perfect person to fulfill his wish." Hiroko paused and chuckled before continuing. "Not only that, Hana, but the number 870 in the Japanese alphabet is *hanamaru*!"[79] A few days later, Hiroko took Hanako to the Honda home. There, they were both delighted to discover that Masujiro Honda's daughter was also named Hanako.

The first project of the Muraokas' new company was a collection of children's stories published under the title *Akai bara* (Red Rose). In the preface, Hanako wrote:

To Mothers,

Morning and evening, my little son, who turns [six] this year, comes running to me, saying, "Mother, tell me a story." Interesting stories, touching stories, long stories, short stories. I am always thinking of stories to tell him. Some are born from my own imagination; others I heard or read as a child to which I have added my own interpretation. It is the stories I told my son and later wrote down that make up *Red Rose*. This book is the product of the joy of one mother and her darling child. With boundless affection, we now offer it to the children of the world.

Its publication was funded solely by readers who responded to our invitation to subscribe. I am profoundly moved whenever I think how many kind-hearted people generously supported the birth of this book.

From the bottom of my heart, I thank my many friends who understood my dream and lent me their support. In addition, I would like to express my gratitude to Miss Azuma Moriya, my esteemed friend, who has written such undeserved words of recommendation for this book. I am also indebted to Gahaku Tomizawa who kindly agreed to undertake the binding.

Taisho 15 [1926]   In Omori   Hanako Muraoka

Recommendation from Azuma Moriya

These days, no one demands a story or wants to read for themselves more ardently than children.

Ever since she was a student at a school for girls, Mrs. Hanako Muraoka has dedicated herself to fulfilling children's desire to read. She has already authored a number of works. Through the publication of *Red Rose*, she seeks to start a movement to create new reading material. I am delighted to contribute to the promotion of this movement. I hope that you, her readers, will also arise to offer your support so that children will have good books to read.

For many years, Mrs. Muraoka has taken on work for the literature department of the Japan Woman's Christian Temperance Union. This book surely represents another step towards the realization of her dream.

Children's Friend   Azuma Moriya

The Price of Happiness

"Listen, Mama," Michio said. "I made a darling-boy song." Dancing around and around, he sang happily, "Here's Mama's darling. Here's Papa's darling. Papa and Mama's darling.'"

Michio, who was almost six, was still quite naughty, causing trouble for the maid Hide, but he also brought his family joy. He liked to make up songs about the things around him, putting these into words just the way he felt or saw them and setting the words to a melody. "Michio," Hanako had told him recently, "you're Mama's darling boy!" She had said this in English, and then translated it into Japanese. Michio had been so taken with the phrase that he wrote his "darling boy" song. He could say his prayers very well, too, and never stumbled when singing "Jesus Loves Me." Reverend Iwamura of Omori Megumi Church, who lived nearby, always called him "my little gentleman."

Hanako tried not to let Michio see their worries and financial struggles. His uninhibited development was a source of comfort and strength for both her and Keizo.

🌺

One morning at the end of August, just before the third anniversary of the cursed earthquake, Michio insisted that his mother accompany him to kindergarten. Hanako did as she was bidden and spent two enjoyable hours watching him show off his skill in various games. Upon returning home in the afternoon, Michio took a nap, which was unusual for him. When he woke, something seemed wrong.

"I think I have a fever," he murmured listlessly.

Hanako put a hand on his forehead. "Oh, my goodness!" she exclaimed.

"You do! And it's quite high." She laid him back down and took his temperature. Then she had him drink castor oil, a purgative, while she waited for the doctor to arrive.

The doctor diagnosed him with severe infantile gastroenteritis, a contagious disease widespread among children at the time. Michio was immediately hospitalized in Fukuda Clinic in Akasaka where he was treated with enemas, Ringer's solution, camphor, serum, and salves. After trying every possible remedy, all that could be done was to wait and hope for him to recover.

All night Michio was tormented by a high fever, but the next day, at three in the afternoon, he woke. He stared around the hospital room with huge, dark eyes. Hanako and Keizo, who had nursed him all night, never leaving his side, drew in a breath.

Joy ran through Hanako. "Michio, you're feeling better now, are you?" she said. "What beautiful eyes you have." Knowing nothing of infantile gastroenteritis, she had no idea that his big dark eyes were a frightening sign, a fatal symptom indicating that the fever had damaged his brain. "Here," she said. "Drink some water." But when she brought a spoonful of water to Michio's mouth, he vomited white foam.

"Michio!" Hanako cried. "Michio! What's wrong?" His little limbs stiffened, and suddenly he was overcome with pain. The doctor shaded the light with a black cloth and pulled the curtains, grimly continuing to do what he could in the darkened room.

With his eyes shut, Michio sometimes called for his mother.

"Mama's right here Michio," Hanako replied.

"Mama, when I call for you, say 'Yes.'"

"Yes, Michio. Mama and Papa are both right here beside you."

Even though Michio's fever dropped, his pulse did not settle, and every thirty minutes the doctor gave him an injection of camphor. Phlegm caught in his throat, and he gasped for air.

Hanako and Keizo prayed desperately.

At dawn, Michio's little frame went rigid. His eyes opened and his lips and fingernails turned purple.

"Michio! Oh, Michio!" Hanako cried. "What do you want Mama to do? Oh, Michio, what shall I do?"

Three times, Michio's lips turned down in a sad expression as if he were going to cry, just the way they did when Hanako scolded him. A small sound escaped his lips.

"There is no more time," the doctor said.

Hanako leaned towards Michio's face, her own deathly pale. The nurse reached out and gently closed Michio's eyes and mouth as Hanako let out an anguished cry.

The nightmare had lasted two days.

Akiko, who was now married to Ryusuke Miyazaki, rushed to the hospital and stayed to comfort Hanako.

❁

Michio died just before his sixth birthday. It was September 1, the same date on which the earthquake had struck three years earlier. From the 1920s until the end of the Second World War, severe infantile gastroenteritis would remain rampant in Japan. The mortality rate was high, making it one of the leading causes of death among children, and for some the symptoms were so acute they succumbed within two days.

On the day of the funeral, each time someone told Hanako, "It was God's will," she rebelled inside. *If God had a heart*, she thought, *why did he take the life of an innocent child?* Why hadn't he listened to their prayers, which had been so desperate their hearts had all but bled? *God, be gone!* she ranted inwardly. *I'm no brave heroine who can endure your heavy blows!*

Throughout the service, she sat in the front pew cursing the God who had ripped Michio from her arms, even while she feared him. *This is not God's will*, she thought. *It's chastisement. He's punishing Keizo for leaving his ailing wife and son, and me for stealing Keizo from them. This is the price exacted for the sin of our union. But to give only to take away is too cruel. Yet it's true we hurt others without regret, ignoring their pain, drunk with our own happiness. Perhaps God will never allow us to live in peace. Must we atone for our sins by carrying this grief for the rest of our lives?*

Hanako, who had lost her only child, had also lost the strength to rise again. Crushed by sorrow, her life an empty void, she wept the days away.

> Was it but a dream,
> my darling boy's sixth summer?
> Just one truth left:
> This little urn of ashes.

> With him,
> life would be the brightest day.
> Without him,
> it's the darkest night.
> My one and only,
> my exquisite, precious boy
> is gone.
> September 23[80]

A hundred days after Michio's death, Hanako's feelings began to shift. In the depths of her despair, she heard a voice murmur in her ear.

"For God so loved the world, that He gave his only begotten son."

John 3:16. A verse from the Bible she had, since childhood, heard and read more times than she could count. But for the first time, the reality of these words touched her heart. God had sent his beloved, his only son, Jesus Christ, as the Saviour of the world. That was how much God had loved humankind. What kind of love had allowed him to relinquish his only son so selflessly?

In the midst of her desolation, Hanako picked up *The Prince and the Pauper* and began to read. Hiroko Katayama had recommended this book to her when Hanako had been expounding on the need for books that could be read and enjoyed by the whole family. It was written by Mark Twain, the father of American literature, who had read each chapter aloud to his two daughters as he finished it. Hanako had been looking forward to the day she could read it to her beloved Michio.

She had not read a book for three and a half months; she had lost even her love of reading. Now, however, she became so absorbed in *The Prince and the Pauper* that she forgot to eat or sleep for two days. When she finished, a thought flashed through her mind like a revelation. As she later wrote:

> I lost my son, whom I loved dearly, and for whom there is no substitute in heaven or earth. That was the bitterest grief I have ever tasted. Yet it was only through losing my son that I realized what it means to truly love a child and became aware of how shallow and transient my own love was. There were times when I thought I was loving him but I was actually seeking to satisfy my own ambitions. Now that I love a child who is no longer here before me, my love has been cleansed. Having been thus refined, it encourages me and guides me to live a meaningful life.
>
> Michio, who left this world at the age of five, was a messenger of God sent to light the flame of motherhood within me. Once lit, that light will never die. Although I'm a mother mourning the loss of a son of whom I was so proud, I have no intention of extinguishing that precious light with tears of sorrow. Instead, I yearn to raise that torch ever higher, illuminating the way for the children of others. Things of beauty are short-lived. Precisely because of this, they leave lasting impressions and powerful emotions that constantly inspire grieving mothers.[81]

I will accept the fate God has decreed, thought Hanako. Although she had lost her own son, she would translate the best literature for the children of Japan. The flame of motherhood that had burned within her grew from that of a mother of her own child to a broader, more universal sentiment. Michio's death became the impetus for Hanako to start anew, aiming for *shinga* before *shoga*, "the true self" over "the small self." Within the depths of her despair, she had discovered her calling, the path given her by heaven: the translation of *katei bungaku*, "family literature."

Hanako's translation of *The Prince and the Pauper* was published by Heibonsha as *Oji to kojiki* in the second volume of the company's world family literature series. Author Akira Maeda and his wife Sumiko Tokunaga were responsible for its editorial supervision, and they supported Hanako throughout the translation process. Both were from Yamanashi prefecture, Hanako's birthplace, and Sumiko, who was five years older than Hanako, was not only a children's book author, but had also lost two of her five children to infantile gastroenteritis.

In the following letter, Hanako apologizes for missing her deadline and asks about payment.

> To Mr. Akira Maeda,
>
> I caught another cold and have had to rest. Perhaps being faint of heart saps the body too.
>
> I am such a pitiful weakling that I get annoyed with myself.
>
> I read your postcard on my sickbed and will send you the manuscript tomorrow morning. There are about nine chapters left, but I will finish these up as soon as I can. I have caused you so much trouble that I am ashamed to look you in the face. I do not think I was so unreliable in the past. But I am surprised by how quickly I run out of energy every time I start to work. This year, I will try to regain a little more strength. The fact that the Taisho era in which Michio was born ended so soon is a comfort. It ended the same year that he died, which helps me believe he was only given a short span of time to live in the first place. I cannot help but brood about such things as fate and destiny.
>
> When I think of all your kindness to [my brother] Kenjiro, it warms my heart. I deeply appreciate all the trouble your

wife has taken to help him too. If I and my husband were still running a business as before, we could have asked others for help, but we are not in a position to do anything for my brother but worry about him.

I would like to consult you about the illustrations and binding for *The Prince and the Pauper* and hope to visit you soon to do so. I wonder what was decided about the royalties. I believe that the conditions were rather complicated, but I have completely forgotten. If possible, I would like to receive this month the portion decided by whatever method everyone agreed upon, but am not sure how to approach Heibonsha about it. I am terribly sorry to bother you but if you could kindly advise me, I would greatly appreciate it. I have not yet received the proofs and would very much like to get them soon. It is still very cold. I hope you are taking good care of your health. I await your reply.

February 2, 1927   From Hanako Muraoka

Hanako's translation of *The Prince and the Pauper* was published on October 15, 1927. Each copy was encased in a box and beautifully bound with a cloth cover in Art Deco style with a gilt top edge. The first page bore the words: *Dedicated to the soul of Michio, my phantom boy*. For Hanako, who had found her calling, these words marked a major turning point in her life.

Chapter 7

In Pursuit of Women's Suffrage: 1928–1938

Age 35 to 45

Women Writers

In the early fall of 1928, Hanako spent an afternoon at Hiroko Katayama's house. Hiroko studied English from Beatrice Lane, the wife of Buddhist scholar Daisetsu Suzuki[82], and went on to translate Irish literature under the pen name Mineko Matsumura. Hiroko's son Tatsukichi and daughter Fusako inherited her literary gift, publishing works under the pen names Tetsutaro Yoshimura and Soei, respectively. Hiroko's husband had died in 1920, so she now lived alone.

Hanako had translated *The Prince and The Pauper* at Hiroko's urging and had poured her heart and soul into the work. Her skillful translation, coupled with the excellence of the original, resulted in favourable reviews, bringing Hanako's ability to the attention of the literary world. She was deeply indebted to Hiroko, who had led her from the dark despair of loss back to the path of literature. In Hanako's words:

> I think that had I not lived near my friend and mentor, Mrs. Katayama, I would have been consumed with just surviving the storms of life that raged about me and could easily have lost my dreams and my love for literature.[83]

The purpose of Hanako's visit on this day in early September was to report on a send-off party in Ueno Seiyoken restaurant which had been held for the highly popular writer Nobuko Yoshiya.

"How was Shigure?" Hiroko asked while pouring Hanako a steaming cup of tea.

"She was in excellent health! Her usual dashing self, always so considerate of everyone!"

Shigure Hasegawa, a senior member of Nobutsuna Sasaki's tanka society, Chikuhaku-kai, as well as a powerful playwright and theatre critic, had organized the farewell party. In July of the same year, she had founded the monthly magazine *Nyonin geijutsu* (Women's Arts) to promote women's liberation. This magazine served as the stage for such prominent women writers as Fumiko Hayashi[84], Kanoko Okamoto, Michiyo Mori, Fumiko Enchi, Ichiko Kamichika, and Yuriko Miyamoto. The contents were highly progressive and included not just literature but also articles that alluded to revolutionary ideas, such as reports on developments in the Soviet Union.

The launching of *Women's Arts* was followed soon after by *Hinotori* (Phoenix), a literary magazine dedicated to works by women writers that was established by Tomeko Watanabe[85], another member of Chikuhaku-kai. Both Hiroko Katayama and Hanako were members of the *Phoenix* coterie.

"Lots of famous people came," Hanako continued. "Of course, Shigure's husband, Otokichi Mikami[86] was there, as well as Soho Tokutomi, Kan Kikuchi[87], and Teppei Kataoka, not to mention Ryutaro Saito from the *Bungei shunju* literary magazine."

At a time when travelling to another country was a major event, Nobuko Yoshiya, Japan's most successful author, was going all the way to Europe, and her send-off attracted over two hundred people. All the leading women in Japan's literary world, including not only authors but also editors, reporters, and critics, were gathered there: women such as Akiko Yosano[88], Hanayo Ikuta, Kuniko Imai[89], Chiyo Uno[90], Yaeko Nogami, Yasuko Miyake, Taiko Hirabayashi[91], and Shizue Masugi.

To describe just a few, Taiko Hirabayashi, a socialist who had been arrested for her activism, wrote proletarian literature that drew on her experiences of severe hardship while living in Korea and Manchuria. Fumiko Hayashi, who had published poetry and children's stories while barely eking out a living with a series of menial jobs, would soon win immense popularity as a fiction writer. Shizue Masugi, a reporter, was just starting out as a novelist, and her lover, the celebrated writer and artist Saneatsu Mushanokoji, had entrusted her with a parting gift for Yoshiya, whose talent he greatly admired.

The array of illustrious guests proved that the age of women writers had finally arrived. The first prominent female author in contemporary Japan was Ichiyo Higuchi, and she was followed by a handful of other outstanding women writers. But Japanese women writers did not begin to flourish until the mid-1920s, when opportunities for women to publish their works increased. They quickly demonstrated their ability and began to assert their presence.

※

"Five yen is certainly a tidy sum just to attend a party," remarked Hiroko when Hanako paused in her detailed report. Hiroko herself had not attended, and her tone was indifferent. In fact, she frequently complained that she was tired of everything and avoided lively gatherings as if she found them distasteful.

Hanako suspected that one reason for Hiroko's world-weariness was the death of novelist Ryunosuke Akutagawa. Acclaimed as a literary genius and the father of the Japanese short story, Akutagawa had been Hiroko's friend and supporter, and his suicide the previous year had dealt her a heavy blow. Hiroko also mourned the demise of pure literature, which Akutagawa's death seemed to symbolize. She disliked the proletarian literature that had risen in its stead, and found it hard to accept the popular trends of mixing literature with political ideologies aimed at overthrowing the current system or portraying the realities of working-class life.

Hiroko's upbringing, as well as her comportment and literary preferences, were clearly distinct from those of up-and-coming writers. Yet Hanako knew that inside she concealed a keen sense of humor, kindness, and ardent enthusiasm. Influenced by Irish literature, she was also a bit of a dreamer.

"When my husband was alive," Hiroko once confided in Hanako, "I was quite swayed by his opinions you know. Often I didn't act on my own ideas. Today, I went for a walk to Magome and threw my wedding ring into Benten Pond. 'This ends my bond with you,' I said. It was exhilarating!"

Uncharacteristically, her face was flushed with excitement during this admission, and the mystical image of Hiroko's wedding ring lying at the bottom of Benten Pond, hidden beneath its cloudy green waters, set Hanako's own heart aflutter.

Hiroko and the author Akutagawa first met at a literary salon Hiroko held at her villa in Karuizawa after her husband's death in 1920. Akutagawa's autobiographical novel *Aru aho no issho* (A Fool's Life), which was published posthumously, contains this passage:

> He met a woman who could match him even in the realm of ability, but narrowly escaped this danger by composing lyrical poems such as "Koshibito."[92] To do so was somehow heartrending, like brushing glittering snow from a tree trunk.

After Akutagawa's death, the poet Tatsuo Hori revealed that the woman who was the subject of the poem "Koshibito" and whom Akutagawa had described as "a woman who could match him even in the realm of ability," was in fact Hiroko Katayama. But Hiroko did not like her literary and spiritual connection with her friend being made an object of curiosity. When Akutagawa died, she quietly expressed her feelings in the following poem:

> On that day at dawn
> I gazed absently at the garden in the rain
> not knowing that somewhere far away
> death had taken him.

Many considered Hiroko to have no interest in the world, but Hanako guilelessly regaled her with news of the event. "Akiko Yosano's speech was marvellous too. But to tell you the truth, what I most wished you could have seen was the dramatic entrance of Chiyo Uno and her friend, dressed in brand new *yukata*."

"How nice," Hiroko murmured, a smile touching her lips. "They must have looked beautiful."

"Beautiful is an understatement. They stole the show. I simply can't help but admire such daring behaviour."

The guest of honour, Nobuko Yoshiya, had worn a white dress to her send-off party while the other women all wore gorgeous, colourful kimonos. The guests remained chatting in the waiting room for some time after the appointed hour when the party was to start. Hanako was talking cheerfully with people she knew, enjoying the lively atmosphere, when suddenly Chiyo Uno, a well-known author and fashion leader, swept into the room with her friend. They were both dressed in white cotton *yukata* and had slipped their bare feet into lacquered wooden sandals. The gathering stared, arrested by the unexpected charm of their appearance, and an exclamation of surprise and admiration rose from everyone's lips.

"I knew you'd all be dressed in formal kimono," Chiyo had explained. "We don't have anything so fancy to wear, but it would be a shame if we couldn't come just because of that. I felt sure we'd be accepted if we came in fresh, new clothes, so we walked up the hill to join you here." Chiyo then made the rounds, greeting everyone in her charming way.

"Just looking at them was invigorating, like drinking a tonic," said Hanako, who had been completely captivated by Chiyo Uno's free spirit. "Surely there's nothing more absurd than to be caught up in old customs and worry about what others might think."

"I'm sure you're right," Hiroko said. "But you know, dear Hana, there are some people whose position in society won't let them ignore tradition so boldly. On the surface, such behaviour appears liberated and refreshing, but what we wear can draw disdain at unexpected times from unexpected people. Personally, I think I'd rather always dress appropriately for the occasion."

For someone raised in the upper class like Hiroko, this was a legitimate view, but Hanako, who was fifteen years her junior, could not help but be intoxicated by the new trends in the literary world, which appeared like a lush garden filled with flowers of varied colours, shapes, and fragrances.

Partly due to the influence of proletarian literature, which remained ascendant throughout the 1920s, many authors were drawn to themes rooted in reality, and novels that questioned the low status of women and social contradictions drew much attention. Fumiko Hayashi's *Aki ga kitanda horoki* (Fall Is Come: Diary of a Vagabond), which was published in serial form in *Women's Arts* in 1928, was an autobiographical novel of her experiences of living in extreme poverty while she switched from job to job and lover to lover. Two years later, it was published under the title *Horoki* (Diary of a Vagabond), and became a runaway bestseller. The portrayal of a young woman who, even in the midst of poverty, loves literature and continues to dream, won many hearts, Hanako's included. She later wrote:

> The women in Hayashi's novels strive with heart and soul to find hope as they stoically endure their fate, and maybe even unwittingly offer great support to those around them. Although delicate and reserved by nature, her protagonists have a strength, a passion for life that makes them struggle to rise again. When I read Hayashi's works, a warmth that is hard to describe surges through my breast.[93]

Hanako Pursues her Calling: Translating Family Literature

Hanako got to know Nobuko Yoshiya through contributing stories to *Shojo gaho* (Illustrated Girls' Monthly), when they were both in their early twenties. Yoshiya's serial novel *Hana monogatari* (Flower Tales) had already won her a wide readership, and she remained an immensely popular author. Hanako, on the other hand, had developed her reputation much more slowly, weathering many hardships in life as she pursued her career in writing and translating books in the family literature genre. But when it came to their views on stories for women and girls and on their high ideals for family literature, Hanako and Yoshiya found in each other a rare soulmate.

Just as households in Japan were ruled by the patriarchal system in which men came first, the world of letters was a man's world. Literature critics and intellectuals contemptuously dismissed girls' novels and family literature as books for women and children. Yoshiya's adoring readers saw her as a charismatic figure, but critics refused to consider her works seriously on their literary merit, declaring them to be "sickly sweet and mawkish and harmful to the minds of young people."

Yoshiya had a generous nature. Women writers trusted her, and she was also popular with male writers, yet for years she struggled with the lack of understanding for the literary nature of her works.

"Don't pay any attention to what the critics say," Hanako consoled her. "Girls growing into women really need what you're writing." Hanako had felt the power of Yoshiya's works to nurture the minds of young people when she was a teacher at Yamanashi Eiwa Girls School. The idealistic and romantic elements in these works enriched the reader's emotions far more than works that were dry and bland. And she was certain that the sordid, erotic love and complicated relationships portrayed in recent novels by popular male writers would be far more harmful.

Just as Hanako was a fan of Yoshiya's works, Yoshiya also loved Hanako's translations. Once she asked Hanako, "Is there any novel in the West that has no romance in it but is still a fascinating read? If there is, please share it with me. But remember, it must be so interesting I can't put it down."

These words stayed in Hanako's mind until it suddenly occurred to her to send Yoshiya *The Prince and the Pauper*. Soon after, she received a thank-you letter.

Written on an evening at the beginning of spring
Tonight I sat by the stove in my little cabin with snow on

the roof absorbed in *The Prince and The Pauper*. Although I started out with a slight sense of obligation, the book was so enchanting, I couldn't put it down. I finished it all in one go. I can see why Mrs. Twain waited impatiently for her husband to finish each page so she could read it, and why she praised it so highly.

I was stunned and even envious to learn that the author, a man in his forties, spent two years writing it, each day looking forward to his wife's response.

I offer this letter with respect for your translation and gratitude for this book.

The next time they met, Yoshiya exclaimed, "That was a wonderful book," and gushed over Hanako's translation.

Translation was not yet considered an independent profession. Rather, it was seen merely as a way for English literature scholars or authors and poets with some foreign language ability to hone their literary skills. In addition, very few people understood the need for translations of the family literature genre, which Hanako valued so highly, and producing such works was relegated to a tiny corner of the publishing world.

In the preface to her translation of Perry Montanye's *The Blossomy Cottage* published by Kyobunkwan at the end of 1929, Hanako wrote:

I gaze with affection at my own courage in sending this innocent, cheerful little tale into the vortex of modern life with its addiction to intense sensory stimulation. I am sure that this humble book *The Blossomy Cottage* will be loved by those who long for beauty, peace and innocence in daily life. I thank the American publisher Abbington and the author Perry Montayne for so generously giving me the right to translate this book.

December 1929 Hanako Muraoka

Compensation for translated works was low, and Hanako continued to write nursery tales and girls' fiction in order to support her family. She worked at her desk until dawn, spurred on by a photo of her son, Michio.

The Women's Suffrage Movement

Female writers, who were still by far a minority, forged bonds that transcended literary styles and genres. One of the factors that united them was the rising women's suffrage movement. The League for the Realization of Women's Suffrage was formed in December 1924 and renamed the Women's Suffrage League the following year. Its representatives were Ochimi Kubushiro of the Japan Woman's Christian Temperance Union and Fusae Ichikawa, who had further broadened her knowledge by visiting leading suffragists in the United States. The invitation to the league's organizational meeting declared:

> Today, when many women are undertaking influential action in every arena of society, today, when daily life, which depends on women, is so intricately related to the life of society and the nation, it is only natural that women should be involved in politics.

The following year, in 1925, however, the Imperial Diet[94] passed the Universal Male Suffrage Law. The law awarded most men over the age of twenty-five the right to vote, yet continued to deny universal suffrage to women. The rage women felt at this injustice motivated writers, activists, and various women's organizations to launch meetings, lectures, and petition campaigns, creating a groundswell that swept up politically aware women from all fields. The battle to raise women's social status became the mission of these feminists who were ahead of their time.

In 1926, as Japan entered the Showa period (1926–1989), women's voices rose to such a height that the government could no longer ignore them, and several times bills for the realization of women's suffrage were presented in the Imperial Diet. Each time, however, they were defeated by the discriminatory view that giving women the vote was incompatible with Japan's traditional family system. In 1930, such a bill came very close to passing, but just before it went through, the all-male Diet was swayed by the baseless remarks of some of its members. Women's suffrage, they claimed, would tarnish the fine customs of Japan, and the bill should be rejected out of respect for women, and in consideration of women's calling and responsibility.

Having studied under Asako Hirooka and the late Kajiko Yajima, the former head of the Temperance Union, who had passed away in 1925, Hanako participated actively in the movement to demand equality. The acquisition of equal rights for men and women was her ardent desire, particularly when she thought of the hardships her mother and her sisters had borne simply because of their gender.

Hanako's youngest sister, Yuki, had married into a farm household in Shizuoka, and as this family was comparatively better off, Hanako's parents had recently moved in with them. Hanako, however, had little time to enjoy the relief this brought her, because soon after she received word from her sister Chiyo, who was in Hokkaido, that their younger sister Umeko was in dire circumstances.

Umeko was eleven years younger than Hanako. Immediately after finishing girls school, she had been hired as a live-in servant by settlers in Hokkaido near Chiyo. But winters in the northern region were particularly harsh, and her employers were so poor that Umeko was forced to work barefoot, even in winter, because she could not afford to buy shoes.

Chiyo, who could not bear to see Umeko suffer so, begged Hanako to help. "I long to help her myself," she wrote, "but as a wife, I have no rights whatsoever in this situation. There's nothing I can do."

Umeko was born after Hanako had entered the dorm at Toyo Eiwa Girls School, and they had had very little contact with each other as children. But still, Umeko was her younger sister, her blood relation. Hanako immediately summoned her sister to Omori to live with her and

Keizo. Freed from her cruel circumstances, Umeko flourished, spending her spare time reading Hanako's translations and the stories she wrote. She went to church with Hanako and Keizo on Sundays, helped Hide with the housework, and made Keizo's meals. Keizo in turn taught Umeko how to fillet a fish and sometimes took her to see kabuki, traditional Japanese theatre.

For Hanako, reading books at school had cultivated freedom of thought. As a writer and translator, she longed to foster young people's aspirations and ideals through books. She hoped each book would become a seed that nurtured happy families and helped create a world in which women could live fully.

In 1930, she and Keizo began publishing a periodical called *Katei* (Home) from Seiransha, the company they had established together in their Omori home. Their aim was to promote family literature that could be read and enjoyed by children and parents alike. The first edition carried Hanako's "Seikatsu-ha" (School of Daily Life) declaration.

> In the realm of literature, I love novels centred in daily life. Through outstanding original works we can assess our own lifestyle objectively. I seek an organic literature where the pulse of daily life itself beats throughout the work. For this reason, I dislike literature which pursues the deformed, the perverted, the erotic or the grotesque. I will pitch my camp in this modest field of "family literature" and advocate for literature rooted in the school of daily life.

In this periodical, Hanako published her translation of Eleanor Hodgman Porter's *Sister Sue*[95] in serial form. Material was also contributed by Nobuko Yoshiya, Tsuneko Nakazato, who would go on to become a prize-winning novelist, Hanayo Ikuta, Sumiko Tokunaga, and Miss Frances Gertrude Hamilton, a Canadian missionary from Prince Edward Island who was serving as the principal of Hanako's alma mater. Readers were invited to submit stories and tanka, the best of which would be printed in the periodical. Byakuren Yanagiwara helped select the winners in the tanka category while Chiyo Kitagawa, a well-known writer of children's literature, assisted with choosing winners in the story category.

When the Greater Japan Union of Women's Associations (Dainippon Togo Fujinkai), an organization under the Ministry of Education, began publishing a magazine of the same name, Hanako and Keizo renamed their periodical *Seiran* (Blue Orchid) from the February edition of 1932 to avoid confusion. They worked hard to produce this publication that bore their company name, instilling in it their hopes and dreams.

During this period, however, the Japanese army's invasion of China, which had begun in 1931, was accelerating, and the conflict between the two countries intensified, much to the concern of many powerful Western nations. When the League of Nations refused in 1933 to recognize Manchuko[96], the puppet state of Manchuria, Japan withdrew from the League in protest.

Meanwhile, in Japan, radicals within the Imperial Japanese Navy stormed the official residence of Prime Minister Tsuyoshi Inukai on May 15, 1932, and assassinated him in what became known as the May 15 Incident. With the death of the prime minister, who had supported the constitution and tried to rein in the military, the military's control over politics increased.

Radio Auntie

In the early spring of 1932, Hanako sat in her parlour staring in stunned amazement at a representative of Radio JOAK (the predecessor of the Japan Broadcasting Corporation, known in Japan as NHK [Nihon Hoso Kyokai]). He had just proposed that she become a regular radio personality. Radios had spread throughout the country with phenomenal speed, becoming an essential fixture in every living room, and JOAK was preparing to launch its first children's program: *Children's Hour (Kodomo no jikan*). It would air for thirty minutes daily from six in the evening and include story readings, a chorus of singers, a music ensemble, and radio plays. A five-minute segment at the end of the program called the *Children's Newspaper* (*Kodomo no shimbun*) would present news content directed at children. Until this time, the general consensus had been that children should not be told what was going on in the world; that they would become better people if they were raised without such knowledge. The radio station, however, was planning to make a radical departure by informing children of the state of the nation and daily newsworthy events, an approach that was in line with the government's new educational policy.

"Yes, of course, I agreed it would be good to have a program to inform children about domestic and foreign news," Hanako protested to her visitor. "But I could never do that myself. I've never done anything but desk work." Several months previously, in response to the station's questionnaire survey, Hanako had indicated that she was in favour of producing a children's news program, but it had never occurred to her that she would be singled out as the voice to convey that news.

Keizo stepped into the room. "What's all the fuss?" he asked.

"The radio station thinks that because the program is for children, it would be better to have a female voice as well as a male voice. But he said they'd like me to do it."

"Really? What an interesting idea. I wonder who recommended you?"

Sensing that he had found in Keizo a powerful ally, the man rattled off some names. "Mr. Sazanami Iwaya and Mr. Takehiko Kurushima. That settled it for everyone at the station."

"I see." Keizo leaned forward with an expression of keen interest. Sazanami Iwaya and Takehiko Kurushima were considered the country's greatest authorities on children's literature and had been dubbed the Grimm and Andersen of Japan. Iwaya was revered as a master story writer, but to Hanako, whose childhood dreams had been nurtured by his *Sekai otogi banashi* (Fairy Tales of the World), he seemed more like a close friend. When she was still a student, he had come to give a talk at her school, and she had gazed up at him with awed affection. As for Takehiko Kurushima, since Radio JOAK's founding in 1925, he had established a solid reputation as a narrator of children's stories. Children loved this expert's rich, melodious voice.

In January 1927, not long after Michio had died, Hanako had spoken into the microphone for the first time in her life. The program was called *Family Hour*, and her topic had been family education through nursery tales. Her talk had been rated highly by everyone involved, and this, coupled with her long career as a story writer and her many contributions to children's culture, had convinced everyone that she was the right person for the job. She had also been strongly recommended by Toyoko Osawa, a former reporter for *Jiji shimbun* (Current Affairs Newspaper) who was now head of women's programming at JOAK.

Yet Hanako was still reluctant. "You have many professional announcers of your own," she protested. "Besides, I couldn't possibly present something like the news."

"But being the first female author to read the news is precisely what makes this so meaningful," Keizo reasoned. "Why not try it? If someone else had already done it, people would have something to compare and judge you by. But no one can criticize you if there's no precedent. You'll be free to develop your own style."

Keizo's ability to embrace new things like this without the slightest hesitation reminded Hanako that he was indeed Heikichi's son and had been raised in the liberal port town of Yokohama. She sent off the messenger from the radio station with the words, "I'll think it over carefully."

❀

Hanako's work was expanding beyond the field of literature. In addition to translation, story writing, and the editing work Tenma Nobechi had passed on to her for *Little Children of Light* and for *Women's News*, she was being invited to participate in an increasing number of discussion meetings and gatherings for various women's organizations. In addition, Toyo Eiwa Girls School had asked her to serve on the board of the alumni association with Chiyo Shiobara and to edit the school's history to commemorate its fiftieth anniversary. She was also giving lectures for teachers at various kindergartens that had been established by Canadian Methodist missionaries. One reason she had hesitated to accept the offer from Radio JOAK was that she did not want to leave Keizo at home alone more than she was already. If she took the broadcasting job, it would keep her away almost every night at dinnertime.

Hanako and Keizo had already been married thirteen years. Together, they had overcome hardships, reinforcing the bond between them. They jointly ran their publishing company, Seiransha, and they spent each evening sharing what had happened during the day and discussing literature. Keizo, who was well-versed not only in English but also in German and Latin and had a deep knowledge of the Bible, served as a valuable advisor for Hanako's translation work. He had been the first to suggest getting a washing machine so as to lighten the burden of housework and had understood the need to renovate the kitchen.

In an era when women in Japan were still expected to walk three steps behind their spouse, Hanako and Keizo walked side by side wherever they went, whether it was the neighbourhood store, the cinema, or the used bookstore. They were known in their neighbourhood as "lovebirds," and people often remarked that the only couple to be seen walking side by side other than the Muraokas were the "swank beggars," an elderly vagabond couple that frequented the Omori and Ikegami districts. They were called by a variety of nicknames, depending on the neighbourhood, such as the "dragging-skirts beggars" and the "uh-huh beggars[97]." They wore every scrap of clothing they could scavenge, which made them look like they were dressed in layers of rags. As the wife was blind, her husband walked solicitously beside her. Despite being vagabonds, they seemed happy, leaving an indelible impression on the minds of those they passed on the street.

Hanako and Keizo were still deeply in love, as indicated by the letter Keizo sent to Hanako on May 4, 1932 while she was away in Nagano giving lectures at Asahi Kindergarten. Hanako was thirty-nine and Keizo, forty-five.

To Mrs. Hanako

May 2nd. Prepared magazines for shipping from six in the morning.[*1] Off to Tokyo in the afternoon, about the business for Mr. [...]mae and Mr. Matsumiya. Returned home and kept packing magazines. Hayashi came to help. Evening. Always the hardest time of day. Sea bream and rice for dinner using the sea bream dear Ume[*2] brought. So lonely I read *Bungei shunju.* But then I couldn't sleep.

May 3rd, morning, off to Tokyo for job with Mrs. Matsumiya. Finished around one o'clock but didn't feel like going home. Watched a movie at Hogaku Theatre. *The Broken Lullaby.* Thought Barrymore's father was the best, then the actress who played his mother. Holmes, who played Paul, and Carroll, who played Elsa, weren't as good.

Made a bath. During dinner, the Nakamura sisters came over, followed by Kenjiro[*3] and Hayashi. They all came to have a bath. Once they were gone, I was all alone again.

But my spirits lift with the thought that with each passing day, the return of my loved one draws nearer. Like a child I count on my fingers, three, four, five, six, seven. Just four more days to endure, I tell myself, and read *Bungei shunju* again.

May 4th. Kenjiro comes. I send off *Akai bara*[*4] (Red Rose) and *Oyama no yuki* (Mountain Snow) in response to two orders by postcard. I prepare packages for Kuniko Imai, Mr. Wang, and Mr. Tsutsumi, among others. Tonight will be mahjong, I think.

The night when I can hold my darling Hanako again draws closer day by day. How my arms long to hold you, and my lips, to give you a hard kiss...I hesitate to put the rest into words.

Darling Hanako. So active, so WONDERFUL!

Come back fit as a fiddle. Without you, work is boring, and I'm bad-tempered. Darling Hanako.

May 4   From Keizo

1 *Seiran* (Blue Orchid). 2 Umeko, Hanako's younger sister. 3 Hanako's younger brother.

4 A collection of Hanako's children's stories published by Seiransha.

That Hanako could balance both work and family was in large part thanks to Keizo's cooperation and unstinted devotion, which had never wavered since the days they courted, and it was from these that she drew her energy. At Keizo's urging, and also in response to the passionate persuasion of JOAK's Toyoko Osawa, who insisted that the presence of women in this field would contribute to women's suffrage, Hanako finally agreed to be the voice for the *Children's Newspaper* segment. The first broadcast was aired on June 1, 1932.

A group of experts, including Sazanami Iwaya and Takehiko Kurushima, as well as authorities on child psychology, health, and education, met regularly to review the content. The main focus of their discussions was how to convey to children the course of the war in China.

Hanako was to read the news every other week, taking turns with Isoji Sekiya, a story narrator who was in charge of the station's children's programming. The Muraokas made a new household rule: supper would be at six-thirty during the weeks that Hanako was not on the radio and at seven-thirty during the weeks that she was.

Hanako's younger sister Umeko, who had lived with them since she had left Hokkaido, had married Iwao Sakata, a budding artist and calligrapher who had been introduced to her by Kokei Kobayashi, an artist who lived in the same area. Hanako and Keizo had built four rental homes on their property. Keizo's younger brother, Noboru, and his family, who had lost their Yokohama home during the earthquake, had moved into one of these, while Umeko and her husband had moved into another.

Noboru and his wife already had three children, one boy and two girls, and Umeko gave birth to a daughter in 1932 on September 13, the same date Michio had been born. Keizo chose her name: Midori. A year and a half later, Umeko gave birth to another daughter, Haruko. Keizo and Hanako, who did not conceive another child after Michio's death, even though they longed for one, doted on their nieces and nephew. Whenever Hanako held these little ones in her arms, she felt motherly love swell once again inside her; especially for Midori. Hanako and Keizo could not believe Midori sharing Michio's birthday was mere coincidence. When they told Umeko and Iwao of their desire to raise and cherish Midori as their own daughter, Umeko and her husband granted their request with a smile.[98]

✿

When it was time for the children's news program, children all over the country installed themselves in front of the radio. Hanako's voice, gentle yet dynamic, won their hearts. She always started with the same greeting: "Good day to you little citizens of Japan! It's your news time." The following excerpts from two different episodes offer a sample of the program's content.

June 1, 1929, the first broadcast: Our Precious Imperial Diet

The Imperial Diet. This topic may seem a bit difficult for our little listeners, but listen carefully because you'll find it in section twelve of the Japanese-language textbook for sixth grade. It's also in the moral lessons textbook. Since 1890, for forty-two years, the Imperial Diet has gathered every year because that's the rule. The rules of this country are called the Constitution of the Empire of Japan[99]. Today, the Imperial Diet will gather for the sixty-second time in its history. The Diet has two parts, the House of Representatives and the House of Peers, and they decide on important matters for the country. The opening ceremony will be held at the House of Peers, and His Majesty the Emperor will depart from the Imperial Palace at ten-thirty-five in the morning to make an Imperial visit and bestow a gracious greeting on the assembled peers and representatives. The Imperial Diet is usually held for three months from the end of the year to the following March. This time, however, the Diet gathered for an extraordinary session and will finish in two weeks, on the fourteenth of this month.

A Lost Crocodile on the Shore of Kyushu
(from a broadcast the following year)

A lone crocodile crawled ashore at Ikitsuki-cho in Nagasaki prefecture on Kyushu. Crocodiles live in hot tropical areas and are so strong they can even beat that king of beasts, the lion. As you can imagine, there was a big uproar. At last, a hunter caught him, but it seems that this creature from the tropics found it very chilly here.

The *Children's Newspaper* delighted not just children, at whom it was aimed, but also adults. It was broadcast at the supper hour, and the whole family listened together. The fact that it was short suited busy housewives well. Whereas the regular news focused on serious topics, such as politics, economics, and military reports, the content of the *Children's Newspaper* was lighter, often eliciting a chuckle from the audience, and included items that would have been found on the local news pages.

Thanks to the radio program, Hanako Muraoka soon became a household name, which resulted in some unforeseen and perplexing problems. At the end of the program, Hanako closed with the words, "Fare you well and good night!" She said it with feeling, conjuring up an image of her listeners beyond the microphone. Her distinctive style was so popular that people began to imitate her. One day she dropped into a variety show at the Hibiya Public Hall only to hear the comedian on stage announce, "And now, here's Kikuko Muraoka" and then proceed to impersonate Hanako's voice. Even though no one knew what she looked like, Hanako left hastily, blushing furiously as laughter filled the hall. The performance must have been a hit, because the comedian went on to repeat it on radio variety programs.

Imposters also appeared. One ordered textile from a clothier in Kanda in Hanako's name, while yet another, who claimed to be "Hanako's husband," requested geisha at a restaurant, and Keizo received the bill.

Letters from listeners arrived daily at the station with messages such as this:

> *Your voice sounded a bit odd today, Auntie Muraoka. Did you catch a cold? Please keep warm and take care of your health. Get better soon.*
> *Goodbye.*

Letters like the above, written in wobbly, childish script, brought a smile to Hanako's face, while others, such as the following, brought tears to her eyes.

> Our child died last week, but she listened to the Children's Newspaper every day, and kept calling you, "Radio Auntie. Radio Auntie."

The knowledge that her voice was a comfort to sick children and the mothers who nursed them strengthened Hanako's sense of purpose in her broadcasting work. At the same time, an increasing number of people wrote to her to consult about their lives, enclosing return postage. Their questions ranged from "I want to study in Tokyo. What would be a good school?" to "Should I remarry or should I stay single for the rest of my life?" As she read these letters, Hanako felt the burden that also came with being a radio personality.

War Approaches

The Second Sino-Japanese War broke out in 1937, five years after the radio program first went to air. Streets in every Japanese town and city were filled with parading citizens bearing lanterns inscribed with the word *hissho*, "victory." The following year, the National Mobilization Law was proclaimed, requiring the citizens of Japan, who guarded the home front, to fully and completely support the military regime.

Hanako when she worked as an editor for the Christian Literature Society of Japan in Tsukiji in 1919. *Toyo Eiwa Jogakuin Archives*

Cherished items Hanako Muraoka kept on her desk.
Toyo Eiwa Jogakuin Archives

Hanako's personal library containing her favourite Japanese and English books that nurtured her through each era, as well as her dictionaries and translated works. *Toyo Eiwa Jogakuin Archives*

Love letters exchanged between Hanako and Keizo. Together, they overcame many hardships and remained devoted to each other to the end of their lives. *Toyo Eiwa Jogakuin Archives*

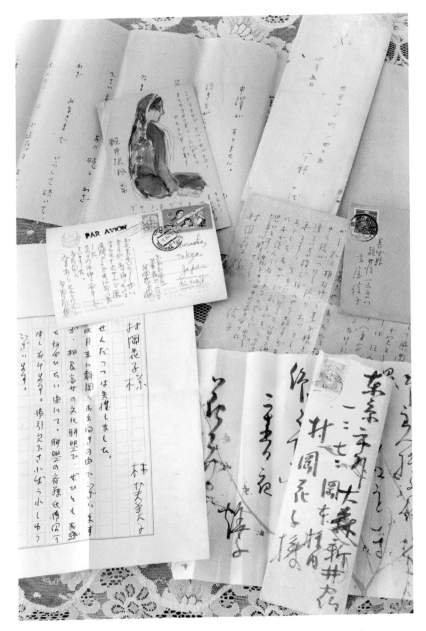

Correspondence with people she loved and admired gave Hanako strength. Letters from such friends as Byakuren Yanagiwara (Akiko Ito), Nobuko Yoshiya, Fumiko Hayashi, Fusae Ichikawa, and Chiyo Uno, all of whom were well-known figures. *Toyo Eiwa Jogakuin Archives*

Hanako's copy of *Anne of Green Gables* received from Canadian missionary Loretta Leonard Shaw, as well as Hanako's handwritten Japanese translation. *Toyo Eiwa Jogakuin Archives*

Passing on her love to her daughter and grandchildren. Summer 1968 at Hanako's home in Omori. From the left: Hanako, her daughter, Midori, and her eldest granddaughter, Mie. Front: Eri, the author of this biography. Hanako passed away on October 25 of the same year. She never realized her dream of going to Canada. *Toyo Eiwa Jogakuin Archives*

Hanako's first trip abroad in 1967 when she visited her daughter, Midori, and family in America. She was seventy-four. From the left: Hanako, Midori, Miyo Shibata, Mie. *Toyo Eiwa Jogakuin Archives*

Hanako's granddaughters: Mie Muraoka (left), a translator, and Eri Muraoka, the author of this book. Hanako always wore kimono, and her granddaughters are holding a kimono sash that was one of her favourites. The sisters reproduced Hanako's study and made it into a memorial room. For many years, they hosted a small open house there several times a month. The memorial room has since been moved to Toyo Eiwa Jogakuin. *Toyo Eiwa Jogakuin Archives*

Various women's associations, which had made remarkable contributions to relief and recovery efforts following the Great Kanto Earthquake of 1923 and had continued to lobby the government to improve women's social status, were reorganized into the Patriotic Women's Association[100], the Greater Japan National Defense Women's Association[101], and similar organizations. Donning aprons and tying back their kimono sleeves with *tasuki* cords, women banded together to make *senninbari* and give soldiers a rousing sendoff when they were mobilized.

Senninbari, meaning "stitches by a thousand people," were protective amulets. Inspired by the legend that tigers could travel a thousand *ri* (about four thousand kilometres) and still come home safely, women took turns sewing one French knot each in crimson thread onto strips of bleached cotton. Each strip would end up with a thousand stitches made by a thousand women. Women born in the Year of the Tiger, however, were asked to sew multiple stitches on each strip because they were believed to bring good fortune. A soldier's mother, sister, or wife would ask women in the neighbourhood to help, as well as strangers passing by. No one would think of turning down such a request as everyone prayed for the safety of the men fighting in foreign lands. Sometimes, women sewed one five-*sen* coin into the cloth to help soldiers pass safely over "the death line," which is pronounced *shisen* in Japanese and is thus a homonym for "four *sen* coins." To help the soldiers win desperate battles, pronounced *kusen* in Japanese, which is a homonym for "nine *sen* coins," the women would sew in one ten-*sen* coin. The *senninbari* cloths were usually wrapped around the soldiers' waists in the battlefield. Women's organizations made many and placed them in *imon bukuro*—"comfort bags" that were sent to the soldiers overseas.

Top priority in resources, both human and material, was given to the war effort, and everyone had to obey the government. Even the Muraoka family's pet dog, Teru, was affected. In the spring of 1938, five-year-old Midori and four-year-old Haruko came running into the study which faced the garden. They rushed over to where Hanako sat translating.

"Have you seen Teru?" Midori said breathlessly. "We can't find him anywhere."

"Teru's gone!" Haruko chimed in. "He was there this morning!"

A year before, a little puppy, white all over except for a brown spot at the tip of his tail and one around each of his winsome eyes, had wandered over to where the girls were playing and followed them home. When he did not leave, they named him Teru and made him a doghouse in a corner of the garden. He grew quickly and was soon a favourite with the neighbourhood children.

Midori and Haruko loved Teru. When they came home from kindergarten, Teru would jump up and down and wave his thin little tail vigorously. But now, he seemed to have vanished, leaving only his chain and collar behind.

Hanako laid down her pen and turned to face Midori and Haruko, who were gazing up at her with worried eyes. Forcing herself to keep her tone cheerful, she said, "Teru has gone to work."

"Work?"

"That's right. Today, some soldiers came and asked him, 'Won't you come with us and serve Japan?'"

"And Teru went with them?"

"Yes. He told me with his eyes, 'I have to go now. Please say goodbye to Midori and Haruko for me and thank them.'"

"But we wanted to say goodbye too!" Large tears rolled down the girls' cheeks for some time, and Hanako had to fight back tears of her own and force herself to smile.

The military had begun to interfere with the lives of ordinary citizens, both men and women, young and old, as well as with children's education. Now they were even recruiting dogs for the war effort, assigning them to guard the camps and carry mail. Teru was just a skinny little dog used to being the family pet. How could he ever survive in battle? But Hanako had no intention of telling the children what would happen to him if he turned out to be of no use.

❁

All throughout dinner, Midori worried, trying with childlike logic to imagine what might have happened to Teru. The next day at the radio station, one of the news items prepared by the staff was about the exploits on the front line of a pet dog that had belonged to a family in Hokkaido. No name was given, but when Hanako faced the mic, on the spur of the moment, she called the dog Teru-go, reporting that he was in good health. (In Japanese, the suffix "go" is added to the names of things such as ships, planes, and machines. To the girls, it probably sounded like Teru had been given a special title for his heroic service to the country.)

Midori and Haruko, who had tuned in to listen, missed the fact that the dog was from Hokkaido but distinctly heard the name Teru-go. The following afternoon, they proudly announced to their friends who had come over to play, "Teru was on the news yesterday!"

"He went to war and is helping the soldiers. What a great dog!"

"That's right. He was given the name Teru-go after going to war. It's a more important name than just Teru."

Midori and Haruko sounded bright and cheerful, and their friends were duly impressed. Inwardly, however, Hanako apologized to the girls, and to her listeners. She knew the war was a serious matter and that she should convey the news accurately to the children. In fact, the military intelligence agency had set up an office in Radio JOAK, and even the *Children's Newspaper* was censored. But Hanako could not bear to rob the girls of hope by telling them the truth. During that period, she wrote:

> I am sure that considering the current state of affairs, many people feel we should be picking more stories from the military and adapting them for children rather than including carefree content. But children in every age have always dreamed beautiful dreams. I believe that the more stressful the times, the more urgent the crises grownups face, the more compassion we should have for the unlimited sensitivity of children.[102]

Popular writers were being assigned as war correspondents to the Pen Brigade and sent off to China to write glowing reports of heroic Japanese soldiers fighting for their country. From the summer of the year the girls' dog Teru was drafted into the army, many of Hanako's close friends and colleagues, including Fumiko Hayashi, Nobuko Yoshiya, Kan Kikuchi, Haruo Sato, and Eiji Yoshikawa, were dispatched to the war, one after the other.

At the same time, women were becoming increasingly visible in society as a whole and had begun to demand a better standard of living as well as more opportunities to pursue cultural activities and other interests. On April 15, 1938, the same year that the Mobilization Law was enacted, the first cultural club was established for women who were not from the upper class. Called the Tokyo Women's Hall, it was located inside the Japan Theatre at Sukiyabashi, Ginza. Dedicated exclusively to enhancing the education and cultural refinement of women from the emerging urban middle-class, the club had no affiliation with a particular ideology or a specific movement.

The club received backing from leaders of the financial sector and cultural circles, most notably the industrialist Ichizo Kobayashi, who founded and successfully developed the Hankyu Railway Company by building entertainment and residential areas along the rail lines, establishing in the process the Takarazuka Revue, an all-female musical troupe, and the City Urban Planning Company. Yasubeh Itakura, president of Lait Cosmetics Company, was appointed as the cultural club's advisor, and Hanako Muraoka was appointed chief director. Other directors included such well-known female writers and activists as Nobuko Yoshiya, Kaoruko Hatoyama, Kotaka Otsuma, Kuniko Imai, Fusae Ichikawa, Azuma Moriya, Aki Fujiwara, Orie Wada, Shigeri Kaneko (Yamataka), Tsuruyo Takeoka, and Byakuren Yanagiwara.

The club's activities were wide-ranging. Lectures, concerts, and theatre performances that nurtured the mind and spirit were presented. Seminars to convey knowledge and skills useful for daily living were organized, and consultations on legal matters and childrearing were offered. Opportunities were provided to learn from the best teachers in many different fields, including flower arranging, tea ceremony, calligraphy, Noh songs, *nagauta* music, dance, Japanese Nihonga-style painting, Western painting, singing, dressmaking, and handicrafts. Inspired by the revolutionary idea of developing diverse skills in women, the club attracted over two thousand members in its first year.

❦

The previous year, Keiko Matsuda, the daughter of novelist Kodo Nomura, known for his work *Zenigata Heiji* (The Casebook of Detective Heiji Zenigata), had published her first book, *Shojo shosetsu monogatari nanatsu no tsubomi* (A Girls' Novel: Seven Buds). Having been raised in an environment that nurtured good taste, Keiko admired such authors as Louisa May Alcott (*Little Women*) and Johanna Spyri (*Heidi*) and began writing her own stories from the age of fifteen or sixteen. Her father, Kodo, read her work for the first time when she was twenty-one. He was impressed by its originality, intelligence, and humour. Although Keiko had not yet had any instruction from Japan's literary circles, Kodo was convinced that if she proceeded in this vein without becoming distracted or influenced by journalism, she could one day become a fine writer; one who could contribute to the nourishment of the human soul. He decided to publish her work himself and asked for Hanako's help. Upon reading it, Hanako perceived within it the same pure and wholesome spirit found in good-quality Western family literature. With her heart throbbing at the excitement of discovering a kindred spirit, she picked up her pen and began to write.

> **Dear Miss Keiko,**
> The first book I read in this new year of 1937 was your *Seven Buds*. Thank you! Thank you! Thank you! I cannot possibly thank you enough. I thank you not just for myself,

but also for the many young women who will read this book. Long ago, when I was your age, I also published my first book. Even now, just recalling that time makes my heart pound with an extraordinary excitement akin to fear. I can imagine that you too must be feeling the same way. I gaze at you, who are wrapped in that same odd feeling, one that could be termed either bliss or terror, with a deep affection, feeling as though the days of my youth have returned. You, who can see the world with a far more penetrating eye than the girls of my era, who can spread the wings of your imagination with ever so much more freedom, have penned a work that conveys a vibrance, a pulsating life such as I have never felt from any other book.... With *Seven Buds*, you have deftly filled in the gaps that were missing from books for girls in this country. How heartening it is to know that this is your maiden work and that you are still young. Before you awaits limitless development. What a blessing that is for the girls of this country. After *Seven Buds*, they can look forward to the glorious blooming of many flowers and a bountiful harvest of fruits....

Within the young Keiko, Hanako had glimpsed at last the birth of a Japanese Louisa May Alcott or Frances Hodgson Burnett. Hanako herself had once held the faint hope of becoming such a figure, but had been unable to realize that dream.

Hanako's letter overjoyed not only Keiko, but also all those who loved Keiko, including her father, Kodo, and her fiancé, the economist Tomoo Matsuda. It was included verbatim in the work's preface. Later, when Kodo visited Hanako accompanied by his beautiful, intelligent daughter, Hanako looked into her clear eyes and confirmed her conviction in Keiko's future as a writer.

In the same year, Chiyo Uno founded the fashion magazine *Style*. Young girls and housewives were delighted by the magazine's stylish layout and the smart fashion sense it conveyed. When it was first issued, Chiyo Uno asked Hanako to take out an annual subscription and provide articles. Hanako happily agreed to both requests. As a token of her gratitude, Chiyo presented Hanako with a sketch, the model for which was most likely Chiyo herself, made by her former lover, the artist Seiji Togo. In 1939 Chiyo married Takeo Kitahara, who collaborated with her on the fashion magazine. Nobuko Yoshiya and the artist Tsuguharu Foujita played the ceremonial role of matchmakers at the wedding, while Hanako served as the master of ceremonies at the reception.

In 1940, the Women's Literature Society was launched in response to a proposal by young female authors interested in pursuing literature. It was formed to provide mutual support in polishing the literary skills of women, regardless of the genre in which they wrote. Nobuko Yoshiya served as its representative, and its members included many familiar faces, including Chiyo Uno and Fumiko Hayashi.[103] Hanako also joined at the invitation of Nobuko Yoshiya.

Although it was wartime, the battlefield was far away, and the people of Japan were optimistic. Daily life went on peacefully.

Chapter 8

Proving Friendship in the Midst of War: 1939–1945

Age 46 to 52

Fumi-e: A Test of Faith

In September 1939, the German army invaded Poland at Hitler's command. Great Britain and France declared war on Germany and were joined soon after by other countries. The following year Japan entered into the Tripartite Pact with Germany and Italy, aligning itself against the Allied nations.

In the late nineteenth and early twentieth centuries, the dominant powers of the West had expanded and consolidated their strength through colonialism. Japan, which lagged behind the Western nations in modernization, sought to gain an equal footing by following the same route of colonialism, expanding its control over Korea, Taiwan, and China, where it sent Japanese troops and settlers. However, the scale of warfare in this new conflict would far exceed that of the First World War. Scientific and industrial developments in the years since had increased the variety and potency of weapons, and the number of armaments had swelled. If Japan was to successfully join the fray, it not only needed to mobilize soldiers, but also to enlist the wholehearted cooperation of all the men, women, and children who guarded the home front to ensure their commitment to their country.

The Japanese government demonized American and British people, calling them "Western brutes," and English was branded an enemy language. Some people threw stones at Hanako and Keizo's house, shouting "Traitors!" and breaking the windows. The stones barely missed Midori. Keizo stopped listening to his collection of classical records, and Hanako, who had always carried several English novels with her when she was out of the house, removed the books from her bag. Midori's primary school gathered the translated works of any authors from English-speaking countries and burned them in the schoolyard.

Burning books! Hanako thought when she heard this. *Imagine that! Twain, Dickens, Alcott, Burnett. All those masterworks thrown into a jumbled heap and set alight, black smoke billowing and ashes dancing in the sky.* Just the thought made her shudder.

❁

About a year before the Pacific War began, people from the Allied countries began packing their bags and preparing to leave Japan. Public opinion was such that even missionaries, who had devoted themselves to the development of Japanese society and culture since the mid-nineteenth century, feared for their safety.

Hanako desperately hoped that, through some feat of diplomacy, Japan might avoid going to war. The teachers at Toyo Eiwa Girls School, who had first taught her about other cultures, were from countries that were now viewed as enemies. Hanako's literary ability and the foundation that formed her character had all been fostered by missionaries from Canada, as well as from England and America.

Twenty-six years had passed since Hanako had graduated from the mission school, but familiar faces rose in her mind one after the other: Miss Blackmore, who had returned home due to advanced age in 1925; Miss Allen, who had supervised Hanako's graduation thesis; Miss Craig, with her kind smile who had passed away in 1923; the late Miss Kobayashi, the model student who became a teacher; Miss Kamo, the dorm mother who was now retired; and Miss Robertson and Miss Strothard from Yamanashi Eiwa. Wherever they might be, Hanako was certain that all the women she had met through Toyo Eiwa must have been deeply distressed by the current situation and the world's obsession with war.

Hanako, Chiyo Shiobara, and other alumni went to the school to bid farewell to the missionaries who had carried on the legacy of such teachers as Miss Blackmore and Miss Craig. Toyo Eiwa had been rebuilt for its fiftieth anniversary in 1934 and was now a modern building designed by American architect William Merrell Vories[104]. The original school uniform, with its wide *hakama* pants, had been replaced by a navy pleated skirt, a sailor top with two gold lines along the collar and cuffs, and a garnet scarf, the colour of Canadian maple leaves in fall. The designer was the school's principal, Miss Hamilton, from Prince Edward Island, who was known for her fashion sense, and the uniform was very popular with the students.

The new assembly auditorium was named the Margaret Craig Memorial Hall in honour of Miss Craig's contributions. The hall's ceiling rose in a high vault, and through the gracefully arched windows poured a gentle light. A stately altar stood in the centre of the stage while on the wall on either side hung large, framed calligraphies, one of the word *keishin* (Reverence[105]) and another of the word *hoshi* (Service[106])—words inspired by the teachings of the Bible. These dynamic works were rendered by Makoto Saito, former prime minister and Lord Keeper of the Privy Seal, whose wife, Haruko, was one of Toyo Eiwa's first graduates. A Christian sympathizer and close advisor to the emperor, Saito was a moderate in his views, which made him a target of the more fanatical members of the Imperial Army. On a snowy day in February 1936, a radical faction attempted a coup. Their plot was to assassinate the prime minister and six senior officials, one of whom was Saito. Young army officers stormed Saito's home and fired forty bullets, killing Saito and wounding Haruko, who had thrust herself before her husband, declaring, "If you must kill him, kill me first." The coup, known as the February 26 Incident, failed, but it gave the military an opportunity to further tighten its grip over the civilian government. Saito's calligraphies, "Reverence" and "Service," were among his last works.

It was the portraits of the emperor and empress at the front of the hall, however, that drew the eye. Although Christianity and English had been the pillars of Toyo Eiwa education since its inception, the school could no longer escape the thrust of the times and had been forced to display the imperial portraits at the government's request. As a symbol of the deified emperor and his consort, they were treated with reverence and placed centre-front. At morning assemblies, everyone bowed to the emperor's image, and if a fire broke out, the portraits had to be rescued. Should they be damaged in any way, the principal would be held responsible. *What, Hanako wondered, would Miss Blackmore have said if she could have seen it.* She remembered how Miss Blackmore had refused to bend to government pressure against mission schools during the Russo-Japanese War or to comply with the notices issued by the Ministry of Education. Instead, she had insisted that Toyo Eiwa would provide the students with a thorough English education.

The Ministry of Education had been urging Toyo Eiwa to install the imperial portraits since 1935. In the face of mounting pressure and of growing public disapproval of mission schools, Toyo Eiwa finally made the decision to comply in September 1938, and the portraits were presented at a special ceremony in February of the following year. Issue Number 38 of the *Toyo Eiwa Newsletter* records two students' impressions of the day the portrait was presented to the school:

> When we entered the classroom, everyone was quiet. I don't know what they were thinking, but they all wore serious expressions as they sat at their desks. I sensed relief in their faces.

> At yesterday's ceremony, the principal said there was no greater honour than this.... Some schools have not yet received the imperial portraits. We should be proud that our school has.

For the students, who had been anxious to see what would happen, the school's acceptance of the portraits was a tremendous relief.

Out of consideration for the safety of their students, the missionaries who were leaving Japan held no farewell gatherings. Instead, they set off quietly, one by one, on the long journey home, their hearts in turmoil. Hanako and the other alumni came to say goodbye, expressing their appreciation for the women's hard work and promising to meet again.

Every foreigner in a position of responsibility from the principal on down was replaced by Japanese, and the school had no choice but to adopt the militaristic curriculum dictated by the Ministry of Education, which included such subjects as The Fundamentals of National Education and the *kokutai*,[107] the Concept of National Polity. The school was required to fly the *hinomaru*, a white flag with a red circle for the sun at the centre. Even the school lunch menu was changed to the *hinomaru bento*, a box of white rice with a red pickled plum in the middle representing the Japanese flag. A few of the Canadian missionaries, including Miss Hamilton and Miss Sybil Ruthena Courtice, remained at the school and continued to pray privately every day.

Christianity had been introduced in Japan in the sixteenth century by the Jesuits, but was banned in the early seventeenth century by Japan's rulers, who saw it as a threat to their power. To weed out any dissidents, people were ordered to step on a *fumi-e*, an image of Jesus or Mary. To step on a sacred object was a form of desecration, and anyone who hesitated was assumed guilty and tortured until they recanted, or they were executed. Some Christians, however, stepped on the image and continued to worship in secret, and Christianity lived on in hiding for two and a half centuries. For mission schools, the decision to accept the imperial portraits and adopt military education was like stepping on the *fumi-e* for those early Christians; they made this painful choice to protect their students and give their schools a chance for survival.

With a determined light in their eyes, Miss Hamilton and Miss Courtice told Hanako that it was impossible for the school to insist on its principles the way Miss Blackmore had done in her time. Miss Hamilton only left on a repatriation ship in 1942 after Japan declared war on the United States and the United Kingdom, while Miss Courtice stayed on, despite the danger, out of concern for her students. Miss Courtice was taken into custody the following year and sent to the detention centre in Kanagawa prefecture for being an "enemy alien." The courage and perseverance the missionaries from Toyo Eiwa displayed in the face of such adversity gave Hanako great strength.

Entrusted with *Anne of Green Gables*

The period was also difficult for the Christian Literature Society in Ginza, the publisher where Hanako had first worked and that was established by missionaries to publish Christian-related books. Miss Loretta Leonard Shaw, Hanako's friend with whom she had co-edited the children's magazine *Little Children of Light*, had continued to work for the publisher, but had returned home as the war between Japan and China intensified.[108]

Born in New Brunswick, Canada, in 1872, Miss Shaw had come to Japan in 1904 as a missionary of the Church of England in Canada. After serving for twenty-seven years at Poole Girls School in Osaka (currently Poole Gakuin), she started working at the Christian Literature Society in 1931. In total, she devoted more than thirty years of her life to educating girls in Japan and to publishing books for women and children. Because Miss Shaw had spent so many years living in a school dormitory, she reminded Hanako of her own teachers, and they quickly became friends.

Miss Shaw regaled Hanako with memories of her life at the school: directing the girls in the play *The Merchant of Venice*, treating her students' chilblains, baking cookies to encourage a sick girl to take medicinal oil, giving a talk on Cain and Abel in Japanese during which she meant to say the two brothers did not get along (*naka ga warukatta*), but instead said they had diarrhea (*onaka ga warukatta*). Within Miss Shaw's anecdotes of the school, Hanko discerned the same spirit that had flowed in her own alma mater. While listening to Miss Shaw, Hanako often felt as if she had actually been there; that Miss Shaw's memories were her own.

On the day Miss Shaw left to return to Canada, Hanako went to see her off. Before they parted, Miss Shaw pressed a book into Hanako's hands. "In memory of our friendship," she said. The book was *Anne of Green Gables* by Lucy Maud Montgomery.

Miss Shaw's copy was quite worn, suggesting she had read and reread it many times, perhaps dreaming of her distant home while living in a foreign land. As the book passed from Miss Shaw's hands to Hanako's, it carried with it Miss Shaw's longing for Hanako to convey the heart of the Canadian people to her own.

In the March 1936 edition of the monthly *Kyobunkwan Bulletin*, Miss Shaw had written the following:

Utopia[109]

Loretta L. Shaw

How the poets and prophets of every age have dreamed of a land where all men should live in peace and happiness! It is to realize this dream that all statesmen work and parliaments make laws. So through the long centuries small groups everywhere have gradually given up their power to a centre, ceased their divisions and made one strong state in order to bring the people greater peace and plenty.... Today through travel and commerce, radio and books, there is the movement toward *international* grouping and this dream of a world Parliament, where the nations may work towards understanding, co-operation, equality and justice, is being fulfilled before our eyes.... There can be no doubt that the most influential book in the west is the Bible and he who would understand English must know the Bible. Then with the Bible comes all the devotional, poetical and biographical literature that has grown up around it. And scientific books also, for it is through the forward looking view of the Christian attitude to life that science has become a hand maid to build our better world. Forge then the link between the nations by introducing the *best books* of each nation to the other.

Miss Shaw had great faith in Hanako, who had known the Bible since she was a child. Feeling the book's weight in her hands, and with it, Miss Shaw's unspoken wish, Hanako resolved to share this story from Canada, the homeland of so many people she loved, with the Japanese. "Miss

1921. Loretta Leonard Shaw (right), who gave Hanako *Anne of Green Gables*, is shown here wearing kimono with a colleague at Poole Girls School in Osaka. *Poole Jogakuin Archives.*

Shaw," she said, "I promise you that one day I'll translate this book for the people of Japan to read."

While hardships intensified and the world moved inexorably towards war, Hanako thus took up the mission of fulfilling the dream of a Canadian missionary.

❀

From the day Hanako first read the book, the story continued to light up her heart. The heroine, Anne, was a skinny little orphan girl with freckles and carrot-coloured hair, whose cultural environment and school life closely resembled Hanako's own. Hanako could even recognize the hair styles and fashions worn by each character. The dress with puffed sleeves for which Anne pined was the same style as those worn by the missionaries who had taught at Toyo Eiwa. Hanako could imagine the very texture of the cloth, as well as the aroma of a pound cake baking in the oven, the taste of candied fruit, the friendly chatter of tea parties, and the ambience of music and poetry recitals. And scattered throughout the book's pages were lines from poems and novels that Hanako herself had loved.

The scenes described brought memories flooding back, causing her hands to tremble. Her friendship with Akiko, which had been like a schoolgirl's crush, the room where she had translated and recited the poems of Tennyson and Browning just to please the friend she admired so much, the throbbing of her heart as she lost herself in those verses. As war marched ever nearer, casting its dark shadow over the emotionally rich world that had nurtured Hanako in her youth, she clung to *Anne Of Green Gables*, a treasure chest of images that reminded her of the school on the hill in Azabu.

The Pacific War Begins

At six in the morning on December 8, 1941, while the world was still dark, the Muraokas' phone rang shrilly. It was from the broadcasting station. "You won't need to come into work today, Mrs. Muraoka," the person said. "We've just received exciting news, and it wouldn't be right to convey it in a woman's voice. Please come tomorrow."

Hanako had finished her turn on the *Children's Newspaper* on November 30, a week earlier, switching with the male announcer, Isoji Sekiya. This was the day she would normally start another week of the program. Wide awake now and filled with foreboding, she boiled some water and made tea, then turned on the radio. Keizo had woken up as well, and together they listened to the special news broadcast at seven.

Japan, they learned, was now officially at war.

"This is a special broadcast," the announcer declared. "At six o'clock this morning, December 8, the Imperial General Headquarters announced that before dawn, the Imperial Japanese Army and Navy declared war on the American and British armies in the West Pacific region."

Japan had attacked Pearl Harbor on the island of Oahu in Hawaii, America's most important naval base in the Pacific. At noon, the imperial edict declaring war against both the United States and the United Kingdom was broadcast, and the news of Japan's entry into the war was repeated throughout the day.

Hanako's first thought was that she needed to protect her family. For the last two or three years, Keizo had been suffering from a weak heart and high blood pressure, and she worried about overtaxing him. Midori was only nine; her youth, the most beautiful part of her life, was still ahead of her. Somehow Hanako had to find a way to guide her daughter safely into womanhood.

With Japan's declaration of war, Hanako quit the radio program she had been involved in for the last nine years. Military censorship had increased, and she had been feeling for some time that she simply couldn't do it anymore. She had written her resignation several times, but had always hesitated to submit it. Now, however, she could do so without any reservations. Entrusting the program to Isoji Sekiya, she quit. As she later wrote:

> I resigned from the Children's Newspaper program the very morning war was declared, silencing the voice that had spoken through the mic. I did so because I knew how much war would grieve Miss Blackmore. Without exception, she and all the teachers from Canada, America, and England, who had guided me through a decade of life at school, were pacifists; women who aspired to high ideals and strove to be good human beings. And behind each one of them was a multitude of others in their native countries who supported them spiritually and materially. When I thought of this, I felt my heart would break. I could not bring myself to convey with my own lips news of war to the children of my country.[110]

From that day on, all news media, including the radio, became mere tools for disseminating information from the army and the government, and the content was censored and managed even more strictly than before.

※

The first air strikes on Japanese soil commenced on April 18 of the following year, 1942. The targets were Tokyo, Nagoya, Osaka, and Kobe. A little after noon on that day, American B-25 bombers attacked the Arakawa, Oji, Koishikawa, and Ushigome districts of Tokyo. Thereafter, blackouts were enforced at night. Neon signs and street lights were prohibited, and Tokyo was wrapped in darkness. Whenever Midori turned the light on to go to the washroom at night, Hanako leaped out of bed to turn it off.

On June 8, the Japanese forces suffered a crushing defeat in the Battle of Midway in the central Pacific. Japan's victories had lasted only half a year after it declared war. Thereafter, Japan racked up one defeat after another. But the Japanese public had no idea, because the true state of the war was never revealed to them. False media reports on military victories stirred the Japanese into a patriotic fervour, and shouts of "Banzai!" ("Long live the emperor!")[111] could be heard everywhere. The people's blind enthusiasm for the war arose partly from the nationalism drilled into Japanese citizens since the Meiji period with such slogans as "rich country, strong army" and "loyalty and patriotism," but it was now magnified by mob psychology and further exacerbated by the military's manipulation of the press. Radio, newspapers, and other media, which should have taken an objective, critical stance, were completely controlled by the government's Information Bureau. Japan's successes were exaggerated, losses were minimized, and details were concealed to fan people's war sentiments. Convinced by these carefully controlled reports that victory was assured, the entire nation was swept up in a surge of pugnacious zeal.

In the beginning, even Japan's leading intellectuals supported the war. Children's board games traced the routes of soldiers in the battlefield, and children's books depicted victorious Japanese soldiers. Various methods were devised and employed in school lessons to instill complete loyalty for the military nation in Japanese boys and girls. Adults and children alike sang rousing anthems to the heroes who were marching off to crush their enemies. Some of the lyrics were penned by such outstanding poets as Yaso Saijo and Kotaro Takamura.

The military regime reinforced the traditional view that a woman's defining role was to take care of the family and bear many children. Suffrage groups had been disbanded or forced to come under the umbrella of organizations that conformed to government policies if they wished to survive, and women's suffrage was no longer even proposed in the Imperial Diet. Faced with this reality and stymied by the war, leading female activists and intellectuals such as Fusae Ichikawa hoped that by collaborating with the government, they could at least use the situation to somehow convince leaders and politicians of women's importance.

Even in more advanced democracies, such as the United Kingdom and the United States, the attainment of women's suffrage had come surprisingly late. The movement gained greater recognition during the First World War through the deliberate participation of suffragists in their respective government's war efforts. The expression "our war," which Hanako had heard the missionaries use frequently when she was teaching at Yamanashi Eiwa, reflected this awareness. This strategy bore fruit, with women finally gaining the right to vote in Great Britain and Canada in 1918 and in the United States in 1920. Following this example, women suffragists in Japan chose the pragmatic route of actively cooperating with the policies of the government's National Spiritual Mobilization Movement, which brought various independent civilian organizations under centralized control and mobilized them in support of the war effort. It was a choice far removed from suffrage ideals, but many suffragists felt that without winning the right to vote, women's voices, including their demands for peace, would never be reflected in government decisions.

The government demanded that writers and authors use their craft to promote its aims, launching the Patriotic Association for Japanese Literature (Nihon Bungaku Hokokukai) in 1942 just ten days after the Battle of Midway. Eiji Yoshikawa, one of Japan's foremost historical novelists, read the following declaration on the occasion of the association's inauguration:

> We who guard the home front and till the same earth can in no way remain idle. For those of us who work in the field of art and culture, our great mission has become even greater. Our country is calling upon us to give our all to the cause of winning complete and certain victory.

The message was clear: the association and its members would cooperate with the wartime regime. The president was Soho Tokutomi, its secretary-general was Masao Kume, playwright and poet, and Kan Kikuchi represented novelists. The Women's Literature Society, which was established before the war, was absorbed into the association as the Women's Literature Division. In addition to established authors, literature students and aspiring young writers also joined.

Formed under the direction of the Information Bureau, the purpose of the Patriotic Association for Japanese Literature was to whip up war sentiment, and the government used the talents of well-known writers and intellectuals to influence the masses, transforming the literary world into a propaganda machine that glorified war.

It became virtually impossible to proclaim antiwar sentiments in public. Socialists and communists were taken into custody as dangerous elements, and the leaders of the United Church of Christ in Japan—the largest Protestant denomination in the country—were rounded up and imprisoned. Writers who balked at lauding Japan's military feats lost any opportunities to publish their works. Not only were they thrown into dire financial straits, but they were at constant risk of being hauled off by the police.

❦

The xenophobia promulgated by the government, and the branding of foreigners as "brutes," was alien to Hanako. While their countries might be at war, the bond between her and the missionaries could never be broken. Though forbidden to say such things out loud, inwardly she longed for the day when she would be reunited with the friends who had been forced to leave Japan.

The suffrage movement, her friendships with the missionaries, her work translating English and American literature—these were things that Hanako had treasured since before the war. In a peaceful world, there would have been no conflict between any of them. But now, the suffrage movement had become intricately enmeshed with the wartime regime, while English literature was outlawed. Moreover, Hanako had a family to protect. As a result, she was forced down a path rife with contradictions.

The members of the Women's Literature Division all wore matching *monpe* work pants. Goods were already being rationed and normally their *monpe* would have been khaki coloured, but at the insistence of the fashionable Chiyo Uno, members were permitted to wear dark purple pants. As a member, Hanako was called upon almost daily to give talks urging women to cooperate wholeheartedly in protecting the home front. She spoke at meetings of such organizations as the Imperial Rule Assistance Association, the Greater Japan National Defense Women's Association, and the Greater Japan Women's Association, as well as at meetings for female student volunteers.

Many people have judged the role these women played in the war from the hindsight afforded by peace. A different picture, however, is presented by author Seiko Tanabe, who lived through the war, fleeing to the air raid shelter with a book by Nobuko Yoshiya clutched to her chest each time the sirens blared:

> The way scholars of women's history tend to judge that history from a contemporary perspective perplexes me. I am referring, for example, to the kind of simplistic reasoning that assumes Nobuko Yoshiya must have been a militarist because she was a war correspondent. That is the careless logic of someone ignorant of the violence with which social currents sweep people along. A country's destiny is like karma; the flow of history is impossible to resist, pushing everything before it in one direction.[112]

Hanako Translates at Great Risk

In February 1943, Japanese forces retreated from Guadalcanal in the southwest Pacific after a series of catastrophic defeats, failing to retake a strategic airfield from American forces. In April, the plane bearing Isoroku Yamamoto, the commander-in-chief of the combined fleet, was shot down

April 1943. Women writers wearing *monpe* trousers gather outside the Military Officers' Club in Kudan. From left: Michiko Yokoyama, Teiko Okada, Shizue Masugi, Fumiko Enchi, Sakae Tsuboi, Nobuko Yoshiya, Hanako Muraoka. *Source: Kanagawa Museum of Modern Literature.*

by American forces. His death dealt a severe blow to the Japanese psyche. Thereafter, one bitter defeat followed another on every battlefront. It was from around this time that air-raid sirens began sounding again in Tokyo even during the day.

Government officials continued to recruit writers like Hanako to give talks and participate in meetings. These sucked away Hanako's time and energy. She had no time even to read, let alone to translate, even if she had been allowed to. Whenever she and her friends got together, they would try to encourage one another.

"Surely this situation can't last forever."

"I'm dying to write something proper again."

"It's just for a little longer. We'll get back to our real work soon."

One day, the members of the Women's Literature Division had an opportunity to look at an American women's magazine. As they turned the pages, Hanako and her colleagues gasped with astonishment. Unlike Japanese magazines, the content wasn't taken up with articles and slogans glorifying war. Instead, it was clear that, even while at war, Americans were still enjoying a prosperous lifestyle. The pages were full of glossy fashion photos, delicious-sounding recipes, hobbies, interests, fiction, and essays.

"How lucky they are…" someone breathed, betraying her inner feelings. Hanako glanced at the bottom of the colourful page she was reading. In small print in one corner were the words "Remember Pearl Harbor." She whispered the words in Japanese: *Paru haba o oboeyo*. Turning the pages, she saw that these same words had been printed in exactly the same spot on every single one. This display of single-minded resolve made her shiver with an inexplicable horror.

❀

Early that fall, Hanako woke to find that her neck under her jaw had swelled to twice its normal thickness. Her throat was excruciatingly sore, and she had difficulty breathing. She had caught diphtheria. She had not been seriously ill since the age of seven, when she had been stricken with a fever for ten days and written her death poem. While she had worried about Keizo's weak heart and high blood pressure, and lived in fear that Midori, like Michio, might get severe infantile gastroenteritis, she had given no thought to her own health.

Diphtheria is an infectious disease, particularly common among children, accompanied by a high fever and sore throat. A membrane-like coating of dead tissue can develop inside the throat, impeding respiration. If the bacteria enters the blood stream, it can cause sudden heart failure or neuroparalysis within four to six weeks after the symptoms first appear. The risk of fatality at that time was one in ten.

Few doctors were left in Tokyo. Many had been sent to war, while many of those who stayed behind had evacuated to rural areas to avoid the air raids. Fortunately, one of Keizo's mahjong partners, Takashi Hayashi, who had a degree in medicine, was able to attend to Hanako. He partitioned off

August 30, 1943. A group of writers gathered at Nobuko Yoshiya's house. Front from the left: Shizue Masugi, Fumiko Hayashi, Lu Guan who was visiting Japan from China, Nobuko Yoshiya, Ineko Kubokawa (Sata), Chiyo Uno, Yasuko Abe (Miyake), Rear from left: Hanako Muraoka, Matsuko Inoue, Fumiko Enchi, Interpreter.

one room of the Muraoka home with sterilized white sheets to quarantine the patient and treated her with diphtheria serum. Due to the risk of infection, family members were forbidden to enter the room and, for about two months, Hanako saw no one but Dr. Hayashi and Dr. Omura, another physician who happened to live nearby. Divorced from all news of the war conveyed by the radio and newspapers and relieved from her duties of giving talks, Hanako relinquished everything and focused on fighting the disease. When the air-raid sirens sounded, she simply lay in bed, bound to the mattress by an unshakable fatigue.

Keizo had never seen Hanako so thin. She had always been round-cheeked with a plump figure, but at less than five feet tall, she looked shrunken when she lost weight.

This blank in her life, however, gave Hanako's exhausted mind and body a chance to rest. While convalescing, she received many letters and gifts from the neighbourhood women and children, even though goods were scarce. Their kind messages helped heal and comfort her. Hanako loved sweets, and Keizo bought some sugar for her on the black market, a precious item rarely found in shops anymore.

As she lay listlessly, plagued by a low-grade fever, Hanako frequently thought of Miss Blackmore and Miss Shaw, recalling the look in Miss Shaw's eyes when she gave Hanako the book. She seemed to be saying, "Hanako, someday peace will surely come. When it does, I want you to translate this book for the girls of Japan."

❀

When Hanako finally rose from her sickbed, she gathered together all the writing paper in the house and began translating *Anne of Green Gables*. *Instead of waiting for peace,* she thought, *I should do this now.*

The freshness of Montgomery's prose and the vibrant world she described cleansed Hanako's soul of the coercive, savage words being spoken all around her in her native tongue. It had been a long time since Hanako had translated anything, and the joy of the work made her heart sing so exuberantly that she forgot English was the enemy language; she forgot even her fear of being discovered by soldiers or the secret police who would imprison and torture her.

Her mind was filled instead with the lush, flower-filled landscapes of Prince Edward Island, the story's setting. Through Hanako, the romantic words that spilled from Anne's lips through the medium of Montgomery's prose were woven into a lyrical and evocative Japanese.

❀

On October 21, 1943, the government held a rally in Meiji Jingu Gaien Stadium to cheer on university students who were being conscripted for the war. Having discarded their pens for guns, the students paraded through a heavy autumn rain before the crowd, which greeted Prime Minister Hideki Tojo's speech with wild enthusiasm. Hanako and Keizo's nephews were also sent off to the front, one after the other.

In 1944, Japan's military budget rose to 85.5 percent of the national budget. Goods disappeared from shop shelves, almost all daily necessities were traded on the black market, and prices soared to twenty or thirty times normal. People no longer spouted the spirited slogans that had been so popular just a year before. Their primary concern was whether they could feed their families the next day, and most conversations centred on the black market. Forbidden to voice their true thoughts, the people of Japan were shrouded in a dark hopelessness.

Intellectuals and writers grew sick of the prolonged war, and their distrust of the military and the government waxed stronger. They had done as they were told, writing what the government demanded, often against their will. The Ministry of Finance continued to issue orders such as "write a novel that will make people save money" or "publish something that will encourage women to be even more frugal," but there was no more paper with which to publish, and many magazines were folding. Although the situation was driving writers out of work, they could expect no help from the government.

One by one, Hanako's friends left the city. Novelist and poet Fumiko Hayashi, who had served as a war journalist since the start of the Second Sino-Japanese War in 1937, had been dispatched as a newspaper correspondent to Singapore, French Indonesia, Java, and Borneo during the Pacific War. On her return in May 1943, she attended a meeting of the Women's Literature Division, but then clammed up completely, contacting no one. In December of the same year, she adopted a baby boy named Tai, and in April of the following year, moved with him and her mother to a hot-spring area in the mountains of Nagano to escape the air raids. There, she began writing children's stories and reading them to the village children while raising her son.

Many people urged Hanako to evacuate too, but she stayed in her old familiar house in Omori. One reason was her reluctance to desert the other members of the neighbourhood women's association. Another was her attachment to her library. Books had been Hanako's lifelong companions, and many of those she owned were Western books. It would be impossible to take her collection with her if she left. After placing them in wicker cases, she had buried them in the garden and hid them in the little dugout they used for an air-raid shelter in their yard.

Soldiers and secret police were watching for suspicious behaviour, and informants were everywhere. Hanako's writer friends warned her that some informants were even posing as fans. Regardless of the danger, however, Hanako continued to translate *Anne of Green Gables*, working in the dim light of a lamp shaded with black cloth, driven by the desire to prove her friendship to the Canadian people. Sitting at her desk in her small study with the book in front of her, she felt somehow protected. To Midori's delight, at bedtime, Hanako shared some of the amusing things the talkative Anne said or the silly mistakes she made.

Air-Raid Days

In June 1944, the Japanese forces suffered devastating losses in the Mariana Islands, culminating with the fall of the strategically significant Saipan in July with heavy civilian casualties. But despite these losses and the likelihood of Germany's defeat, Japan's Supreme Council for the Direction of the War[113] decided to resist to the bitter end.

When the government abruptly announced that everyone should prepare to defend their homeland from invasion, the people of Japan were thrown into consternation. To the last moment, the government had insisted on distorting Japan's war achievements in the press, and the ordinary Japanese never dreamed that their country's might was inferior to that of its enemies. Removing any children remaining in Tokyo to places of safety became a pressing concern, and the evacuation of schoolchildren began in earnest. On August 22, Hanako sent Midori, who would soon be twelve years old, with Haruko to stay with relatives in Kofu city, Yamanashi prefecture. After they left, Hanako wrote:

At night I listen
to the crickets' song,
having sent my child away.

On August 27, she received her first letter from Midori, which was dated August 23.

> **Dear Mother,**
> **Thank you for your letter.**
> **We started going to school today. I am in class 4, grade six. My teacher's name is Matsudo. The classroom is on the second floor, so the scenery is beautiful and it is very cool. The principal met us specially. He told us to take care of our health, to study hard and to become good Japanese. I have made friends already so please don't worry. We will have a holiday from the 27th to the 30th. Please give my love to Father.**
> **Goodbye.**

On November 1, 1944, the first B-29 reconnaissance plane appeared over Tokyo. This was the same type of aircraft that had been bombing northern Kyushu, Chugoku, Shikoku, and the Ogasawara Islands since the summer of that year. It was just one plane, flying high in the clear autumn sky, trailing a single white thread of cloud behind it. Staring at the bright form, which looked like a small bird, Hanako remembered the day she had first seen an airplane.

It had been a clear day many decades earlier, when she was living in the Toyo Eiwa dorm. The girls had rushed into the schoolyard, crying out in delight as they stared into the air and watched the brilliant flight of this new machine, an American airplane visiting Japan. Miss Blackmore gazed up at the sky with them, one hand shielding her eyes from the glare. "Hanako," she said, "the development of the plane will either lead us to peace or make war more miserable. How will mankind try to use these machines? For peace or for war? This is the question that now hangs over all of us. You should think about it too." At the time, Hanako had never imagined that planes would one day be used to bomb and kill.

The eerie reconnaissance planes continued to come, and the air-raid sirens announcing their presence set people on edge, wearing away at their nerves. On November 20, Hanako received a letter from Midori that threw her into turmoil. It was a heartrending appeal, unlike anything Hanako had heard from her before.

> Dear Father and Mother,
> Are you well? I am well.
> Mother, when are you coming to see me? I am looking forward to it.
> The track suit reached me on the 15th.
> Please tell me how to read the Chinese characters I sent with this letter. They are hard for me to read, but Auntie refuses to tell me what they say. She's mean. I don't like that. Sometimes I get very homesick. I thought Uncle was nice at first, but now he is very unkind. At night, they send us to bed early and then stay up and say bad things about us while eating fruit. At those times, I'm so homesick I cry. They put so little in our lunch boxes that we get very hungry.
> Today is a lovely day but it is very cold.
> I put my test paper in with this letter. Please look at it.
> It is getting colder so please take care of yourselves.
> Goodbye.
> November 18   From Midori

Hanako put down the letter and turned to Keizo. "I'm going to fetch Midori and Haruko tomorrow."

Keizo looked at her in surprise. "How can you say something so silly?" he said. "They'll be bombing us soon, you know. Weren't you the one who said that a mother must be patient, no matter how much she misses her children? That the lives of the children must come first?"

"Yes," Hanako replied. "But here, read this letter. The poor things are miserable. Once the bombing starts, who knows if other parts of the country will actually be any safer? They may be my relations, but I'm afraid they won't think twice about Midori and Haruko if their own lives are in danger."

Keizo read the letter and cocked his head. "Even so, it's still much safer in the countryside. Midori's just a child. She may have written like this because she's homesick."

But Hanako was not convinced. The fear of what might happen if she and Keizo died, leaving Midori all on her own, tormented her. Families, she thought, should never be separated. She managed to convince her sister Umeko, Haruko's mother, and the two of them set off for Kofu, brushing aside the protests of Keizo and Umeko's husband, Iwao.

Although startled by Hanako and Umeko's sudden appearance in Kofu, their relatives showed no sign of guilt or shame. "Why don't you stay a little while since you've come all this way?" they suggested, but Hanako and Umeko politely declined. Thanking their relatives, they took their daughters to Kofu city and spent the night in Takeya, a local inn. The next day they returned to Omori.

Ironically, after a two-and-a-half-year hiatus, the bombing of Tokyo commenced on November 24, the day after the four came back from Kofu, as if they had timed their homecoming to coincide with the bombing. Air-raid sirens blared with a pre-raid warning, followed soon after by the signal for an imminent attack. B-29 bombers appeared, flying in formation. There were at least eighty planes. Throwing quilted air-raid hoods over their heads, the Muraokas turned off the gas and filled the water tank and buckets with water.

"Midori, hurry!" Hanako cried, grabbing her by the hand. In the other, she clutched a tightly tied *furoshiki* cloth which contained *Anne of Green Gables* and her half-finished translation. She, Midori, and Keizo fled into the dugout in their yard.

A munitions factory and the surrounding neighbourhood in Tama were attacked, and bombs were dropped on Shinagawa, Ebara, and Suginami. Until recently, Japan's battles had been fought in enemy lands. As their homeland had never become a battlefield, the lives of ordinary Japanese citizens had never before been directly threatened. Now, for the first time, the people of Tokyo experienced the terror of war.

Thereafter, B-29 bombers attacked every two or three days. No one knew when bombs might fall on the area in which they lived. Hanako implored Keizo and Midori to take *Anne Of Green Gables* and her translation, which were the most precious things in her life next to her family, to the shelter should she be out. The day after each attack, American reconnaissance planes flew over the city in midday to review the damage, setting off the air-raid sirens. Hanako later recollected:

> Although groaning in anguish under the ravages of war, the people of Japan were fed nothing but glowing reports. In retrospect, I think within those circumstances the only "truth" they could trust with any certainty was the mutual support of parent and child, husband and wife, brother and sister, who banded together to protect one another.[114]

American soldiers died too, downed in mid-flight over Tokyo by the anti-aircraft corps and homeland defense units.

On January 27, 1945, the city's residents were plunged even deeper into terror. Rather than targeting military plants on the city's outskirts, for the first time, bombs rained on central Tokyo. The attack began at two in the afternoon, just as a train pulled into Yurakucho Station. Over 100 passengers died. Also damaged were Taimei Primary School, the Imperial Hotel, The Asahi Shimbun Company, and the Japan Theatre. With 1,451 dead and wounded, the attack claimed far more civilian casualties than those before it, and the damage was compounded by the fact that in the middle of the air raid someone mistakenly sounded the all-clear signal. This sowed more seeds of grievance against the army.

On February 25, while Tokyo lay buried under a heavy blanket of snow, the likes of which had not been seen since the February 26 Incident in 1936, the city was bombarded by 130 B-29 bombers and 600 carrier-based aircraft. The first incendiary bombs used on Tokyo hit Shitaya, Asakusa, Kojimachi, Akasaka, Fukagawa, Katsushika, Edogawa, Joto, and Arakawa, leaving 627 casualties and destroying over 20,000 buildings. This attack was followed on March 10 by the Great Tokyo Air Raid, which commenced at midnight and razed the entire Shitamachi area of central Tokyo bordered by the Fukagawa district and the Sumidagawa and Arakawa Rivers, before the bombers fanned out to target surrounding areas. For two and a half hours, low-flying planes pelted the city with incendiary bombs. Strong winds whipped the flames into a maelstrom of fire, killing over 100,000 people.

The End of the War

Subsequent air raids followed in quick succession. Starting at eleven o'clock on the night of April 13, a team of one hundred and seventy aircraft bombed Tokyo for four hours, burning the districts of Shiba, Shinjuku, Nakano, Oji, Yotsuya, and Kojimachi. Although the raid was comparable in scale to that of March 10 and over 210,000 buildings were destroyed, the number of casualties was only 2,459. This was thanks to the fact that there was no wind and that the people, who had learned a bitter lesson from the Great Tokyo Air Raid, fled rather than trying to put out the fires with bucket relays.

Omori was first targeted by the B-29s on April 15. Fortunately, the block where the Muraokas' house stood was spared from the fires. But when Hanako and Keizo thought of those who had lost their homes, they could not rejoice. And who knew when their own home might be destroyed? The members of the women's association cooked and distributed food as well as blankets to people whose homes had burned and to orphaned children.

On May 24, at one-thirty in the morning, as Hanako was polishing her translation of *Anne of Green Gables*, she heard the air-raid siren. She had had a feeling the bombers might come soon. She laid down her pen. Just as she rose from her desk, the house shook with an ear-splitting roar, and a firebomb smashed through the roof, landing in the living room next to the room where Keizo and Midori were sleeping. Another plunged into the well in the garden. Fortunately, they failed to ignite, and Hanako, Keizo, and Midori took refuge in the dugout in their yard.

Soon after, an alarm alerted them to a fire in the neighbourhood, and they scurried out of the shelter. Flames consumed two houses that had been directly hit. That day, two hundred and fifty B-29s attacked the districts of Ebara, Meguro, Omori, and Shinagawa. When Hanako and her family returned to their house near dawn, they saw that the room that had been struck had collapsed like a tumbledown shack, leaving the interior exposed to view from the outside. The washroom had also been damaged, and the smell of oil permeated the house. Members of the civil defense unit dug up the ground under the floor to remove the bomb, which was filled with napalm. From the dirt emerged Keizo's treasured mahjong tiles, each ivory piece charred and blackened.

"The wall must have collapsed on the bomb before it could fully ignite, smothering the fire perfectly," one of the men said.

The Muraokas' private library had escaped destruction. Dazed, Hanako and Keizo began gathering the mahjong tiles, which had taken the brunt of the blast in their family's stead. The thought of what would have happened if the bomb had ignited sent a chill down Hanako's spine.

The next day, Matsuya, Mitsukoshi, and the Yomiuri Shimbun Company buildings in Ginza burned, and the greater part of numerous other districts were reduced to ashes, including Yodobashi, Koishikawa, Nakano, Ushigome, Shibuya, Shiba, and Akasaka. This was the last major air raid on Tokyo.

On the morning of May 29, just when Hanako and her family had managed to clean some of the dirt from their house, a lone B-29 strayed from a raid on the city of Yokohama and, as if on some fickle whim, dropped a firebomb into the Muraokas' garden. Hanako was at her desk in her study, which looked out onto the yard, when she was assaulted by a deafening roar and a shower of earth.

The maid, Fumi, rushed into the room shouting, "Quick! Get down, Madam! You'll be hurt!" They crouched down and counted to three, then ran into the garden and began throwing buckets of water on the fire. Although the flames were not very strong, they slipped around the garden like will-o'-the-wisp. When they touched the daphne bush, the leaves burst into flames with a whoosh. With the neighbours, who had come running to help, Keizo and Midori rushed back and forth to the bathtub to get water. Without bothering to take off their shoes, they refilled and emptied their buckets until they finally extinguished all the flames.

The B-29s that had burned much of Tokyo to the ground moved on to other regions of Japan. The city in Yamanashi where Midori and Haruko had been sent for safety was bombed, and Hanako's relatives were burned out of their house. This news, which Hanako only received after the war, assuaged some of her guilt for having exposed the two girls to such danger by bringing them home.

On June 23, the Japanese army on Okinawa was routed. On August 6, an atom bomb was dropped on Hiroshima; another was dropped on Nagasaki on August 9. Six days later, on August 15, Japan finally conceded defeat.

Gathered before the radio, tears streaming unchecked down their cheeks, Keizo, Midori, and Hanako listened to the emperor announce the end of the war. They experienced no rush of joy to know the war was finally over. Were their family and friends safe?

※

A month later, Hanako received news that left her shattered. Kaori, the son of her friend Akiko and Ryusuke Miyazaki, had been dispatched as part of the student corps. On August 11, just four days before Japan surrendered, Kaori had been killed during an American air raid on Kushikino, Kagoshima.

Akiko's profound grief can be glimpsed in a poem she wrote upon receiving the news of her son's death.

It is just the wind
that beats on my door tonight.
Oh, won't you come and
surprise me, my son,
by telling me you're home?

The war had devastated Japan and all its people. What had sustained Hanako throughout was her family and the mission entrusted to her by Miss Shaw: the translation of *Anne of Green Gables*.

"… my future seemed to stretch out before me like a straight road," Anne says when her life changes unexpectedly. "Now there is a bend in it. I don't know what lies around the bend, but I'm going to believe that the best does." Encouraged by Anne's optimism, and buoyed by the belief that peace would surely come, Hanako had managed to finish the translation.

How she longed to share this story with children who had lost their parents and parents who had lost their children in the air raids; with all those people who now wandered through this desolate landscape. She had no idea if the day when she could fulfill her promise to Miss Shaw would ever come. But on her desk lay Miss Shaw's copy of *Anne of Green Gables* and Hanako's translation, a stack of more than seven-hundred pages with no one to publish it.

Chapter 9

The Long Road to Publication: 1946–1952
Age 53 to 59

Like Portia

Soon after Japan's surrender, Hanako visited Toyo Eiwa Girls School. When she reached Toriizaka in Azabu and saw her school silhouetted against the blue sky, the only building left standing amid the rubble and scorched earth, she could not suppress tears of joy. Inside, the imperial portraits and the *hinomaru* flag, which had been displayed so prominently during the war, had been removed by order of the GHQ, the General Headquarters of the occupation government in Japan.[115]

The following year, Canadian missionaries began to return and lay the groundwork for reconstructing the mission schools. They focused first on rebuilding the Yamanashi Eiwa and Shizuoka Eiwa Schools, which had been destroyed by air raids. One of the first to return was Miss Courtice, who had been arrested as an enemy alien and imprisoned in the foreigners' detention centre in Kanagawa in September 1943. That same month, she had been evacuated on the last repatriation ship to Canada.

Hanako was overjoyed to be reunited with Miss Courtice. From her, Hanako learned that Miss Hamilton, who had returned to Canada in 1942, had stayed in British Columbia rather than returning to her home in Prince Edward Island, spending the remainder of the war caring for Japanese Canadians, who had been forcefully relocated to internment camps. According to Miss Courtice, none of the missionaries who had served in Japan had forgotten their girls, praying for them continuously in their churches throughout the war. But Hanako's heart was filled with sorrow when she heard the news that Miss Blackmore, grief-stricken by the enmity between Japan and Canada, had passed away in 1942.

The occupation government launched a new school system at the start of the Japanese school year, in April 1947. This coincided with the start of Midori's third year of junior high, and she took this opportunity to transfer into Toyo Eiwa, donning the school's sailor-suit uniform. Unlike in Hanako's school years, students now took their own lunches to school. At Hanako's request, the maid, Fumi, prepared Midori's lunch every morning. About a month after she began attending Toyo Eiwa, however, Midori told Hanako that she wanted to pack her own lunch box. "Fumi's lunches look so unattractive," she complained.

"It can't be helped," Hanako said. Food and goods were even scarcer than they had been during the war. With rations alone, they could not possibly get enough ingredients to make a varied menu, and black-market prices were prohibitive. Still, Midori insisted that a poorly packed lunch box was just too embarrassing, and she began getting up early every morning to arrange the food herself.

"When they saw my lunch today, the other girls were very impressed," she reported. "'Oh my! Did Mrs. Hanako Muraoka make that?' they said. Of course I told them you did, because everyone's convinced you're the kind of woman who can balance work and homemaking."

"How kind of you!" Hanako said with a laugh, but inside she bowed her head in self-reproach. She was so busy these days, she felt bad for Midori.

※

The Patriotic Association for Japanese Literature established by the wartime government had been disbanded on September 20, 1945, after Japan accepted the terms of the Potsdam Declaration, which called for Japan's surrender, and the Women's Literature Division was dissolved along with it. Soon after, however, the Women's Literature Society, which was established before the war and later absorbed by the league, was revived with Nobuko Yoshiya as a driving force. After enduring years of bleak misery, women writers shared the joy of being free once again to write.

From the fall of 1945, editors began visiting Hanako one after another. Some were former colleagues with whom she was delighted to renew old bonds, while others were new. All of them stared hungrily at Hanako's bookshelves, filled with her collection, which had miraculously survived the war intact. Many writers and scholars had lost their personal libraries, the thing they prized most next to life itself.

Even though people's most compelling concern was how to put food on the table, they still longed for dreams and for books. The stories Hanako had written and her abridged translations of English works were reorganized and republished, albeit with skimpy bindings and coarse, low-grade recycled paper called *senkashi*, the only kind to be had during the supply shortages that followed in the wake of the Second World War. In 1946, her unpublished translation of *Uncle Tom's Cabin*, which she had completed before the war, was published as *Dorei Tomu monogatari* (The Story of Slave Tom). She also wrote a novel for young girls, *Haru no uta* (Spring Song), and published a collection of essays, *Shin-nippon no josei ni okuru* (For the Women of the New Japan).

In the New Year of 1946, Hanako appeared on a special children's radio program four nights in a row. It had been five years since she had quit speaking through the mic for the *Children's Newspaper* program. Many listeners were moved to write messages to the radio station sharing memories of listening to Hanako in the past.

"I am now a university student," wrote one listener. "When I heard your familiar voice, I felt as happy as if my aunt had come all the way to visit me."

The thought that young people who had listened to her when they were children felt as if she were family made Hanako very happy.

During this same year, teachers in Hiroshima, which had been flattened by the atomic bomb, began publishing two children's educational tabloids, both called *Gin no suzu* (Silver Bell) in Japanese, one for children in lower primary grades and the other for children in upper primary grades. The aim was to provide fun and educational reading material to children traumatized by war, and Hanako also contributed stories. These publications were later taken over by Hiroshima Library, which combined them into one eighteen-page monthly magazine. Published for seven years, it was distributed to children all over the country.

Keiko Matsuda, the young writer Hanako believed would one day be the Alcott or Burnett of Japan, had died of peritonitis in 1940, just three years after publishing her maiden novel. She was only twenty-three years old. In 1941, Keiko's work *Shion* (Aster) was published posthumously with a preface by Hanako, in which she mourned the loss of a gentle-natured writer endowed with exceptional talent that never reached fruition. The book also included postscripts by Keiko's father, Kodo, and her husband, Tomoo. This volume was followed by the publication of *Chiisaki ao* (Small Blue) and *Safuran no uta* (Song of Saffron). Along with Nobuko Yoshiya's girls novels and the magazine *Shojo no tomo* (Girls' Friend), Keiko's works nurtured the dreams and longings of adolescent girls during the war. For many, the treasure they had clutched in their hands as they dashed for the air-raid shelter was one of Keiko's books.

In 1947, the artist Junichi Nakahara established the Himawari-sha publishing company and began publishing *Himawari*, a girls' magazine, as well as continuing to publish the women's magazine *Soleil*, which he had launched the previous year. In addition to a foreword by Nobuko Yoshiya, the first issue of *Himawari* carried an essay by Hanako and the first installment of Keiko Matsuda's posthumous series *Ningyo no uta* (Doll's Song). In response to the fervent wishes of Keiko's fans, pocketbook versions of her works, illustrated by Junichi Nakahara, were republished as Himawari Library Pocketbook Editions.

�❀

Postwar Japan was in a state of turmoil. Some Japanese became informants, reporting suspicious behaviour to the GHQ. One evening, an old friend came to consult Hanako and Keizo because someone had informed on her husband.

"They told the GHQ that my husband was making a lot of money on the black market," she said. "Soldiers raided our house, searching all over and confiscating a lot of things."

His worst offense, however, was not dealing in black-market items, but the possession of a naval officer's ornamental short sword, which the soldiers had discovered in their house. Japanese were forbidden to possess weapons of any kind, and the woman's husband was being tried in a military court for violating this law.

"I know he shouldn't have been involved in the black market," the woman said. "But having that short sword appears to be an even worse crime. Who knows what will happen if they decide he's guilty? Some people have said that he could be sent to Okinawa and forced to do heavy labour as punishment. We hired a lawyer, but he doesn't speak any English. And the court interpreter is a Japanese American who doesn't seem to understand what the lawyer is saying. My husband's resigned to his fate, but he feels it's unfair to be punished without being able to properly defend himself. Especially as he only bought the dagger to celebrate our grandson's first Boys' Day. I'm so sorry to trouble you like this, but his last court appearance is tomorrow. We would be so grateful if you...." Tears choked her voice, and she could not continue.

Hanako and Keizo remained silent for some time. Finally Keizo asked, "Has the blade ever been sharpened?"

"I don't know...but I doubt it. I can't check because they took it away, but I'm sure it was just a decoration." The woman looked at him imploringly.

Keizo nodded. "If it was a decoration, then I doubt it was sharpened. And in that case, it can't be considered a weapon. After all, in Japan, there is an entire profession devoted to sharpening swords. Only when a blade has been sharpened well enough to cut can it be called a weapon. Which means the short sword you owned was 'sleeping armour.' Anything can become a weapon if we decide to use it that way. Even a fountain pen or an ornamental hairpin. But we don't call such things weapons."

Keizo turned to Hanako. "My dear," he said, "that's the argument you must use tomorrow. Tell them it can't be called a weapon because it's just an ornament. It may not work, but it's worth giving it a try. Do your best and see what happens."

The next morning, steeling herself for the encounter, Hanako headed off to the Shinagawa Police Station with the couple, their daughter, and their lawyer. A sign over the entrance bore the words *American Military Court*. The lobby was crowded with people waiting to be interrogated. At last, Hanako's friends were summoned into the courtroom. After a superficial interrogation by the court, which was conducted in English, Hanako rose to her friend's defense and clearly expounded Keizo's "sleeping armour" argument.

When it was time for the verdict, everyone rose. Hanako's friend's husband received a stern reprimand and a ten-thousand yen fine for dealing in black-market goods. As for possession of the short sword, he was given a suspended sentence in view of extenuating circumstances. Hanako had heard the term "probation" before, but not "suspended sentence." Nevertheless, she realized that the American judge appeared to have accepted her argument. Just as she was breathing an internal sigh of relief, the judge turned to her. "Are you a lawyer?" he asked in English.

"No sir, I know nothing of the law," Hanako answered boldly. She felt compelled to show him that while some Japanese women might cozy up to American soldiers, the majority of them were both proud and sensible.

The man looked at her with a twinkle in his eye and cocked an eyebrow in mock surprise, his expression transforming him from the stern judge of moments before into someone completely different. Hanako and her friends bowed and turned to go when the judge stopped Hanako again. "You're just like Portia," he said. "Do you know who Portia is?"

Portia, the heroine of Shakespeare's *Merchant of Venice* who saved her husband's friend by disguising herself as a man and arguing his defense with scintillating wit to defeat the scheming Sherlock.

Hanako looked up at the judge and smiled. His words, which bore the sweet scent of literature, melted away the tension that had gripped her heart.

❀

With Japan's defeat, democratization proceeded rapidly under the American occupation. Women's suffrage was realized the year the war ended. Fusae Ichikawa, along with Ochimi Kubushiro and Shigeri Yamataka, had organized the Women's Committee on Postwar Policy ten days after the war ended to lobby the Japanese government and each political party for women's suffrage. But while the Japanese government dawdled, the GHQ awarded women throughout Japan the right to vote. Hanako, however, did not see this as a "gift" bestowed upon Japanese women by the Americans. Rather, for the sake of those who had died before witnessing the realization of women's suffrage, as well as for the women of the future, she wanted to believe it was the just reward for the sacrificial efforts of three generations of women who had fought for women's rights from the late nineteenth century through to the end of the war. In 1946, the GHQ also passed a law abolishing licensed prostitution, a cause for which the Japan Woman's Christian Temperance Union had worked for decades.

As part of the country's democratic reform, the GHQ issued an edict prohibiting those who had played leading roles before and during the war from holding public office. In 1947, Fusae Ichikawa was subjected to this purge. But those women who had known and worked with Fusae knew very well the cause for which she had always fought. They collected more than 170,000 signatures on a petition requesting that she be exempted from this order and submitted it to the GHQ and the Japanese government.

In 1950, the prohibition on Fusae was lifted, and she became president of the League of Women Voters of Japan. From 1953, she was elected for three consecutive terms as a member of the House of Councillors, the upper house of the National Diet.

Hanako's first love, Renzo Sawada, who had served as vice-minister of foreign affairs during the war, was purged from public service in 1948. A month later, he and his wife, Miki, the granddaughter of Yataro Iwasaki, who founded the Mitsubishi Financial Group, started the Elizabeth Saunders

Home[116], an orphanage for biracial war orphans, in Kanagawa. Although Japanese society was sympathetic towards Japanese war orphans, it turned a cold shoulder to the "mixed-blood" children fathered by American soldiers and abandoned by their Japanese mothers. Discrimination was so strong that local people refused even to allow these children to play on the nearby beach in Oiso. Instead Sawada got permission from his hometown in Tottori prefecture to take the children to Uradome Beach, which was about five hundred kilometres away, for the summer.

The Muraoka and Sawada families gradually became close. Hanako often visited the Elizabeth Saunders Home, where she came to appreciate Miki Sawada's strong sense of justice and enthusiasm. Sawada was reinstated as a diplomat in 1953 and appointed as ambassador extraordinary and plenipotentiary to the United Nations. As the representative of a defeated nation, Sawada was given no opportunity to speak or to vote, but he bore this treatment patiently while working for Japan's inclusion as a member of the United Nations.

☙

Hanako's sister Umeko and her family, as well as Keizo's younger brother Noboru and his family, were still living in the rental houses that the Muraokas had built beside their own home in Omori. After the war, Hanako invited her brother Kenjiro and his family to live there as well, because their home had been destroyed during the air raids. This blow had been compounded by the death of Kenjiro's eldest son of tuberculosis at the age of twenty-one, soon after Japan's defeat. Kenjiro's daughter Mariko, who had loved her brother dearly, became so despondent that Hanako invited her to stay with her for several days, sleeping in the same bed to comfort her. In every part of Japan, families pulled together like this to help one another through the chaos of the postwar period.

Perhaps because paper had been in such short supply during the war, Hanako could not bring herself to discard manuscript paper when she made a mistake. She often had to scrap a page after writing only one or two lines, but rather than throwing it out, she would cut off the ruined piece and use strips of the remainder to paste over mistakes she made on other sheets. Then she bound the finished manuscript with paper string called *koyori*. For Hanako, *koyori* was an important part of daily life. It was also inextricably tied to memories of her father.

Hanako's father, Ippei Annaka, came from a family of tea merchants, and they had used *koyori* to seal the bags of loose tea. When she had lived in Shinagawa as a child, *koyori* was the only thing Hanako's family had had in plenty. After her father quit the business, Hanako had received paper string from a nearby tea shop or made her own by twisting strips of scrap paper. Even now, she twisted her own paper string. It was just the type of chore that kept her hands busy whenever she reached an impasse in her translation work.

Hanako's parents had spent the war living with their fourth daughter, Yuki, who had married into a family in Shizuoka, the area where Ippei was born and raised. He died there in 1947 at the age of eighty-eight. Ippei had been a book lover and an idealist who had pursued his dreams at the expense of his family. For Hanako, he was certainly far from being a perfect father of whom she could feel proud.

Several months after his death, Hanako and the rest of her family were astounded by an unexpected visitor: Shozaburo, Hanako's brother, six years her junior, who had vanished without a trace after being apprenticed many years earlier. Where he had been and what he had done, no one knew, but his unwholesome demeanor and disheveled appearance, down to the tattered gaiters[117] that soldiers had worn during the war, frightened even his own siblings. After consulting Keizo and other family members, Hanako got Shozaburo a job at a bread factory. But he could not adjust to this new way of life and flew into a rage if there was no liquor to be found. One day, the family noticed he had not come home, only to discover that he had dropped dead, poisoned from drinking ethanol disinfectant.

The pitiful death of her brother was another shock for Hanako. Her mother had aged noticeably, and Hanako had not even told her yet that Shozaburo had reappeared. Although he was the eldest son, poor

Shozaburo had been ignored by his father and had lacked love ever since leaving home. Having been forced down such an unhappy path, he was truly a victim of his father.

Yet perhaps their father had also been a victim of the times. Although endowed with exceptional curiosity and a love of learning, Ippei had been too poor to receive an education, and his involvement in socialist activities made it impossible for him to escape the poverty of his parents' generation. After the High Treason Incident of 1910, which had dashed his dreams of creating a better future through social reform, Ippei had lived like a fugitive for thirty-seven years. Did he perhaps feel some remorse towards the end of his life for the suffering he had caused his children? The war years would certainly not have been easy for an elderly man.

Even when Ippei had been actively involved in the socialist movement decades before, the government had seen him as a mere cog in a wheel and had dismissed his zealous assertions. In the eighth volume of a collection of documents and records found among the belongings of Takashi Hara, prime minister from 1918 to 1921, there is the following brief reference to Ippei Annaka:[118]

> [Ippei Annaka] met and became a socialist through Mr. K, a socialist who lives in Kita Shinagawa and is engaged in textile dyeing. [Annaka] has no sound knowledge. Nothing worthy of note in his words or actions. Merely a blind follower of socialism.

But Ippei's dream of equal educational opportunity for all had set Hanako on the path of scholarship. She had absorbed the ideals he had pursued in his youth. Shozaburo, on the other hand, had been denied the opportunities Hanako had enjoyed. Faced with the tragedy of his fate, Hanako vowed that she would not let her brother's death be in vain. Employed part-time by the Ministry of Education, she became actively involved in educational reform to open up opportunities for all children.

She was also invited to offer her opinions as a member of various committees working on postwar revisions of the civil code. She used these forums to advocate for the necessity of a new, democratic family law that would abolish the existing inequitable system, ensuring that spouses would respect one another, could jointly own property, and would be encouraged to share the responsibility of childrearing.

An Auspicious Encounter

Hanako's translation of *Anne of Green Gables*, which, along with Hanako and her family, had escaped the flames of war, was still sitting in Hanako's study, bundled up in a *furoshiki* cloth. As stability returned to daily life, Japanese admiration for the Western lifestyle grew. This orientation was reflected in the publishing world, and many editors came to Hanako looking for newly translated works. They showed no interest, however, in *Anne of Green Gables* or Lucy Maud Montgomery, a Canadian author they had never heard of. When it came to children's and family literature in particular, publishers could not shake their conservative approach. They wanted works that were certain to sell, so they chose to publish new arrangements of proven classics: things like *Little Women*, *Little Lord Fauntleroy*, *A Little Princess*, or *Heart* (*Cuore*) by Italian author Edmondo de Amicis.

It did not help that in 1950, the GHQ abolished paper rationing and introduced free competition into the publishing world, making it even harder to secure capital or paper for publishing projects. Publishers were struggling for survival, and their editors would never be permitted to gamble on an unknown writer even if they wanted. Although Hanako introduced *Anne* to many different editors, she received no favourable responses.

One day in 1951, Kiko Koike, an editor from Mikasa Shobo Company, came to visit Hanako at home. Before and during the war, Koike had been an enthusiastic primary school teacher, as well as an avid scholar of history and social studies. In 1948, however, he and many other educators were forced to quit teaching, owing to the so-called education purge, which aimed to remove anyone opposed to occupational policies from the teaching profession. Koike joined Mikasa Shobo Company as an editor in 1951, the very year the expulsion edict was lifted.

Mikasa Shobo had been founded in 1933 by Michinosuke Takeuchi—known for his translations of Scottish novelist Archibald Joseph Cronin—and his wife, Tomiko. Their aim was to publish literature in translation. The company produced many translated literary works, such as a complete collection of Dostoevsky and of Herman Hesse. They also published Yasuo Okubo's translation of Margaret Mitchell's *Gone with the Wind* in 1937.

Around 1940, as militarism tightened its grip on Japan, many of Hanako's previously published translations, including *The Prince and the Pauper, Pollyanna Grows Up, Sister Sue*, and *The Exile: Portrait of an American Mother*, had been condemned as enemy literature. Mikasa Shobo's Japanese edition of *Gone with the Wind* met the same fate, and soon after, Japan launched the Pacific War. When the war finally ended and Takeuchi had rebuilt the company, he republished *Gone with the Wind*, which became a sensational bestseller. In addition to their admiration for American culture, postwar Japanese readers were enthralled by the tenacity of the heroine, Scarlet O'Hara, as she surmounted suffering and hardship in the context of the American Civil War. The book also captured the hearts of far more women readers than any previous translated literature. Hanako had read the book, both in the original and in Yasuo Okubo's translation.

As Koike explained the purpose of his visit, Hanako could see that he had great faith in Mr. Takeuchi. "Our president wants to maintain this focus on our female readership," Koike said. "That's why I came to you. I thought you might know of some new work that could follow up on the success of *Gone with the Wind*. Can you think of anything?"

Mikasa Shobo was seeking novelty, Hanako thought. Their approach was to translate and publish original new works soon after they came out overseas. *Anne of Green Gables* was by no means new. It had been written in 1908, when Hanako was fifteen, and more than forty years had passed since then. It also lacked the vivid drama that characterized *Gone with the Wind*. Instead, it followed the ordinary life of an orphan girl as she grew and matured. Yet this novel was studded with words and phrases that transformed the ordinary into something that shone. Within it, Hanako perceived an ordinariness so refined it was extraordinary. But still.

"No, I'm sorry. I don't," Hanako said.

Koike left disappointed, but continued to drop by and chat with Hanako about different topics. He was particularly passionate in his views on the future of children's education. In the winter, about half a year after his first visit, they were sitting in Hanako's study sipping tea when he suddenly said, "You're a Christian, aren't you?"

"Yes, I am. Why do you ask?"

"Because I noticed you have so many bibles on your shelves," he said, pointing to the bookcase. One section was devoted to Japanese and English bibles and hymnals published by Fukuin Printing Company.

"Oh, those."

"Do you think a good knowledge of the Bible is necessary to deeply understand British and American literature?" Koike asked. He had never read the Bible.

"Well yes, just as we need to know Buddhism to understand the Oriental arts. The Bible is the basis of everything in Western philosophy and lifestyle, so a knowledge of it is essential for people studying English literature. Regardless of whether one believes in it or not, it would be better to have read it. The language in the Book of Proverbs and the Book of Psalms in the Old Testament is really beautiful. When I was young, I memorized many of them in English. I can still recite them word for word." She recited part of a psalm for him on the spot.

"How did you learn your English?" Koike asked.

"At school. I lived in the dorm of a school established by Canadian missionaries."

"A mission school."

"Yes. I thought that if I could just learn English, that would be enough. Now I realize how narrow-minded that was. At the time, I read every

English book they had in the school library. When I was about seventeen, they expanded it. One of the Canadian teachers told me they needed a bigger one because I'd read all the books. She was joking of course."

"Have you read all the books here?" Koike asked as he ran his eyes over the spines of the English books on the shelves.

"Yes, I have. Some were given to me by foreign teachers when I was studying or teaching, and others are ones I collected myself. But they aren't new books of the kind that you're looking for."

"May I?" Koike asked. He stood up and took a book off the shelf. It was *Through the Looking Glass*, the sequel to *Alice's Adventures in Wonderland*, which Miss Blackmore had sent to Hanako when Hanako worked at Yamanashi Eiwa. Koike picked up books one by one. *A Dog of Flanders*, *The Nürnberg Stove*, *A Christmas Carol*. Each was adorned with beautiful illustrations. When he picked up Tennyson's "In Memoriam," with its dignified binding, it opened at a page that contained a tricoloured violet wrapped in thin, silk-like paper. Passionate words written by a young Hanako remained inscribed in the margin.

"What a beautiful book," said Koike with a sigh.

Hanako was reminded suddenly of words she had heard long ago. "It's my goal to produce ones as beautiful as those in England." She recalled her brother-in-law, Hitoshi, whose life had been cut short before he could realize his dream of creating beautiful books. The Great Kanto Earthquake seemed so far in the past. The blow dealt the publishing industry by the air raids had been even worse than the destruction wreaked by the earthquake. Publishers that had managed to rise from the ashes of war were struggling desperately to survive.

"Mr. Koike," she began tentatively. "You know, I might have something that would interest you."

Koike raised his face, eyes wide, and stared at Hanako silently.

"But it's not new," she continued, "and I know you're really looking for new works." She opened the glass doors of a book cabinet and took out the copy of *Anne of Green Gables*, which she had received from Miss Shaw, and her translation, still wrapped in the *furoshiki* cloth. She placed them in front of him.

"Here," she said.

"May I?" Koike asked.

"Please. Go ahead. It was written in 1908, which is forty-three years ago now. Your company wouldn't want to take the risk of publishing a work totally unknown in Japan, would they? I mean, you'd have no way of knowing if it would sell or not. But I can tell you this: It's loved by many American and Canadian readers."

She showed him the copyright page. The first printing was listed as June 1908 followed almost every month by a new printing. Hanako's copy had been printed in December 1908 and was the seventh edition.

Koike narrowed his eyes at that. "You're right," he said.

Hanako told him the story of how the book had come to her, and showed him Miss Shaw's signature, which was written at the edge of the first page in small letters. She told him what had driven her to translate the book during the war, and of the special meaning it held for her. All the while, Koike listened motionlessly, his expression intent.

"I see," he finally said. "Let me take this and speak with the president."

Hanako handed it to him a little reluctantly. "If he says no, please bring it back right away," she begged him.

"I'll do everything I can to make sure we publish it," said Koike. He strode briskly off, cradling the bundle in his arms as though it were very precious.

The Birth of *Akage no An* (Redheaded Anne)

Hanako waited breathlessly for the decision. Several days later, an elated Koike appeared at her door. "I consulted Mr. Takeuchi," he said. "We're going to publish it!"

Hanako could have danced for joy. At long last, this Canadian story would be published in Japan. The whole family had protected it through the war, and Midori and Keizo clapped when they heard the news.

After repeated polishing, the manuscript was ready for printing. Then they hit a snag. The English title was *Anne of Green Gables*, but no one in Japan was familiar with a gabled roof. Hanako thought up numerous alternatives that sounded romantic in Japanese, such as "Dreamer Girl," "Girl by the Window," and "The Girl Gazing out the Window." After much discussion, Hanako finally decided on the latter. After she returned home that evening, however, she got a call from the president of Mikasa Shobo himself.

"Hello," he said. "About the title, Koike wondered about changing it to 'Redheaded Anne.' What do you think?"

"Redheaded Anne?" Hanako repeated. She did not like it. It was too direct, leaving no room for the imagination. She was sure that Anne, the romantic, would have hated it. "Absolutely not. It won't do at all," she said emphatically and hung up the phone.

While drinking tea with her family after dinner, Hanako told Keizo and Midori that they had decided on "The Girl Gazing Out the Window" for the title. "But you know Mr. Koike?" she added indignantly. "He suggested calling it 'Redheaded Anne.' Honestly!"

"Redheaded Anne?" asked Midori, who was now twenty.

"That's right. It's so plain, isn't it?" Hanako said.

"Do you really think so, Mother?" Midori asked. She rolled the words over her tongue. "Redheaded Anne. Why, it's wonderful! Mother, 'Redheaded Anne' is much better! It's the perfect title. 'The Girl Gazing Out the Window' sounds strange!"

Although Hanako had scorned the editor's suggestion, Midori's unexpected opposition jolted her back to her senses. This book was for young people. A young person's opinion just might be right. As the book was to be sent to the printers the very next day, Hanako rushed to the phone and called the company president.

"Hello, Mr. Takeuchi?" she said. "I'm terribly sorry for being so rude earlier. My daughter has just told me she thinks 'Redheaded Anne' is perfect, and she won't back down. I've decided it's better to trust a young girl's sensibility in this case. So please, change the title to 'Redheaded Anne'!"

❀

The grief of losing loved ones during the war and scenes of desolation were still fresh in people's minds, but tensions triggered by the Cold War were rising on the Korean peninsula and preparations for another conflict were already evident in Japan, which had been integrated into America's military strategy. In June 1950, the Korean War began, pitting pro-communist forces in northern Korea against pro-Western forces in the south. In Japan, a police reserve force, which would later evolve into Japan's self-defense forces, was formed.

Hanako's friend Akiko Yanagiwara, whose son Kaori had been killed just before the end of the Second World War, started the International Association of Grieving Mothers (Kokusai Hibo no Kai), an organization dedicated to promoting peace that was led by mothers who had lost children in the war. After the Korean War broke out, Akiko wrote:

> I believe we no longer need borders. The seas and land of this earth are the common property of the entire human race, a bounty bestowed by nature on all alike that should never be monopolized by a single nation or people. To use violence in the supposed pursuit of human survival and happiness is pointless, for these can only be achieved through peaceful means. Many Japanese have suffered as victims of the recent war, yet our nation has offered them no relief. The same government that deceived its people and spurred them on to fight is herding us yet again towards war. The end result will be nothing but chaos, insurrection, butchery, and finally, extinction.[119]

At the end of April 1952, the Treaty of San Francisco came into force, re-establishing peaceful relations between the Allied nations and Japan and bringing to a close the American-led occupation of Japan and the GHQ. Despite Japan regaining its status as an independent nation, the Japanese people were in no mood to celebrate. Instead, on May Day, demonstrators paraded through the streets. Bearing placards that said *Stop Re-armament* and *No More War*, they clashed with the police.

It was within this social context that the Japanese version of *Anne of Green Gables* debuted on May 10. The Japanese people yearned for freedom, ideals, and peace, and Anne appeared as a symbol of hope. The cover, which bore in red letters the title *Akage no An* (Redheaded Anne), featured a girl with strawberry blonde hair and a serious expression. Not even the most prejudiced eye could have claimed that this girl resembled the book's heroine. The illustration was in fact the painting *Ethel* by British artist Ralph Peacock, which had been introduced in a feature on famous paintings in the February 1940 edition of *Girls' Friend*. Hanako, who had been closely involved with the magazine since around 1935, saw this publication as a beacon of hope that had accompanied Japanese girls through the changing times. Knowing that many fans of the magazine would read the book she had translated, Hanako had quietly taken that picture and placed it on the cover. She did so as an expression of love for all the girls and women who had lived through great hardship.

Compared to the translations Hanako had published before the war, such as *The Prince and the Pauper*, *Pollyanna Grows Up*, and *The Exile: Portrait of an American Mother*, the binding was of very poor quality. But she could not complain. Being able to publish at all was worthwhile and brought her immense joy. The price was 250 yen per copy. At a time when a bowl of noodles with broth cost only 13 yen, the book's price was steep indeed.

Hanako took a copy just off the presses before the publication date. Inside the cover, she wrote, *For my beloved Midori, from Mother* and gave the book to her daughter. Miss Shaw had died in Canada in 1940, while the author, Lucy Maud Montgomery, had passed away in 1942. But Hanako had carried on the spirit of these two women, and the Japanese version, *Akage no An*, was the result. In the afterword of the first edition, Hanako wrote:

There is something within the story of Anne, a young girl wrapped in a world of daydreams, that breathes with the pure innocence of girlhood, an innocence which is never lost but lives on in our longing for it, even in the age of the airplane, even though television has become a familiar part of daily life.

Although the country of Canada extends north from the United States of America, the Canadian people have a cheerfulness and simplicity that sets them apart from the Americans or the British. I learned English from Canadian missionaries at Toyo Eiwa Girls School, which was founded through the collaboration of Canadian missionaries and the Japanese, during one era of that school's seventy-year history. From that time to the present, the Westerners I have met have mainly been Canadians. My desire to introduce this work by a Canadian author stems from my gratitude for the warm friendship extended to me by many Canadians. Now, when the publishing industry of Japan suffers from a dearth of wholesome family literature, it is with great joy that I dedicate my translation of *Anne of Green Gables*, the eternal heroine of the younger generations, to the memory of my youthful days at my alma mater on top of the hill in Azabu, and to the younger sisters of my heart who continue to study there.

Spring 1952 In Omori, Tokyo

Hanako Muraoka

Anne of Green Gables captured the hearts of young women all over Japan, quickly becoming a bestseller and far exceeding the expectations of both Hanako and the publisher. Although the Japanese were materially poor, through Anne's words, readers knew the joy of using their imagination, and their admiration for the heroine extended to Anne's homeland, Prince Edward Island.

Readers sent Hanako letters, some of which, like the following, were influenced by Anne's style of talking, making Hanako smile.

"Mrs. Muraoka, who gave me this marvellous book, won't you be my bosom friend?"

Soon after the first edition was published, Koike came to consult Hanako about translating a sequel.

❀

After publishing Hanako's translation of *Anne of Windy Poplars*, the fifth volume in the Japanese *Anne* series, in 1957, Mikasa Shobo went out of business. Although the company was later resurrected, Koike, who had played a leading role in the birth of the Japanese *Anne*, was no longer there. Unable to give up his passion for education, he had moved to Hokkaido and become a social sciences teacher at Kitami Hokuto High School in 1953.

To those who knew Mikasa Shobo in the early days, Hanako often spoke of Koike, the editor who first recognized the value of *Anne of Green Gables*, with fond nostalgia. "To be the first is truly great," Hanako declared. "Koike's discernment was impressive. I'll never forget him. I'm sure he's using his keen perception to teach his students."

Koike quickly demonstrated his ability as an enthusiastic history teacher, pulling information from a wide range of sources to make fact-filled sheets for his students. He was also in charge of the ping-pong club, playing the game himself, and he led the school team to victory several times in the prefectural championships. In his spare time, he devoted himself to the study of popular history based on vigorous field studies, writing numerous books[120] about such subjects as the villagers of Yanaka who were displaced by pollution from the Ashio Copper Mine, prison labour and the rights of prisoners, the digging of the Jomon Tunnel in Hokkaido, and the way of life of Japanese socialists at the turn of the twentieth century. His contributions in this field were remarkable, shedding light on the history of those hidden in the shadow of modern social development, such as the marginalized labourers who were exploited in the development of Hokkaido, minority ethnic groups like the Ainu and the Orok, and Korean and Chinese wartime labourers.

Michio's Library

The summer that Hanako's translation of *Anne of Green Gables* was published, Hanako decided to reorganize her library with the help of Midori, who was now a university student and on summer vacation. While they were working, Hisayuki, the eight-year-old son of the Nishikawas, who lived next door, dropped by. His face was darkly tanned from playing out in the sun.

"What're you doing, Auntie?" he asked.

"Hello there, Hisayuki," said Hanako. "I'm reorganizing my bookcases because they're too full."

"They sure are," Hisayuki agreed. He was the boss of the boys in the neighbourhood, and he and his older brother Seiji were always running about in just shorts and undershirts with clean-shaven heads. Every day, Hanako could hear the sounds of them quarrelling loudly and their mother scolding them from their house. After watching Hanako and Midori for a while, Hisayuki suddenly said, "Auntie, can I borrow some of your books?"

"You mean manga, right?" Hanko teased him. "I'm afraid I don't have any of those. How about one of these nursery tale collections? Why don't you give them a try? They're fun."

Hisayuki kicked off his muddy canvas shoes and jumped up into the room with a grin. For some time he immersed himself in the mountain of books, scouring their titles. Finally, he announced, "I'll take this one!" He held up a collection of nursery tales by Hirosuke Hamada which, as was common in books for children in lower elementary grades, was written entirely in *kana*, a simple script of phonetic symbols without any Chinese characters. Early the next afternoon, he appeared again. "Hello Auntie. I came to return this," he said.

"Surely you haven't finished it already, have you?"

"Yes, I did. There weren't any pictures, but it was still interesting. Can I borrow another one?" he asked, his eyes shining. He picked another from the pile.

"Next time, bring your brother too," Hanako said.

Hisayuki shrugged. "I'll think about it. See you!" He ran off with the book tucked under his arm.

Midori waved goodbye. Turning to Hanako, she said, "Mother, why don't we start a library for the neighbourhood children? You've got all these books of Michio's and mine that I don't read anymore. It seems a waste to just line them up on the shelves. I could run it if you like. What do you think?"

There were no public children's libraries in Japan yet, and few families had any children's books. "That's a great idea!" Hanako exclaimed. "It would make the books happy too."

❁

Fourteen years earlier, in 1938, Hanako had had the idea of building a little children's library in the yard. She had noticed that girls from upper elementary grades who lived in the neighbourhood used to come by almost every day and ask to play with Midori, even though she was only in grade one. Curious, Hanako had taken a peek at what they were doing and had found each one engrossed in a magazine or book that they had picked off the shelves. Because she had so many books, Midori had become an important person in their lives.

Children really want to read, Hanako thought. *I wonder if we couldn't scatter simple little children's libraries all over Japan.* She envisioned building a small two-storey structure in the garden with a meeting room on the second floor and a children's library on the first. There would be a sink for washing their hands when they entered and, once inside, they could sit quietly and read books and magazines. She could put in a little kitchen and washstand on the first and second floors. All the children living nearby would be welcome there. She would give them membership cards, and they would be free to enter whenever they wanted. The only rule would be no talking. Sometimes they could have events for the children on the second floor: not just talks by good speakers, but also discussions, consultations, and even debates run by the children themselves with an adult there just as a supervisor. If there were one such children's library in each district, how happy the children would be!

Of course, it would be even better to have a large, well-equipped library, but Hanako's vision was to start small by creating neighbourhood children's libraries, which would be less work. When she published an essay about her dream, she received a letter from Momoko Ishii, an editor fourteen years her junior. Ishii wrote that she had had exactly the same idea and was actually preparing to start up a children's library in the home of author Takeru Inukai, whom Ishii had gotten to know through her work, using his personal collection. The war, however, intervened before either of their dreams could be realized.

By the time the war ended, Midori, as well as Hanako's nieces and nephews, was much older, and Hanako had forgotten her idea. With the appearance of Hisayuki, however, her dream was revived. Moreover, it was Midori who suggested it, a fact that brought Hanako much joy.

Although Hanako's original concept had been quite small, the children's library she and Midori hastily put together was even simpler. They started by arranging on shelves in the corridor and in the garden shed the picture books that Hanako and Keizo had collected for Michio, their son who had died before his sixth birthday. His books were stamped with the words *Michio Books*. As they all used old-style *kana* readings for Chinese characters that no longer matched modern pronunciations, postwar children could not read them, but Hanako still placed them on the shelves in memory of Michio. Books that Midori had read when she was small were stamped with

1953. Children reading books in Michio's Library, Japan's first home library for children.

the words *Midori Books*. When they added to these the books that Hanako had been involved in publishing and the many books that she had received as gifts, they had close to one thousand children's books, enough to make a respectable home library. They called it Michio Bunko (Michio's Library), and Midori was the chief librarian.

Japan was in the midst of the postwar baby boom, and the library was a great success, its membership rapidly multiplying. Early one morning, a boy in grade two dropped by. "I've come to get my dictionary," he said.

"Your dictionary is here?" Hanako asked.

"Yes," he said. "I thought if I leave it here, then everyone can use it." This made Hanako so happy, tears welled in her eyes.

Looking for someone to assist with the library, Hanako singled out Shigeo Watanabe, a university student boarding with Hanako's neighbours, the Masui family. A member of the newly established librarian course at Keio University, he went on to become a leading figure in the Japanese children's book world, writing stories such as *Mori no Henasoru* (Henasoru of the Forest) and translating works such as *My Father's Dragon* and *Harry the Dirty Dog*. Hanako had met him soon after the war while at a friend's house in Shizuoka where she had been invited to give a talk at Shizuoka Eiwa Girls School. When Watanabe later moved to Tokyo for university, he had ended up boarding very near Hanako. As he later wrote:

> Mrs. Muraoka was overjoyed when I told her that I intended to join the library science division at university and focus my studies on children's libraries and children's literature. Because of our connection, I started visiting the Muraoka home. There were two low bookshelves placed in the corridor between the parlor and the living room, and the neighbourhood children came to borrow books from these. Younger brothers and sisters would tag along after the older girls, who led them by the hand. Midori always treated each one very kindly.... The users of the library belonged to the Michio Club of which Midori was the president. Before I knew it, I was

helping out too. I brought along some classmates from Keio, and they helped me organize new books that Mrs. Muraoka got for the library and get them ready for lending.[121]

As news of Michio's Library spread by word of mouth, journalists from newspapers and children's magazines began coming to see it. Each time, the children appeared dressed in their best clothes and with their hair neatly cut.

Michio Club members gathered every Saturday after school to play and study, and they looked forward to the snacks that Fumi prepared for them. Watanabe was enthusiastically involved, coming up with different ideas for activities, while Hanako participated whenever she could find time in her busy schedule. The library featured storytelling, excursions, debates, and English study, as well as Christmas parties, which were held on the premises of a nearby kindergarten. For Christmas, each child received a card and a book with their name written in it.

Late 1950s. Women writers gathered in spring and fall for enjoyable events at Higashi Kurenaikai. At a carp-fishing event, Nobuko Yoshiya (second from right) is stylishly dressed in Western clothing. Hanako (fifth from left) always wore kimono, even after the war.

Upon graduation, Watanabe went to study in America. In his stead, a teacher from the neighbourhood school, Iriarai Daini Elementary School, began helping with the library. As he was aiming to become a writer, he taught the children how to write stories.

Michio's Library closed in 1967 when Hanako had cataract surgery, and the book collection was donated to two nearby elementary schools.

As for Momoko Ishii, the first to support Hanako's concept of children's libraries, she translated A. A. Milne's *Winnie the Pooh* which was published by Iwanami Shoten Publishers in 1940. In 1951, her book *Nonchan kumo ni noru* (Nonchan Rides on a Cloud) became a bestseller. In 1954, Ishii spent a year in the United States, where she studied children's literature and library science. In 1958, she launched a children's library called Katsura Bunko in a room in her house in Ogikubo.

Hanako and Momoko Ishii, along with Shigeko Tsuchiya, who promoted the reading movement, started the Home Library Research Society for the study and dissemination of home libraries. At their meetings, members reported on their activities and discussed ideal features of children's libraries. Momoko Ishii provided knowledge and information gained while studying children's library science in America and made significant contributions to the development of children's literature in Japan and the establishment of public children's libraries. By the early 1960s, the society's members included children's book publishers, elementary school teachers, and housewives who had established home libraries. Children's libraries were spreading throughout Japan.

Chapter 10

Cherished People, Cherished Books: 1953–1968
Age 60 to 75

Peaceful Days Return

Hanako and Keizo's house was always lively, a hub for relatives and friends. Hanako's mother began living at the house at the age of eighty, after Hanako brought her to Tokyo in 1951, a few years following Ippei's death. Hanako cared for her mother with the help of her siblings. From afternoon until evening, neighbourhood children dropped by Michio's Library; around the time they left, Hanako's nieces and nephews would stop by the house. Sometimes they were joined by the children of Keizo's youngest brother, Kiyoshi, who lived in Setagaya. Once or twice a week, there would be an evening mahjong party with Hanako's younger brother Kenjiro, and Keizo's friends, including Seishiro Iwamura, the Omori Megumi Church pastor. Sometimes Midori or the Muraokas' nieces and nephews would join, but not Hanako. With all her translation and writing work, she simply had no time. Yet she loved to have people over and to hear the house filled with cheerful conversation.

Unexpected visitors were frequent. Young women majoring in British and American literature at university came to consult Hanako, asking earnest questions about how to become a translator of her calibre. Sometimes they even brought a sample of their work. Moved by their enthusiasm, Hanako would lay down her pen and listen. As she did so, she realized that although they were all highly motivated and excelled at English studies, unlike Hanako at that age, they felt no need to hone their Japanese writing skills. "You don't have to use difficult words," she would tell them. "But in translation, you need to choose the right words, ones that bring out subtle nuances, and to do that, I believe you need a rich vocabulary and a sensitivity in your mother tongue. That's at least as important as, and perhaps even more important than English-language ability. When you look at the many expressions in the Japanese language for the seasons, nature, colours, and emotions, when you think of the language's rich history, surely you can see how important it is to expose yourself to Japanese classical literature and poetry, such as tanka and haiku." The young women invariably looked taken aback by Hanako's advice, as though she had somehow disappointed their expectations.

Hanako remembered the days when she had studied under Nobutsuna Sasaki with the sincere intent of becoming a poet. Although now over eighty, Nobutsuna was still vigorously pursuing his study of the classics. When Hanako considered his students, even just the ones she knew personally, regardless of whether they were famous or not, she recognized that many were true artists of the Japanese language. Recently, Hanako had run into several former members of Chikuhaku-kai, Nobutsuna's tanka society, which no longer existed. Nobutsuna, they told her, was very pleased with her achievements. These words, however, made Hanako want to crawl into a hole with embarrassment. Although she had given up her dream of becoming a poet, she had never lost her respect for verse. "I'm completely unworthy of having been his disciple," she protested. "I now write nothing but prose." Still, she had clung desperately to her pen through all the vicissitudes of life. The one thing of which she was certain was that, from her school days to the present, she had never given up translating.

Keizo and Midori often went to the theatre or the movies together. They also did most of the shopping, not only for daily necessities, but also for items that would add beauty to their home—a task Hanako mainly left up to them. She was frequently out most of the day attending meetings or giving lectures, so the only time she could really sit down to focus on writing or translation was after eleven at night, when Keizo and Midori went to bed. From this time on, the world was Hanako's domain. When she sat down to sip a cup of tea or coffee she had made in the kitchenette using the little electric burner, she finally felt free to do as she liked. Surrounded by shelves crammed with books, she tackled her work, which was at times delightful and at times gruelling.

She was by nature a night owl, and would end up working until dawn if she wasn't careful. This happened about three times a week. She did not start out with the intention of staying up, but by the time she thought about going to sleep and glanced at the clock, it was already four or five in the morning.

"You should drink milk," Keizo told her. "It's excellent, a complete food, you know." Having suffered from poor health during the war, Keizo began drinking milk daily when he heard it had health benefits. Worried about Hanako, who kept such irregular hours, he urged her to try it too. Hanako hated milk, but she drank it just to please him.

On December 17, 1954, Hanako's mother, Tetsu Annaka, passed away at the age of eighty-three. Although Tetsu had been baptized, Hanako gave her a Buddhist funeral. She knew that it was only because Tetsu's husband, Ippei, had become a Christian that Tetsu had abandoned her family's Buddhist religion and begun going to church. Christianity had never had any reality for her. After Ippei's death, she had talked constantly about the teachings of Buddha. Intuiting her final, unstated wish, Hanako gave her mother, who had never asked for anything in life and had always obeyed her husband with a smile, a fine Buddhist memorial service.

The causes for which Hanako had worked through the Japan Woman's Christian Temperance Union had been realized, including women's suffrage, the abolition of licensed prostitution, and the banning of alcohol and tobacco for minors. Longing for a society where everyone, including women and children, could live happily, Hanako had gone on to serve as vice-president of the National Federation of UNESCO Associations in Japan. Through this organization, she addressed social problems and engaged in welfare projects. She also supported the activities of the feminist Fusae Ichikawa, and, as a member of government committees

1958. A gathering with the wife of the Philippine ambassador. Hanako is on the far right, beside Fusae Ichikawa.

tackling such issues as juvenile delinquency and prostitution, Hanako sometimes argued heatedly with male committee members. But she was also mature and generous of spirit, always reaching out with a friendly smile to the other members when the debate was over. She studied politics and economics earnestly, conversing and exchanging views with leading figures in the postwar reconstruction of the Japanese economy. These included such men as Hisato Ichimada[122], president of the Bank of Japan; Aiichiro Fujiyama[123], who, despite being a private citizen, served as Japan's foreign minister in the Kishi Cabinet; and entrepreneur Hisakichi Maeda[124]. Hanako was also frequently called upon to interpret for social activists and other guests from overseas. She never stinted in her efforts to contribute to the betterment of society.

⚘

On October 30, 1952, Margaret Higgins Sanger visited Japan from America at the age of sixty-nine. Founder of the birth control movement, she had devoted forty years of her life to the cause. Two days after her arrival, she took part in a discussion on Radio Tokyo (currently the Tokyo Broadcasting System) with Shidzue Kato[125], who pioneered the birth

1955. Hanako conversing with Hisato Ichimada, who devoted himself to Japan's postwar economic revival and was able to debate on an equal footing with General Douglas MacArthur, an American five-star general known for his persuasive debating style.

control movement in Japan. Hanako served as their interpreter. Sanger's motivation for promoting birth control was the death of her mother, who had been so depleted from child-bearing and from poverty-induced malnutrition that she had contracted tuberculosis and died giving birth to her eleventh child. While serving as a nurse in a poor working-class district, Sanger witnessed the tragedies poverty and excess births caused women like her mother. To prevent unwanted births, she began advocating contraception, which was considered taboo by Christians because it violated God's domain. She also began devising different contraceptive methods.

Rather than refusing to have children, Sanger's movement advocated choosing to have only the number of children a person felt capable of responsibly raising in view of their economic capacity and physical health. Her approach, however, was greeted with harsh criticism, and she was imprisoned for breaking anti-obscenity laws. Despite this, she had

November 1, 1952. A lecture by Margaret Sanger hosted by Radio Tokyo. From the left: Margaret Sanger, Shidzue Kato, Interpreter Hanako.

gradually gained the support of other women and has since become hailed in America as a heroine who changed the course of that nation's history.

When Hanako first met her, she found Sanger so calm and gentle that she wondered where this woman concealed the strength to endure being imprisoned or the courage to stand up for her beliefs in the face of so much scorn and opposition. Once Sanger began to speak, however, her passion poured forth with eloquence. As she interpreted the words of this woman who had fought against persecution for the realization of her ideals, Hanako was galvanized by Sanger's unshakable spirit.

✹

On May 28, 1955, every Japanese newspaper carried a feature on the visit of Helen Keller, who was hailed as an "angel with a triple handicap." Keller's renowned teacher, Anne Sullivan, had died in 1936, and Polly Thompson, who carried on Sullivan's spirit, accompanied Keller instead. This was Keller's third visit to Japan, her first being in 1937 and her second in 1948, just after the war. She was seventy-five years old. Hanako had

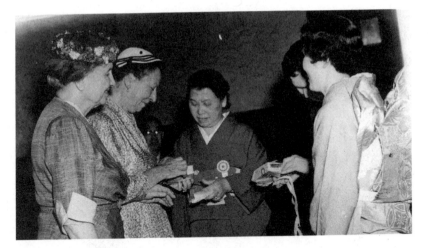

May 1955. Hanako (centre) learns tactile fingerspelling from Miss Thompson at a welcome reception for Helen Keller (far left).

heard her speak at the Hibiya Public Hall during her second visit. Deeply moved by Helen's words, Hanako wrote a biography of Helen Keller for children based on two books, one of which was *The Story of My Life*, related by Helen herself.[126] Hanako's book was published in 1950 by Kaisei-sha Ltd.

During Keller's third visit to Japan, Hanako was able to meet and talk with her at a welcome reception held in the Imperial Hotel. On May 30, she also interpreted for Keller's lecture at the Iidabashi Fujimicho Church. In this lecture, Keller appealed to the Japanese people to show understanding for those who were visually impaired and expressed her hope that Japanese society would come to embrace them. She also strongly encouraged visually impaired people not to give up on their fate. In the second edition of Hanako's biography of Helen Keller, Hanako shared her impressions of coming into contact with such a remarkable soul, as well as the words Keller had spoken.

In 1932, Azuma Moriya, who was on the board of the Japan Woman's Christian Temperance Union, had established a welfare facility for people with physical disabilities. Even in the 1950s, however, the general public still had very little compassion for or understanding of people living with disabilities, who were relegated to the background in society. Helen Keller's third visit to Japan helped to deepen people's understanding and led to actions that would spur changes in Japanese society, including the expansion of a welfare system and improvements in education for the deaf and visually impaired. The Blue Bird Movement (Aoi Tori Undo)[127], which was started to commemorate Helen Keller's visit, spread nationwide, and the Tokyo Helen Keller Association was founded at the time to support people living with disabilities, work that the organization continues to this day.

🟊

After *Anne of Green Gables* was published in Japanese, Hanako had continued to translate the sequels, encouraged by the ardent letters of the book's many fans who longed to read more. Within the span of seven years, she completed the entire *Anne* series of ten novels. The complete series translation was published by Shinchosha Publishing Co., Ltd., while the abridged translation was published by Kodansha Ltd. The series included *Anne of Green Gables, Anne of Avonlea, Anne of the Island, Chronicles of Avonlea, Anne of Windy Poplars, Anne's House of Dreams, Anne of Ingleside, Further Chronicles of Avonlea*, and two books that shift the focus from Anne to her children, *Rainbow Valley* and *Rilla of Ingleside*.

In *Rilla of Ingleside*, life on Prince Edward Island during the First World War is depicted through the eyes of Anne's youngest daughter, Rilla. Anne and Rilla support their country from the island, praying fervently for the safety of Anne's sons and Rilla's older brothers, who have gone to war. They receive news, however, that Walter, who had inherited his mother's poetic nature, was killed in France. Through her portrayal of Anne and Rilla's profound grief, Montgomery conveyed her hope for peace.

Having survived the era of Japanese imperialism by participating in the Japan Patriotic Writers League, Hanako was still plagued with remorse. Recalling the anguish of all mothers and sisters who mourned the loss of loved ones killed in the Second World War, Hanako translated the last volume of the series, *Rilla of Ingleside*, as a plea for an end to war.

Memories of Friends

Hanako's study was filled with cherished mementos from her friends. On her writing bureau sat a poem penned on a square card by the poet Kuniko Imai, which Kuniko had given Hanako when she finished renovating her study before the war.

> Always bringing forth new life,
> like water springing from a mountain valley
> thick with cedar.

Kuniko's prim, kimono-clad appearance belied her determination and passion. A Christian, she had run away from home at the age of nineteen in protest against a marriage arranged for her by her parents. She became a newspaper reporter and two years later married a fellow journalist. Discovering that her husband was cheating on her after a decade of marriage, she left him and their two children and got a job as a house cleaner. She returned home, however, for the sake of the children. She died of a heart attack in 1948 at the age of fifty-nine.

Writing is a difficult art: the ebb and flow of emotions makes it hard to sustain one's passion, yet without passion, it is impossible to perform one's work properly. The poem was Kuniko's prayer that Hanako would always find new inspiration, like water springing from a mountain and gushing through a valley. It was also a prayer for Kuniko herself.

Adorning the wall of Hanako's study was another poem, this one penned by her friend and junior in years, Fumiko Hayashi. It was the poem that contained the famous lines "A flower's life is short." The distinctive round letters of Fumiko's handwriting were written in fountain pen on lined manuscript paper.

The wind blows,
the clouds shine.
The joy of living
bobs like a seagull
on the waves.

You know
the joy of living,
I know it too.
A flower's life is short.
Only bitterness abounds.
Yet still,
the wind blows,
the clouds shine.

Fumiko was originally a poet. After her novel *Diary of a Vagabond* became a sensational bestseller, she wrote mainly fiction, but her innate poetic spirit breathed through her works to the very end. In 1951, she died suddenly from a heart attack. She was only forty-seven. Called the "darling of the media" because her tumultuous life gave reporters so much to write about, she was also in demand as a journalist, writing investigative articles for a variety of magazines. She escaped the grinding poverty into which she was born through sheer effort, writing constantly. Eventually, she gained every material thing she could have wanted. Yet even after establishing herself as the most popular writer in Japan, she always seemed driven and was a stranger to peace of mind.

Nasty gossip plagued her. Some people claimed that she had interfered with a rival publisher, while others said that she had spread false rumours. Some even sneered at her for having the vulgar tastes of the nouveau riche.

But the only Fumiko that Hanako remembered was her dear friend: the Fumiko who wept and ranted that her friends misunderstood her; the Fumiko who puffed away on cigarettes and scoffed at "family," even though deep down she really cared about her family; and the Fumiko who had introduced her mother to Hanako saying, "My mother's a huge fan of yours." *If Fumiko had been steadier emotionally,* Hanako often thought, *she might not have died so young.* But it was precisely because Fumiko felt things so keenly that her works touched people's hearts. More than her social reputation, more than her words and actions, the poem that hung framed on Hanako's wall revealed Fumiko's inner truth.

❀

In a prominent spot in Hanako's bookcase was a copy of *Tokasetsu* (Candlemas), a collection of essays published in 1953 by Hiroko Katayama, whom Hanako greatly admired both as a writer and a woman. Hiroko had lost her son, Tatsukichi, just before the war's end. Tatsukichi had been a literary critic who wrote under the pen name Tetsutaro Yoshimura, and Hiroko had great expectations for his future. His death at the age of forty-four plunged her into loneliness and economic hardship. The following letter from Hiroko to Hanako, written on April 6, 1949, indicates the difficulties Hiroko was facing.

> At last, the cold has given way to the season of blossoming flowers. Iwako conveyed your kind words the other day. Thank you so much. I want to do something, but the thought of my advanced age is so daunting I feel paralyzed.
>
> Hard times are coming, however, and I cannot afford to wait idly, doing nothing. I know that I must try to do something commensurate with my capacity. It would make me very happy if you could suggest any work that someone like me could do. There is no hurry, so please think about it when you have an opportunity.
>
> I hope to pay you a visit in Omori this month, but if we could perhaps speak on the phone, that would be wonderful. I apologize for only writing to ask for your assistance.
>
> In haste.
>
> Hiroko

In the past, Hiroko had accepted no payment for her writing, never treating it as a job. Now, however, she picked up her pen and began to write as a means of livelihood. In 1955, *Candlemas* won the Third Essayist Club Prize, while her poetry collection *No ni sumite* (Living Among the Fields), which was published in the same year, also won high acclaim and was nominated for the Japan Art Academy Award. The following year, however, Hiroko collapsed from cerebral anemia and passed away one year later at the age of seventy-nine. She was deeply admired for her noble character, and many writers attended her funeral.

The death of Hanako's beloved friend and mentor, who had accompanied her through turbulent times, forced Hanako to ponder how she should spend the remainder of her life. Family literature, the necessity of which Hanako had first recognized while still a student, was gradually gaining social recognition in postwar Japan, and Hanako was considered a pioneer in the field. There were times when she wondered if translating family literature was truly the work she should have done. She had wanted to write more original stories and novels. But agonizing over it was pointless; she could not turn back now. Her path in life, she decided, was the way she had come thus far. She should see it through.

She continued to translate the stories she had read in her youth for the people of Japan: Gene Stratton-Porter's *A Girl of the Limberlost* and *Freckles*, Kate Douglas Wiggin's *Mother Carey's Chickens*, Mark Twain's *Huckleberry Finn*, Louisa May Alcott's *An Old-Fashioned Girl*, and Charles Dickens' *A Christmas Carol*.

A Letter from Canada

On April 26, 1959, Hanako's daughter Midori married Mitsuo Sano, a physicist who had studied at the prestigious Kyoto University. A small reception officiated by Shinji Iwamura, the pastor of Omori Megumi Church, was held at the International House of Japan across the street from Toyo Eiwa Girls School. Hanako turned sixty-six that year. Blessed with good health, she was strong in both mind and body.

After the wedding, Hanako turned Midori's room into an extension of her study. She had a penchant for reorganizing rooms, and this tendency was particularly pronounced when it came to her study. She would change the position of the furniture and bustle about moving things around during the busiest times, or more accurately, just before she became swamped with work. But Midori's bookshelves, filled with Midori's favourite books, which she had read over and over, seemed sacred, and Hanako could not bring herself to touch them until over half a year had passed. Finally, she began removing them one at a time, starting with the top shelf.

Midori had read a lot of good books. She had transferred from Aoyama Gakuin Women's Junior College to the English literature department of the four-year Aoyama Gakuin University where she had studied under the well-known English literature scholar and first president of Aoyama Gakuin University, Minoru Toyoda, and English literature scholar and author Makoto Kuranaga. There she had read all the British and American classics and modern literature that Hanako also loved. But Hanako had not read many essays by T. S. Eliot, a writer Midori appeared to admire. As for Japanese authors, Midori's copies of works by Yasushi Inoue, Tatsuo Hori, and Sei Ito were well worn, as were the poetry collections of Jun Takami and Magoichi Kushida.

The expressions on Midori's face when she had read these books rose in Hanako's mind as she perused them, one by one, while sitting or sometimes lying on Midori's bed. Midori's books were like a path leading Hanako through her daughter's mind in each period of her life. As she turned the pages, Hanako held a prayer in her heart for Midori that she would create her own happy family and home.

The neighbourhood children still came to borrow books from Michio's Library. Fumi had taken over Midori's job of lending the books, but the library seemed a little lonely without her. Midori had moved to a housing complex in Kumegawa, which was near Tanashi and the Tokyo University Institute of Nuclear Study, where Midori's husband worked. Midori had also served as Hanako's secretary, and when she moved out, Hanako hired Reiko Yagi instead. Frank and dependable, Reiko was an editor with experience in journalism in whom Hanako had complete confidence. Midori also came once or twice a week to help, travelling an hour and a half each way. Each time, she gazed wide-eyed around her old room and said, "You've changed it again."

One day, Midori found books and manuscript paper spread out over her old desk. "Mother, you're keeping very busy, aren't you?" Midori said.

"Yes, I've started a new translation. Another Montgomery book," Hanako answered, keeping her voice bright and cheerful to reassure Midori that she had nothing to worry about; that her mother was still actively pursuing her career. Hanako pointed to the book on her desk, Montgomery's *Kilmeny of the Orchard*, which she had ordered from Canada through Maruzen Bookstore. Like the *Anne* series, it was set on Prince Edward Island.

While translating the book, Hanako received a letter from Miss Hamilton, who had served as the principal of Toyo Eiwa before the war. Miss Hamilton had retired in 1956 and returned to Canada, after devoting herself for forty years to girls' education. Although the letter had been sent from Toronto, Miss Hamilton was originally from Prince Edward Island. After the war, she and Hanako had taught in the early childhood education department at Toyo Eiwa Junior College. Each time they met, Miss Hamilton would extol the beauty of the island and tell Hanako about Lucy Maud Montgomery, urging Hanako to go and see the place in which *Anne of Green Gables* was set. Miss Hamilton's letter read as follows:

> July 31, 1957[128]
>
> Dear Hanako,
>
> Just one week ago today, I went to Prince Edward Island and visited Green Gables, the model for Anne's story. How I thought of you! I could not help but wish from the bottom of my heart that you were there with me and so could see it too. I

cannot even begin to imagine how fascinating and meaningful that house and its surroundings would have been for someone like you, who knows everything there is to know about the Anne books. In commemoration of my visit to Green Gables, I am sending you a small parcel from the island with some postcards, a spoon, and the anthem of Prince Edward Island. L. M. Montgomery wrote the words.

On the cover of the musical score of *The Island Hymn* was a photo of Green Gables, beneath which was written "Home of Anne of Green Gables, Prince Edward Island National Park." These were the lyrics:

The Island Hymn

Fair Island of the sea,
We raise our song to thee,
The bright and blest;
Loyally now we stand
As brothers, hand in hand,
And sing God save the land
We love the best.

Upon our princely Isle
May kindest fortune smile
In coming years;
Peace and prosperity
In all her borders be,
From every evil free,
And weakling fears.

Prince Edward Isle, to thee
Our hearts shall faithful be

Where'er we dwell;

Forever may we stand

As brothers, hand in hand,

And sing God save the land

We love so well.

Hanako gazed at the postcards, recalling episodes related to each photograph: Haunted Forest, Lovers Lane, White Way of Delight, the rooms of Anne and Matthew at Green Gables. More than any place on earth, Montgomery had loved Prince Edward Island—the island called Abegweit by the Mi'kmaw people who first settled there, meaning "cradled on the waves.[129]"

❀

On February 1, 1960, Midori gave birth to a baby girl, and she and her husband named her Mie. Keizo and Hanako were ecstatic at the birth of their first granddaughter. Two months before Mie was born, Midori and her husband temporarily moved back to the Muraoka home in Omori, and Midori stayed for two months after the birth, while Hanako helped her care for Mie. Hanako brought both the cradle and the baby bed into her study and spent many happy hours watching her daughter and granddaughter. For her daughter, who was experiencing motherhood for the first time, Hanako wrote *Wakaki haha ni kataru* (Talking to a Young Mother) and *Mama to kodomo: Mama e no chumon 12 sho* (Mother and Child: Requests to Mothers: 12 Chapters). For her granddaughter, as a wish for her healthy growth, Hanako began translating Virginia Lee Burton's *Choo Choo: The Story of a Little Engine Who Ran Away*, which was published as *Itazura kikansha chu* by Fukuinkan Shoten.

In the fall of the same year, Pearl Buck visited Japan. Hanako, who deeply admired Buck's work, had translated *The Exile: Portrait of an American Mother* and was delighted to be invited to dinner with the author. They spent a satisfying evening, stimulated and moved by each other's conversation. Joy welled up inside Hanako as she entered this period of fruition.

Parting with Keizo

Although the first day of spring had passed, the cold had lingered as though winter had finally decided to show its true form. After dinner, as always, Hanako and Keizo had sipped a cup of tea together and conversed about the day's events. Keizo was about to go to bed, and Hanako to return to her study, when Keizo was suddenly seized by a severe pain.

"Keizo! Papa!" Hanako cried out. "What's wrong?"

Keizo had always had a weak heart, but it had become even weaker over the last two years, and he had been lying down more often during the day to rest. Hanako had had a loved one wrenched from her arms before. Even as she moved into action, shouting Keizo's name, rousing Fumi from her bed, and calling the doctor, deep inside she knew she was confronting fate; something ordained by a force she could not defy.

On February 6, 1963, two hours after his heart attack, Keizo Muraoka, Hanako's partner of forty-four years, the man she had never stopped loving, drew his last breath. He was seventy-five years old.

🌼

Face pale, Midori rushed over with her husband and Mie. For Midori, Keizo had been a kind and loving father, the one who had taken her to kabuki, the movies, and shopping instead of her busy mother. For Hanako, Keizo was husband, lover, and comrade; truly her other half. Together, they had moulded the person known as Hanako Muraoka.

After the funeral at Omori Megumi Church, the grief-stricken Hanako cried for almost three days and three nights. When she finally succumbed to exhaustion, she slept so deeply she did not wake until morning. She lay for a while in bed, feeling the aching reality of emptiness. *He's gone*, she thought.

Every day, she changed the water in the vase of flowers placed like an offering in front of Keizo's photograph. She trimmed the stems, one by one, before returning the flowers to the vase. With each snip of the scissors, she heard Keizo's voice: *They say it's best to cut the stems a little each day. It makes the flowers last longer.* For over a month, she trimmed the stems and changed the water as though she were a flower guardian. As she wrote during that time:

> Every day, I notice things I'd like to share with him. And each time I think, "If only I had done it sooner." But that's the nature of selfish desire. I will carry this regret as long as I live. To say he lives on in memory is far too mild an expression. Keizo is my memory, an inextricable part of my life. As such, he is always with me. I must admit that I am blessed. As I change the water in the vase, I savour the joy of loving.[130]

Keizo permeated Hanako's life. She just needed to carry on within the daily life he had left for her. On top of a swivel stand beside her desk sat the imposing *Webster's Third New International Dictionary of the English Language, Unabridged,* a gift from Keizo. This not only assisted Hanako greatly in her translation work, but it was also her favourite reading material. She loved to dip into it whenever she had a little extra time. It was so extensive, offering unlimited enjoyment—just like Keizo.

Hanako Travels Overseas

People were always shocked to hear that Hanako had never been abroad. Anyone who saw her joking or conversing animatedly with foreigners in fluent English simply assumed that she must have lived overseas. More than twenty years had passed since the end of the war. By now, almost everyone Hanako knew had visited other countries. The foundation of Hanako's language ability had been bequeathed to her during her ten years at Toyo Eiwa Girls School by Canadian missionaries. Her five years as a teacher after graduation and her work as a translator had polished both her English and her Japanese. After the war, she had been called upon to participate in talks with, and interpret for, visitors to Japan. She had thus been blessed with countless opportunities to hone her English without ever going abroad.

She had been given several chances to travel outside Japan, both before and after the war, but had declined them all, claiming she was too busy. After the publication of the Japanese version of *Anne of Green Gables*, she had been particularly busy, producing one translation after another in response to her readers' yearning for sequels. The real reason she had refused to travel, however, was because of Keizo. When she thought of his weak heart and how he was prone to sickness, she could not bring herself to leave him behind and cross the ocean. Although Hanako was always ahead of her times, the more her sphere of activity expanded, the more concern she showed Keizo, her staunchest supporter.

In 1966, Midori's husband, Mitsuo, was invited to a research institute at Cleveland State University in Ohio, and Midori and Mie moved with him to the United States. From there, Mitsuo transferred to the University of California, Davis, along with his family. Midori frequently begged her mother to come and visit. At first, Hanako protested that the freedom to go anywhere she liked made her feel lonely, but, at the age of seventy-three, she finally made up her mind. She would go visit Midori with Miyo, a young girl not yet twenty who had been helping her since Fumi, the Muraokas' maid for many years, had retired.

Midori phoned from the States. "I would have loved to show you our house in Cleveland on the shores of Lake Erie, Mother," she said. "It was wonderful. But Davis is a great city too. It's a student town and full of young people. I'm sure you'll love it. And Mother, if you're coming all this way, let's go to Prince Edward Island too. I'm making lots of plans for when you come next year."

✻

For quite a few years, Hanako had been working on Montgomery's Emily trilogy, the most autobiographical of Montgomery's works, particularly of her youth. After translating the first book, *Emily of New Moon*, Hanako's cataracts had worsened, impeding both her work and reading. Still, she continued on, taking two years to complete her translation of *Emily Climbs*. When that was finished, she finally had cataract surgery. Although she did not regain her eyesight fully, she decided that the operation had been well worth it. Gazing at the soft light falling through the curtains the morning after, she realized how precious her health was: without it, she couldn't work.

At the end of June the following year, Hanako and Miyo landed in San Francisco airport. While Japan was in the midst of the dreary rainy season, San Francisco was dry and clear, with a bright blue sky overhead. They were met by Midori, Mitsuo, and seven-year-old Mie. Plus one more: A new life was stirring in Midori's womb.

Hanako had left her work behind and come for two whole months just to enjoy herself. She had once met an American professor in Japan who was travelling around the world for his sabbatical. Having worked continuously all her life, she was surprised to learn that in the States professors got a year-long holiday every seven years. The trip to visit Midori was her first long vacation in fifty years. She had not taken an extended holiday since she had begun working as a teacher at Yamanashi Eiwa Girls School.

Japan was now a peaceful nation. It had undergone a remarkable economic recovery, and its people enjoyed a comfortable lifestyle. America, on the other hand, was once again at war; this time in Vietnam. Even in Japan, America's iniquitous policies regarding Vietnam were criticized, but in the United States, young people had arisen in protest throughout the country. From the car window during the ride from the airport to Midori's place, Hanako saw many protesters bearing antiwar placards.

The car sped smoothly along the road. Davis was about a fifteen-minute drive from the capital of Sacramento and was home to many people who worked at University of California, Davis. As a visiting professor, Mitsuo and his family enjoyed the middle-class lifestyle of the average American. Hanako went shopping with the family, went for walks in parks or on the university campus, and dropped into the local library. Every day, the weather was fair with no sign of rain. The midday sun felt as hot as summer, but in the evening a cool breeze began to blow, and by night, it felt chilly.

On the street, passersby often did a double take when they saw Hanako, an elderly woman dressed in kimono, and gave her a smile. Hanako returned their smiles and spoke to them. It was unusual enough to see a tiny, kimono-clad woman, but to hear her speak fluent English was an even greater surprise. Hanako found their reactions entertaining and stopped to chat animatedly.

Hanako took her young companion, Miyo, and her granddaughter, Mie, to Disneyland. She also bought a mink stole, something she had always wanted, in San Francisco. Midori bought a camel coat with a mink collar. Although Hanako was on holiday, it made her uneasy not to take any work with her, and at the last minute, she had stuffed into her suitcase the final volume of the Emily trilogy, *Emily's Quest*, along with a thick pad of manuscript paper. She had been planning to start translating it when she returned to Japan in the fall. No matter how unusual the place, however, there were bound to be moments when she was bored. At such times, she spread out a sheet of paper, placed *Emily's Quest* beside it, and translated. Without the many interruptions she would have had at home, she could concentrate more easily, and the work proceeded much faster than she had expected. The pleasure this gave her made her glad she had brought the book.

The highlight of Hanako's visit was to be a trip to Prince Edward Island. One morning, however, Hanako suggested they scrap their plan.

"But you were looking forward to it so much," Midori protested. She had seen the trip to Canada as the best way to express her love for her mother. "Besides, I want to go too," she added. "I've always wanted to step on to Prince Edward Island with you, Mother. What is it? Are you worried about me?"

"Yes, I am," Hanako said firmly. "It wouldn't do if something happened that affected you and the baby. And I'm really very content, Midori.

Besides, things have changed. I can go anytime I want now, so let's postpone it this time."

While translating *Anne of Green Gables* in the midst of the grey desolation of war, Hanako had woven the words of Montgomery into a vivid landscape of natural beauty that she channelled through her pen into her translation. To go with her daughter to Prince Edward Island, the birthplace of *Anne of Green Gables* and its author, would be a dream come true. Yet to witness reality might mean the loss of the imaginary world in her mind that she loved so dearly. Deciding to keep her dream for a little longer, Hanako wrote to Miss Hamilton and her other friends in Canada to let them know that she wasn't coming this time after all, and promising to visit them in the near future.

Hanako's Affinity for Montgomery

Hanako returned to Japan in early September and poured her energy into her translation of *Emily's Quest*. When she finished, she was filled with a pleasant sense of achievement. Of Montgomery's twenty-one novels, Hanako had translated a total of sixteen, including the entire Anne series, as well as *Kilmeny of the Orchard*, *Jane of Lantern Hill*, *Mistress Pat*, and the Emily trilogy.

Due for a second eye operation, Hanako decided to close Michio's Library, which had been run out of her home since 1952. Her favourite books from Michio and Midori's childhood quietly joined her private collection. She donated the others, which included nursery tales, biographies, and books on science and social studies, to the neighbourhood elementary schools, Iriarai Daini and Iriarai Daiyon, giving four hundred volumes to each. On November 7, 1967, *The Asahi Shimbun* carried an article about the library's closure, and on the day she was discharged from hospital, Hanako received the following letter from Momoko Ishii, who ran the Katsura Bunko home library.

November 16, 1967

To Mrs. Hanako Muraoka,

I was laid low with a strange cold when I opened the newspaper and saw your photo. What a surprise. You were smiling and looked very young and beautiful. But the caption seemed so contrary to the picture that I caught my breath. "Second Eye Operation," it said. "Michio's Library Closes." The article evoked so many emotions that after reading it, I sat staring at your photo for some time. Your bright, cheerful expression captured you so perfectly; you who have transcended so many hardships without ever complaining. The article said you would be released from hospital on the fifteenth so I assume you must be back in Omori by now. I am praying that the operation was successful.

Michio's Library may have closed, but it has fulfilled its purpose very well, showing us the way and giving us strength, and for that I am very grateful. Thank you for keeping it going for so long. Please wait until you are fully recovered before launching back into your work. I hope to come and visit soon. I will contact you to confirm when is best for you.

Please take good care of yourself.

Momoko Ishii

The following year, Hanako made the bold decision to take a whole ten days off before starting a new translation project. She wanted to visit Midori and her family in Ikeda City, Osaka where they had moved after returning from America. This time she left all her work behind so that she could devote the full ten days just to being with her grandchildren. While there, she napped every afternoon after lunch, which was unusual for her. The rest of the time she played with nine-year-old Mie and eleven-month-old Eri. At night, after the children had gone to sleep, she sat with Midori and her husband, drinking tea and talking.

One day, Midori went out shopping while Eri was taking a nap, and Hanako stayed home to babysit. After a little while, Eri opened her eyes and began babbling away, clearly in high spirits. Suddenly, she stopped and looked intently at Hanako's face, then burst into tears. Hanako tried everything to comfort her but Eri only cried louder. Her shrieks were so loud that Hanako worried what the neighbours would think. At last, Eri began to tire and started nodding off. Hanako lay down beside her and patted her on the back, singing a lullaby that she had not sung for years: *nennen korori yo, okorori yo* (Sleep, sleep, lie down now and sleep.) As she gazed at her granddaughter's face, Hanako thought, *It would be unthinkable for Midori to leave this little child behind.* Hanako had started planning another trip to Canada. It was to be a short one of a few weeks, but she had intended to take Midori as her assistant. As Hanako wrote soon after:

I abandoned my plan then and there. How could I possibly separate this darling, helpless baby from her mother? My overseas trip could go to the devil. I knew I could never take this child's mother away.

At that moment, Midori rushed in breathlessly. "Sorry to keep you waiting," she said.

My granddaughter slept soundly. "It's all right now, Eri," I whispered in her ear.[131]

The morning Hanako left for Tokyo, Midori and her family came on to the bullet train to say goodbye. "We'll come and see you at Christmas," Midori said.

"I had a wonderful time," said Hanako. "Thank you so much, Midori. As for you, Eri dear, please don't forget me before Christmas. And Mie, see you soon."

As the train pulled away, Midori and her family stood on the platform waving to Hanako until she was out of sight.

❀

On October 20, Hanako began translating her seventeenth Montgomery work: *Pat of Silver Bush*. Sitting down at her desk, she opened the book, picked up her fountain pen, and began to write, just as she always did.

Although she had translated numerous authors, Hanako felt a special affinity for Montgomery. She had studied English under Canadian women of Montgomery's generation and had been raised within the Canadian culture and customs of that era. The background and the spirit of the work embedded between the lines spoke to Hanako's senses.

Montgomery's view of life also resonated deeply with Hanako. *Anne of Green Gables* had brought Montgomery fame and popularity, and she had been showered with praise by such literary greats as Mark Twain and Rudyard Kipling. Yet Montgomery had stayed in her village to nurse her ailing grandmother, who had raised her, and continued to work at the post office. Even after her grandmother's death and her own marriage to Reverend Ewen Macdonald, Montgomery continued to write and to advocate for better status for women. At the same time, she did not neglect her duties as the wife of a minister and the mother of two children. Having lost her own mother very early in life and her father when he remarried and moved away, Montgomery never forgot the gratitude she owed her grandparents for raising her, and she dreamed of having a warm and loving family.

Hanako understood painfully well Montgomery's dilemma. They had both been caught between their dream of being a writer and the demands and responsibilities of life. In the shadow of her father's ideals, Hanako's family had suffered and been torn apart when Hanako was still very young. The family bonds that she had painstakingly nurtured since then were a treasure just as precious as having realized her dream to earn her living by her pen.

Within the protagonists of Montgomery's stories, Hanako could see the author's approach to life. When Matthew, who first took her in, dies, Anne gives up her scholarship and returns to Prince Edward Island to work as a teacher so that she can take care of Marilla and Green Gables.

Emily, who aspires to be a writer, strives to understand others even while rebelling against the old-fashioned conventions that bind them. Both Anne and Emily choose the welfare of their loved ones over their personal aspirations. However, this choice is not made from despair or bitter martyrdom. Rather, these young women go on to discover happiness along the new path they have taken, even though it is a roundabout route to their dreams. In doing so, they gradually melt the stubborn hearts of those around them, who discover in these girls a source of comfort and support.

The choices these women made in their lives rang true for Hanako. Few people could pursue their dreams without encountering a bend or two in the road. No matter how perfect a society's laws and systems might be, the unexpected was bound to occur in life. Trying to push through one's dreams regardless only resulted in hurting others or running into a dead end. Montgomery's stories were precisely what Hanako had always sought: stories imbued with a message that would bring happiness to readers of any era. They could be enjoyed by adults and children alike and portrayed the ordinariness of daily life so exquisitely that it bordered on the extraordinary. The profoundest meaning, the richest harvest in life was to be found within those hours spent with loved ones, just laughing, crying, or walking together. The preciousness and the evanescence of daily life: this is what Hanako wanted to convey to the younger generations through translating Montgomery's works.

※

On October 25, the day after Hanako and Keizo's forty-ninth wedding anniversary, Hanako tackled a backlog of work with help from her assistant, Reiko Yagi. She wrote replies to fan letters from readers of *Anne of Green Gables*, graded the reports of seventy students from Toyo Eiwa Junior College, and dictated papers for courses produced by NHK Gakuen, the public broadcasting corporation's high school correspondence school, even though they were not due until November 1. In the evening she sat down to dinner with her maid, Miyo, but collapsed from a stroke. She never regained consciousness, and died two hours later.

Midori and her family rushed from Osaka to Tokyo, arriving late that night. Midori and Umeko, Hanako's younger sister, placed in Hanako's coffin her pen, sheets of manuscript paper, and a Japanese copy of *Anne of Green Gables*, into which Hanako had poured her soul.

A wake was held for three days in Hanako's home. On the night of October 28, an elderly woman came bearing a bouquet of white chrysanthemums. Blind, she was led by a boy of about ten. The woman wept and prostrated herself before the bereaved family. Two days before Hanako had passed away, she told them, Hanako had sent her a message of encouragement for blind people for a Braille pamphlet they were making. The woman held out a copy, tied with a simple ribbon. "Thanks to that," she said, "we were able to include her kind message and print it." She asked the boy to read it aloud, after which they left.

✿

The funeral was held on October 29 at Omori Megumi Church and was attended by over one thousand people. Eulogies were given by Michio Namekawa, who represented the world of children's literature, Kenji Takahashi, president of the Japan Society of Translators, Nobuko Yoshiya, who represented Hanako's friends, and Mako Kaneko, president of Sankei Gakuen. Fusae Ichikawa, who was now a member of the House of Councillors, and Tamiko Yamamuro, a feminist activist and the daughter of Salvation Army founder Gunpei Yamamuro, also gave speeches expressing their gratitude for Hanako's contributions.

At two o'clock, just as the funeral was about to start, lightning flashed in what had been a clear blue sky, and it started to pour. After Hanako's favourite hymns, the choir began singing "God Be with You Till We Meet Again"[132] while people placed flowers in the coffin. As the refrain reverberated through the church, the rumbling thunder faded and the rain abruptly ceased. The sun setting in the west lit up the sky.

1951. Hanako in her study in her home in Omori.

Afterword

Translators played a vital role in introducing Western culture and thought to Japan from the Meiji period onwards. Yet little light has been shed on the process of how they came to translate or what motivated them to do so.

※

Hanako Muraoka was born in 1893 and died in 1968 at the age of seventy-five. She translated many literary works from English into Japanese, including the Anne series by Lucy Maud Montgomery, as well as works by such authors as Charles Dickens, Mark Twain, and Pearl Buck. The scope of her activities was wide-ranging, and she was well known not only as a translator but also as a writer of children's stories, an essayist, a commentator on women's issues, and a radio personality.

Although Hanako Muraoka is my grandmother, I was born in 1967, a year before she died, and thus have no memories of her. The first and only time I appeared in her writings was in an essay she wrote two days before her death. In it, she described how I fell asleep in her arms as she sang me lullabies. Of course, I treasure that essay, but while my sister, who was born eight years before me, received many picture books with messages penned by my grandmother, I received not even one, and as a child, that seemed most unfair.

For more than ten years after her death, my grandmother's study, which was in our house, remained untouched, as if she had been working there until just moments before. My mother used to sit with my sister and me in that room and share her memories. As she did so, I found myself drawn to the owner of the study, the kimono-clad woman who had always worked into the wee hours of the morning, foregoing sleep.

There are so many questions I would have liked to ask her. Women with their own career were highly unusual in those days. What obstacles did she face in that male-dominated society? What had she liked about my grandfather? How did it feel to translate a book from an enemy country in the middle of the war? What impelled her to take such a risk?

Fortunately, my grandmother's house survived both the Great Kanto Earthquake of 1923 and the air raids of the Second World War, leaving us with a mountain of letters, diaries, manuscripts, and other documents, as well as her personal library. My journey back to the era through which my grandparents had lived was a journey of discovering my own roots. Through the warp of history, I wove the actions and feelings of my grandparents, the people of that era who were closest to me, sharing their joys and sorrows and experiencing this most recent modern history, one that cannot be found in any textbook. As I did so, I became aware that the circumstances in which we live—the social systems, rights, and peace that we take for granted—were hard won through the tears and earnest prayers of the previous generation and of those who came before them.

❊

My grandmother was blessed in the people she met, in her teachers and in her friends. The decade she spent in the dormitory of the girls school known as Toyo Eiwa Jogakuin was particularly influential. The education she received from Miss Blackmore and the other Canadian missionaries, her English-language ability, her Christian faith, and the spirit of service she acquired at Toyo Eiwa, determined the course of her life. Her translations, her children's stories, and her social activism all sprouted from the seeds these Canadian women had sown in the heart and mind of young Hanako. These seeds set firm roots that anchored Hanako through life's savage tempests, allowing her to grow strong and true, even with a few twists and bends. Using her power of expression to nurture women and children, my grandmother dedicated her life to repaying the gift these Canadian women gave her.

I have quite a few Canadian friends of my own, and they have all asked me the same question. "Why do the Japanese love *Anne of Green Gables* so much?" The easy answer is that the story, even after a century, retains a freshness that still captures the heart, and its characters never lose their appeal. But just as each individual experiences joy and sorrow differently, there is no all-embracing answer. Nor is everyone in Japan a fan of the Anne books. In fact, many have not even read them, particularly as far fewer young people read books in Japan these days.

I think it is not the number but rather the passion of Montgomery's readers that gives Canadians this impression. Anne's story attracts readers who become fans for life, who are such ardent admirers that they read and reread the whole series and are even moved to travel to Prince Edward Island, halfway around the world, just to see the place where the story was set.

I believe part of the answer is also that the timing of the translation's release in Japan was perfect. It was published as *Akage no An* (Redheaded Anne) on May 10, 1952, when the country was just beginning to rise from the mire of defeat. Government policies were being democratized and people's lifestyles were becoming Westernized. Anne, a hot-tempered, disadvantaged orphan who was by no means pretty yet who brimmed with a bubbling vitality, was the perfect democratic heroine for this new age.

Readers let their imaginations run free, just like Anne, conjuring up images of puffed-sleeved dresses, raspberry cordial, and layer cakes. Inspired by Anne, Japanese women found joy and beauty around them in their daily lives. They studied hard so as not to be bested by boys. They were emboldened to express their thoughts and encouraged to respect themselves, even while fretting about their flaws. They gained the energy to live, the freedom to dream, and the happiness that comes with contentment.

Japanese women in their sixties, seventies, and eighties tend to be the most ardent *Anne of Green Gables* fans. It seems that the world of the Anne series resonates closely with the way things were in Japan when these women were young. The Japanese translation gained indisputable status in the postwar Japanese publishing industry, and its popularity has been passed down through the generations. The ongoing support is thanks in part to the influence of animated and live-action adaptations of the story, as well as to Anne's "bosom friends," who have encouraged their children and grandchildren to read the books. That Hanako Muraoka's translations of the Anne series continue to be loved and reprinted, despite significant changes in the Japanese language over the intervening years, gives both my sister and me great joy.

❀

From the moment I began writing this book, I longed to introduce to the world not only my grandmother, but also her friends, contemporaries, and—above all—the Canadian teachers who had such an impact on the person Hanako Muraoka was to become. The original Japanese edition of this book, which you now read in English as *Anne's Cradle*, was published by Magazine House in Tokyo in 2008 and received an enthusiastic response. It was Akifumi Ikeda, president of Toyo Eiwa University, who first proposed that the book be published in English and so reach readers in Canada and other countries from which the missionaries who taught my grandmother had come. With the support and understanding of the university and Toyo Eiwa Jogakuin, the English publication of *Anne's Cradle* was adopted as a joint project for the commemoration of Toyo Eiwa Jogakuin's 135th anniversary and Toyo Eiwa University's 30th anniversary. I am profoundly grateful to Mr. Ikeda and to everyone else involved with this project at Toyo Eiwa for their understanding and assistance.

For their unstinting support, I am also deeply indebted to Kimihiro Ishikane, Ambassador of Japan to the United Nations, who was Japan's Ambassador to Canada in 2008 when the Japanese original was published; to Dr. Elizabeth R. Epperly, the foremost scholar on Montgomery; and to Dr. Takako Hikotani, associate professor of modern Japanese politics and foreign policy at Columbia University. Due to the kind offices of Ambassador Ishikane, my sister and I had the honour of attending the commemoration of the 90th anniversary of diplomatic relations between Japan and Canada in 2019. It is a memory we will cherish forever.

The greatest good fortune for this project was finding Cathy Hirano, an excellent translator. The backdrop for *Anne's Cradle* is the modern history of

Japan. Even for Japanese people, it can be hard to grasp the atmosphere and emotions of that time. Through meticulous research, however, Cathy delved deep into the background of this story as she translated it. The sincerity and sympathy with which she approached her work were manifest in the questions and suggestions she conveyed in her correspondence, reminding me that translation is not a simple process of substituting words in one language for those in another. What is really needed is an understanding of the culture and history embedded in each word, the ability to draw close to those who live and breathe within the story, a depth of humanity, and a rich imagination. A translator is a messenger who, through the medium of a book, connects people of different cultures, and I am deeply grateful to Cathy for taking on that role.

I would like to express my gratitude here as well to Patricia Sippel, professor emerita at Toyo Eiwa University, who, as a scholar of the history of early modern and modern Japan, provided invaluable advice on the English translation of historical terms and shared precious information concerning the timing of the missionary Loretta Leonard Shaw's return to Canada. I would also like to thank Michiko Urata at Japan Uni Agency for her expert handling of the many procedural details and Whitney Moran at Nimbus Publishing for her unfailing encouragement. Finally, I would like to express my appreciation to the many others who have so faithfully supported the publication of this book from behind the scenes. If *Anne's Cradle* conveys the outstanding achievements of those women who came to Japan as missionaries and contributes to the understanding and study of Japan and its people in the English-speaking world, my dream will have been fulfilled.

Due to the pandemic, the world remains in a state of uncertainty. We cannot travel even within our own countries, let alone internationally. Instead, I have been using this time as a period of quiet preparation, holding fast to the belief that after the long winter, spring will surely come, and we will once again enjoy the warmth and fellowship of being together. I offer you my heartfelt prayers for your health and wellbeing.

February 2021

Special Thanks

Kazue Suemasu, Fuki Miyazaki, Yukiko Yoshiya, Eiko Ichimada, Kayo Koike, Yui Arisawa , Haruko Ubukata, Mariko Kitabayashi, Michiko Muraoka, Yasuteru Ono.

Toyo Eiwa Jogakuin, Yamanashi Eiwa Jogakuin, Shizuoka Eiwa Jogakuin, Japan Women's University Naruse Memorial Hall, Meiji Gakuin University Library, Poole Gakuin Archives, Yamanashi Prefecture Museum of Literature, Japan Christian Women's Organization, League of Women Voters of Japan, Ichikawa Fusae Centre for Women and Governance.

Kyobunkwan Publishers, Shinchosha Publishing Co., Ltd., Seron Jihosha Publishing Co., Ltd.

Embassy of Canada in Japan, Destination Canada, Atlantic Canada Tourism Partnership, Tourism Prince Edward Island, and Kate MacDonald Butler/Heirs of L.M. Montgomery Inc.

Chronology of Events in Hanako Muraoka's Life

Note: Only Hanako Muraoka's published translations that could still be purchased as of May 2008 have been included in this chronology. The ten books of Montgomery's *Anne* series translated by Hanako Muraoka are currently published by Shinchosha Publishing Co., Ltd. under its Shincho Bunko label. An abridged version of the series is also published by Poplar Publishing Co., Ltd. while Kodansha Ltd. publishes *Anne of Green Gables* under its Blue Bird Library label.

1893 June 21 Hanako is born to Ippei and Tetsu Annaka, the first of eight children. Named Hana, she is baptized as a Christian at the age of two.

1898 Age 5. Hanako and her family move to Tokyo. The following year, Hanako enters Jonan Elementary School.

1903 Age 10. Hanako transfers into Toyo Eiwa Girls School, a mission school established by Canadian Methodists. Hanako lives in the school dormitory for the next ten years.

1904 Age 11. Miss Isabella Slade Blackmore, a Canadian missionary, becomes the principal of Hanako's school and provides strict instruction in both academic studies and daily life.

1909 Age 16. Hanako is introduced to the poet Nobutsuna Sasaki by Akiko Yanagiwara, the daughter of a count who transferred into Toyo Eiwa in 1908 and later becomes known as the poet Byakuren. Hanako joins Nobutsuna's poetry society, Chikuhaku-kai, where she composes tanka and studies such Japanese classics as *The Tale of Genji* and the *Manyoshu* under Nobutsuna's tutelage. Nobutsuna introduces Hanako to the poet Hiroko Katayama, who becomes Hanako's lifelong friend. Hanako, who has spent her days reading British and American literature in the original English, is deeply moved by Ogai Mori's Japanese translation of Hans Christian Andersen's *The Improvisatore* and begins to dream of becoming a translator.

1910 Age 17. Through the Japan Woman's Christian Temperance Union, Hanako is exposed to such social issues as licensed prostitution. She edits and submits tanka, essays, short stories, and translations to the Union's *Fujin shinpo* (Women's News), a job she continues until 1935.

1913 Age 20. Hanako graduates from the collegiate course of Toyo Eiwa Girls School.

1914 Age 21. Hanako is hired as a teacher at Yamanashi Eiwa Girls School. While teaching English at the school, she also writes for the *Fukuin shinpo* (The Evangelical News) under the direction of the pastor Masahisa Uemura. This year also marks the outbreak of the First World War.

1916 Age 23. Hanako begins writing children's stories and fiction for *Shojo gaho* (Illustrated Girls' Monthly), a magazine for teenage girls. Nobuko Yoshiya, a popular author three years younger than Hanako, also writes for the same magazine. That summer, Hanako meets Fusae Ichikawa through the businesswoman Asako Hirooka.

1917 Age 24. Hanako publishes her first book *Rohen* (Fireside), launching into a lifelong pursuit of family literature, books that can be enjoyed by children and adults alike.

1919 Age 26. Hanako quits her job as a teacher to translate children's and women's literature for the Christian Literature Society of Japan in Tokyo. (The Society will merge with the publisher Kyobunkwan after the Great Kanto Earthquake.) On October 24 at Tsukiji Church, Hanako marries Keizo Muraoka, a Christian and the branch manager of Fukuin Printing Company. The newlyweds move into a house in Omori, Tokyo.

1920 Age 27. The Muraokas' son, Michio, is born.

1923 Age 30. The Great Kanto Earthquake strikes, forcing Fukuin Printing Company into bankruptcy and leaving Keizo and Hanako with a large debt.

1926 Age 33. Hanako translates and edits for the Christian Literature Society of Japan. She and Keizo launch Seiransha Shobo, a publishing and printing company, in their home to promote wholesome family literature. Their son, Michio, dies at the age of five of severe infantile gastroenteritis.

1927 Age 34. Hanako's translation of Mark Twain's *The Prince and the Pauper* is published as *Oji to kojiki* by Heibonsha.

1928 Age 35. Hanako becomes a founding member of *Hinotori* (Phoenix), a literary magazine dedicated to works by women writers that was established by the poet Tomeko Watanabe.

1930 Age 37. Hanako participates in the Japan Women's Suffrage Conference held by the Women's Suffrage League and is an active supporter of the women's suffrage movement. The Muraokas' company, Seiransha, begins publishing the periodical called *Katei* (Home). Hanako's translation of Eleanor Hodgman Porter's *Pollyanna Grows Up* is published as *Pareana no seicho* by Heibonsha. (It is subsequently renamed *Yorokobi no hon*. Later, it is republished as *Pareana no seishun* by Kadokawa Shoten Publishing Co., Ltd.)

1932 Age 39. Hanako begins working part-time for Radio JOAK, the forerunner of the Japan Broadcasting Corporation, as an announcer for *The Children's Newspaper*, a segment of a radio program to present news to children. She becomes known nationwide as Radio Auntie, and her closing words, "Fare you well and good night!" become a hit with listeners. She continues this job until the beginning of the Pacific War. Hanako's younger sister Umeko gives birth to her first child, Midori, whom Hanako and Keizo later adopt as their own daughter.

1938 Age 45. Hanako is appointed the chief director of the Tokyo Women's Hall (Tokyo Fujin Kaikan), Japan's first culture centre for women. (The name is changed to Sankei Gakuen after the Second World War.)

1941 Age 48. The Pacific War begins.

1945 Age 52. The Second World War ends. Hanako finishes translating *Anne of Green Gables*. She receives an increasing number of opportunities to officially present her opinions through her appointment to the Temporary Committee for the Investigation of Legal Systems (Rinji Naikaku Hosei Chosa Iinkai), serving as a member of two of its subcommittees: the Council for Revision of the Judicial System (Shiho Hosei Shingi Iinkai) and the Legislative Council for the Revision of the Civil Code (Minpo Kaisei Yoko Shingikai). Together with such women's rights activists as Yayoi Yoshioka and Shigeri Yamataka, Hanako establishes the Japan Women's Collaboration Committee (Nihon Fujin Kyoryokukai), a women's organization under the Ministry of Health and Welfare that addresses such issues as war victim relief and the treatment of women by soldiers of the Occupation Army. Hanako is also appointed head of the Japan Progressive Party's women's division.

1946 Age 53. Hanako works part-time for the Ministry of Education, assisting with communications between the United States Education Mission to Japan and the Japanese government and contributing to educational reforms that promote equality of educational opportunity.

1952 Age 59. Hanako's translation of *Anne of Green Gables*, is published as *Akage no An* on May 10 by Mikasa Shobo Company. Over the next seven years, Hanako translates and publishes ten volumes of the Anne series. In the summer of 1952, Hanako opens Michio's Library in her home, the first home library in Japan.

The home library movement, in which people lend books to children in the neighbourhood and offer related cultural activities, gradually spreads throughout the country. In November 1952, Hanako serves as interpreter for Margaret Higgins Sanger, founder of the birth control movement, during Sanger's visit to Japan.

1953 Age 60. Hanako is appointed vice-chair of the Special Committee on Countermeasures for the Problem of Prostitution (Baishun Mondai Taisaku Tokubetsu Iinkai).

1954 Age 61. Hanako's translation of *A Dog of Flanders* by Ouida is published as *Furandasu no inu* by Shinchosha Publishing Co., Ltd.

The rights to *Akage no An*, Hanako Muraoka's Japanese translation of *Anne of Green Gables* which was published by Mikasa Shobo Company in 1952, are acquired by Shinchosha Publishing Co., Ltd..

1955 Age 62. Hanako is appointed director of Sankei Gakuen (formerly, Tokyo Women's Hall) and is also appointed to the board of directors for the Japan Juvenile Writers Association (Nihon Jido Bungeika Kyokai). In May, Hanako serves as interpreter for Hellen Keller. Hanako's biography of Harriet Beecher Stowe, *Sutou fujin*, is published by Kodansha Ltd. (It is subsequently republished as *Harietto B. Sutou* by Dowa-ya Co., Ltd.)

1957 Age 64. Hanako becomes the director of the Home Library Research Society (Katei Bunko Kenkyukai) and vice-president of the Japan Society of Translators.

1958 Age 65. Hanako's translation of Eleanor H. Porter's *Pollyanna* is published as *Kurige no Pareana* by Kodansha Ltd. (It is subsequently published as *Shojo Pareana* by Kadokawa Shoten Publishing Co., Ltd.)

1959 Age 66. Hanako's daughter, Midori, marries Mitsuo Sano, a physicist. Hanako's translation of Montgomery's *Emily of New Moon* is published as *Kaze no naka no Emiri* (subsequently renamed *Kawaii Emiri*) by Akimoto Shobo. Over the next ten years, Hanako finishes translating the Emily trilogy, concluding with her translation of *Emily Climbs (Emiri no motomeru mono)*. The trilogy is later published by Shinchosha Publishing Co., Ltd. under its Shincho Bunko label. In 1959, Hanako's translation of Mark Twain's *Huckleberry Finn* is published as *Hakuruberi Fin no boken* under the Shincho Bunko label.

1960 Age 67. Hanako receives the Blue Ribbon Medal, which is awarded for significant achievements in public service, from the government of Japan. Her granddaughter Mie is born.

1961 Age 68. Hanako's translation of Virginia Lee Burton's *Choo Choo: The Story of a Little Engine Who Ran Away* is published as *Itazura kikansha chu* while her translation of James Daugherty's *Andy and the Lion* is published as *Andi to raion* by Fukuinkan Shoten Publishers, Inc.

1963 Age 70. Hanako's husband, Keizo, dies on February 2.

1964 Age 71. Hanako's translation of *The Happy Lion* by Louise Fatio with illustrations by Roger Duvoisin is published as *Gokigen na raion* by Fukuinkan Shoten Publishers, Inc.

1965 Age 72. Hanako was awarded The Order of the Precious Crown 4th Class for her contributions to society.

1966 Age 73. Hanako's translation of *A Christmas Carol* by Charles Dickens is published as *Kurisumasu karoru* by Kawade Shobo. (It is subsequently republished by Shinchosha Publishing Co., Ltd.)

1967 Age 74. Hanako visits her daughter, Midori, and family in the United States. It is her first trip overseas. Her second granddaughter, Eri, is born.

1968 Age 75. Hanako dies of a stroke. Her translation of *The Bremen Town Musicians*, a fairy tale from the Brothers Grimm, is published as *Buremen no ongakutai* by Kaisei-sha Ltd. and illustrated by Chiyoko Nakatani.

The Story Continues

From 1954 to 2020, Hanako Muraoka's translation of *Anne of Green Gables*, *Akage no An*, has undergone 153 printings with a total of 2,984,000 copies printed.

Due to circumstances in the industry when the translation was first published, portions of the translation were abridged. In 2008, the centenary of the publication of *Anne of Green Gables* in English, Shinchosha Publishing Co., Ltd. published a new edition of Hanako's translation. It included those portions previously omitted, which were translated by Mie Muraoka, Hanako's granddaughter (and the author's elder sister), who is herself a translator. Mie also updated some of the outmoded language used in her grandmother's translation.

In addition, Mie's translation of L. M. Montgomery's *The Blythes Are Quoted* was published by Shinchosha Publishing Co., Ltd. as *An no omoide no hibi*.

Hanako Muraoka's abridged translations of the Anne series for children continue to be published by Kodansha Ltd. and Poplar Publishing Co., Ltd., with new printings every year.

Glossary of Japanese Terms & People

Japanese terms

bancha tea: a low-grade tea that is pungent and twiggy.

banzai: literally "ten-thousand years." From about 1868 until the end of the Second World War, the word was used to mean "Long live the emperor!" Now its use and meaning are similar to "hooray" in English.

bunko: can mean a library or a pocket edition of a book.

furoshiki: a square piece of fabric used to wrap, store and carry things.

haiku: a Japanese style of poetry consisting of an unrhymed verse of three lines with 5, 7, and 5 syllables respectively.

hakama: wide, pleated trousers tied at the waist.

haori: a short coat worn over kimono.

kabuki: a traditional Japanese theatre art dating back to the early seventeenth century. It combines dance, drama, and acrobatics and uses elaborate costumes, stage sets, and special effects.

kana: a simple script of phonetic symbols without any Chinese characters

katei: "home." Used by Christian socialists in the late nineteenth century to convey the Western concept of "home" and "family."

katei bungaku: "family literature," books that can be read and enjoyed together as a family.

Kyobunkwan: a publishing company producing and selling Bibles and Christian literature.

maru-obi: stiff brocade sash, ornately embroidered, 4.5 metres long and 70 centimetres wide which is worn with a formal kimono.

Meiji period (1868–1912): A period during which the emperor was restored as nominal ruler of Japan and the nation underwent rapid modernization.

monpe: a specific style of baggy pants tied at the waist and ankle that were ubiquitous during the war.

shinga: "the true self."

shoga: "the small self."

shogun: first used in the eighth century as the title for a general. From the end of the twelfth century until the mid-nineteenth century, it became the title of the hereditary military ruler of the country. Although it was the emperor's prerogative to appoint the shogun, in reality, the emperor had little political influence.

shogunate: the government of the hereditary military ruler called the shogun.

Showa period (1926–1989): During the first two decades of this period Japan became more nationalistic and militaristic, leading to the invasion of other Asian countries and the Pacific War.

tabi: Japanese socks that button up the side and are separated between the big toe and the second toe. The socks are sewn from cloth, not knitted.

Taisho period (1912–1926): A period during which democracy surged and various movements arose to demand political and social change.

tanka: a Japanese style of unrhymed poetry consisting of five lines. The first and third lines have 5 syllables and the others have 7 syllables for a total of 31 syllables. The first 3 lines usually describe an image while the remaining 2 lines often reveal what the poet thinks or feels about the image.

tasuki: a sash used to tie up the long sleeves of a kimono while doing tasks or exercise.

tatami: thick rectangular flooring mats made of tightly woven straw.

yakuza: Japanese gangsters and their Mafia-like organized crime syndicates.

Yoshiwara: a popular red-light district in Tokyo.

yukata: a light cotton summer kimono.

People

Akutagawa, Ryunosuke: Famous author who was considered the father of the Japanese short story.

Annaka, Ippei: Hanako's father.

Annaka, Tetsu: Hanako's mother.

Byakuren: Akiko Yanagiwara's penname.

Chiyo: Hanako's younger sister who married a farmer in Hokkaido (four years younger than Hanako).

Egawa, Sachi: Keizo's first wife.

Fumi: Hanako's second maid.

Hajime: son of Hitoshi and Tomoe Muraoka.

Haruko: Umeko and Iwao's daughter, Hanako's niece.

Hayashi, Fumiko: Hanako's friend. A highly successful novelist and poet.

Hide: Hanako's maid. She was 16 years old in 1923.

Hirooka, Asako: a prominent businesswoman and promoter of women's education. Founder of the first women's university in Japan.

Hitoshi: Keizo's younger brother who inherited the printing business with Keizo.

Ichikawa, Fusae: Hanako's friend whom she met at Asako Hirooka's summer retreat. A leading feminist and politician.

Iso: Hanako's younger brother.

Ito, Denemon: a coal tycoon from Kyushu who married Akiko Yanagiwara.

Jutta: Keizo's oldest brother who adopted Keizo's first son Yoshio.

Kagawa, Haru: Heikichi Muraoka's niece who married the pastor and social activist Toyohiko Kagawa. They dedicated their lives to helping the poor.

Kamo, Miss Reiko: Hanako's dorm mother at Toyo Eiwa Girls School.

Kaori: Akiko Yanagiwara and Ryusuke Miyazaki's son.

Katayama, Hiroko: Hanako's mentor and friend. A leading poet and translator of Irish literature.

Kazuho: Umeko and Iwao's son, Hanako's nephew.

Kenjiro: Hanako's younger brother who later lived next door.

Kiyoshi: Keizo's younger brother.

Kobayashi, Miss Tomiko: teacher at Toyo Eiwa Girls School who interpreted for the principal, Miss Blackmore.

Koike, Kiko: editor with Mikasa Shobo Company in charge of publishing Hanako's translation of *Anne of Green Gables*.

Kunihisa: Hanako's younger brother.

Mariko: Kenjiro's daughter.

Michiko: Noboru's daughter, Hanako's niece.

Michio: Hanako and Keizo's son.

Midori: Hanako and Keizo's daughter.

Miyazaki, Ryusuke: a lawyer and social activist. Married Hanako's friend Akiko Yanagiwara after she divorced Denemon Ito.

Miyo: Hanako's third maid.

Moriya, Azuma: Hanako's friend from the Japan Woman's Christian Temperance Union. A leading woman's liberationist and social activist.

Muraoka, Eri: Midori's second daughter, Hanako's granddaughter. The author of this book.

Muraoka, Heikichi: Keizo Muraoka's father.

Muraoka, Keizo: Hanako's husband.

Muraoka, Mie: Midori's first daughter, Hanako's granddaughter.

Nishimura, Tomoe: Hitoshi's wife, Hanako's sister-in-law.

Noboru: Keizo's younger brother who later lived next door to Hanako and Keizo.

Okuda, Chiyo (later Shiobara): Hanako's friend and senior at Toyo Eiwa Girls School who helped her fit in.

Sakata, Iwao: Umeko's husband, an artist and calligrapher.

Sano, Mitsuo: a physicist, Midori's husband, Hanako's son-in-law.

Sasaki, Nobutsuna: A poet and scholar of Japanese literature who taught Hanako. She was a member of his literary society, Chikuhaku-kai.

Sawada, Renzo: Hanako's first love. A diplomat. Married Miki Iwasaki.

Shozaburo: Hanako's younger brother, Ippei Annaka's eldest son.

Shunji: Keizo's older brother who was adopted by the Matsuno family and became a tailor.

Umeko: Hanako's younger sister who later lived next door.

Uno, Chiyo: A prize-winning author, trend setter and fashion leader.

Yanagiwara, Akiko (Byakuren): Hanako's "bosom friend." A famous poet whose penname was Byakuren.

Yoshiko: Keizo's sister who married Seichi Sano.

Yoshio: Keizo's son by his first wife.

Yoshiya, Nobuko: Hanako's friend and fellow writer. A highly popular author of adolescent girls' fiction.

Yuki: Hanako's youngest sister who married a farmer in Shizuoka.

Yukiko: Keizo's younger sister who was adopted by the pastor Seigoro Minakami.

A Selection of Canadian Missionaries at Toyo Eiwa

Allen, Annie Whitburn (1878–1973): Born in Montreal, Quebec. Came to Japan as a Methodist/United Church missionary in 1905 and served there until 1940. Worked at Toyo Eiwa Girls school from 1905 to 1907 and from 1912 to 1915. Hanako's English thesis supervisor.

Blackmore, Isabella Slade (1863–1942): Born in Truro, Nova Scotia. Arrived in Japan in 1889 as a Methodist missionary shortly after finishing teacher training. Served as the principal of Toyo Eiwa four times (1890–1891, 1896–1900, 1904–1912, 1922–1925). Devoted herself to evangelism, the education of women, and the development of social welfare services in Japan.

Courtice, Sybil Ruthena (1884–1980): Born in Porter's Hill, Ontario. Taught music at Toyo Eiwa from 1911 to 1934 and served on its Board of Trustees from 1934 to 1943. Interned in a detention centre in Kanagawa in 1943 and sent back to Canada the same year aboard a repatriation ship. Returned to Japan in 1946 and worked at Toyo Eiwa until 1949 when she went back to Canada.

Craig, Margaret (?–1923): Born in Montreal, Quebec. Graduated from McGill University. Arrived in Japan in 1903 where she taught at Toyo Eiwa and was one of Hanako's English teachers. Served as the eleventh principal (1912–1916) and the thirteenth principal (1918–1922). Returned to Canada in 1922 due to ill health.

Hamilton, Frances Gertrude (1888–1975): Born in Prince Edward Island. Served as the fifteenth and seventeenth principal of Toyo Eiwa Girls School during the period from 1925 to 1938. Returned to Canada in 1942 on a repatriation ship. Worked with Japanese-Canadian youth in an internment camp in Lemon Creek, British Columbia. Returned to Japan in 1947 where she stayed until 1956.

Shaw, Loretta Leonard (1872–1940): Born in Saint John, New Brunswick. Studied modern languages and trained as a teacher. Came to Japan in 1904 as a missionary and taught at Poole Girls School in Osaka (currently Poole Gakuin) from 1905 to 1919 and from 1923 to 1932. From 1932, worked at the Christian Literature Society of Japan where she became friends with Hanako. Returned to Canada before the start of the Pacific War and gave Hanako *Anne of Green Gables* as a parting gift.

Endnotes

Prologue

[1] Lucy Maud Montgomery (1874–1942) was a Canadian author from Prince Edward Island who is best known for *Anne of Green Gables* (1908).

[2] Under the National School Order of 1941, elementary schools were renamed *kokumin gakko*, which literally means "national people's schools," and the emphasis on nationalistic indoctrination was further increased. The system was abolished in 1947.

[3] The Tokugawa period, also called the Edo period (1603–1867), was a time of internal peace, political stability, and economic and cultural prosperity under the Tokugawa shogunate, a military dictatorship founded by Ieyasu Tokugawa (1543–1616).

[4] The name of this school at the time was Toyo Eiwa Jogakko. It was later renamed Toyo Eiwa Jogakuin, which is its current official name. Both *jogakko* and *jogakuin* mean "girls' school." With the author's permission, the translator has used Toyo Eiwa Girls School throughout the main text for ease of reading in English.

Chapter 1

[5] The *kazoku*, or "peers," newly created by a law promulgated in 1869, were ranked below members of the Imperial Household and above the former samurai. At first, the term only applied to those with the rank of court nobles and lords, but in 1884 a government decree expanded the rank to include meritorious retainers from the Meiji Restoration. Later, entrepreneurs were also added and awarded one of five titles: duke, marquis, count, viscount, and baron in descending order of rank. In 1947, after the end of the Second World War, this class system was abolished with the enactment of the new constitution.

[6] Keisuke Otori (1833–1911) was a statesman from the late Edo period through the Meiji period. He studied Western sciences and military strategy under Koan Ogata and Tarozaemon Egawa. During the Boshin War (1868–1869), he fought and lost the Battle of Hakodate with Tokugawa admiral Takeaki Enomoto against the forces of the newly formed Meiji imperial government which replaced the shogun with the emperor. After being released from prison, Otori was given a post in the new government and served as ambassador to China and Korea, playing a key role in negotiations before and after the First Sino-Japanese War (1894–1895). He was also an advisor to the Privy Council.

[7] Sazanami Iwaya (1870–1933) was a children's writer and haiku poet. His real name was Sueo Iwaya but he used the pen names Sazanami Iwaya and Sanjin Sazanami. He founded a writers' society called Kenyusha with author and poet Koyo Ozaki, and subsequently published original children's stories such as *Koganemaru*, for which he is best known. He also devoted his talents to retelling and performing traditional folktales and nursery tales.

[8] Christianity had been banned since the early sixteenth century in Japan, and freedom of religion was only introduced in 1871. Most Japanese people were Buddhist and Shinto, and it was therefore unusual for Hanako to have a Christian father.

[9] Canadian Methodism: Methodism is a Protestant denomination of Christianity that had its roots in a revival movement with the "Holy Club" founded by British theologian and evangelist John Wesley (1703–1791) and others in Oxford, England. In 1795, Methodism was officially recognized as separate from the Church of England. It spread worldwide, particularly in the United States. The Wesleyan Methodist Church in Canada chose Japan as the site of its first foreign mission in 1873 and dispatched two missionaries.

[10] From "Shogakusei no koro" (My Primary School Days), *Oya to ko* (Mother and Child).

[11] The Society of Commoners (Heiminsha), was a socialist organization established in the late Meiji period by Shusui Kotoku and Toshihiko Sakai, who quit the Yorozu Choho Newspaper company in 1903 in protest at the approaching Russo-Japanese War. The Society published the *Heimin Shimbun* (The Commoners' Newspaper). It was shut down in 1905 by the authorities, and although it was revived in 1907, it was shut down again after only three months.

[12] The Japan Socialist Party (Nihon Shakaito) was established by Toshihiko Sakai and Kojiro Nishikawa in 1906 and was the first legally recognized socialist party in Japan. The following year it was disbanded by the Public Order and Police Law (Chian Keisatsuho).

[13] Although families that were destitute were often forced to sell or indenture their children if they could not feed them, Ippei and his wife did not exchange their children for money. They were hoping to give them a better chance. Kenjiro, for example, was given up for adoption to a family that had no male heir on the condition that he would be given an education. He eventually graduated from university and worked for a publisher.

Chapter 2

14 This is the original title of the piece by Robert Schumann and the one used in the Japanese. It may be better known in English by the title "Dreaming."

15 The Imperial Rescript on Education (Kyoiku Chokugo) was issued on October 30, 1890 under the name of Emperor Meiji. It declared that the basis of education was Japan's unique system of imperial government based on *kokutai* or "national polity," and placed the virtue of filial piety, and by extension loyalty to the emperor, at the centre of national education. The Imperial Rescript on Education was annulled in 1948.

16 The Private School Ordinance (Shiritsu Gakkorei) was proclaimed on August 3, 1899, by the Ministry of Education and came into effect on August 4. Responding to a treaty revision with Western powers that mandated opening Japan to unrestricted foreign residence, the ordinance aimed to increase government control over schools operated by foreigners.

17 The Ministry of Education Order No. 12 (Monbusho Kunrei Junigo) was enacted at the same time as the Private School Ordinance (see note 16). It banned religious education and religious rituals not only in public schools but also in private schools. At the same time, it declared that Shinto was "not a religion" thereby exempting it from this ordinance. Any school that wished to continue a Christian education would be classified as a "miscellaneous educational institution" (*kakushu gakko*) and its graduates would lose the privilege of advancing to higher levels of education and exemption from conscription into military service.

18 This is from the hymn "Jesus Bids Us Shine." There are multiple versions with slightly different lyrics. The English version quoted here is the same version used in the Japanese book. The Japanese text also includes a Japanese translation attributed to Hanako Muraoka.

19 The first English-Japanese dictionary was completed in 1867 by James Curtis Hepburn (1815–1911), an American lay missionary and physician, who compiled it while studying Japanese and treating fishermen. It is unknown which edition of this dictionary Hanako used during her school days.

20 *Uncle Tom's Cabin*, a novel by Harriet Beecher Stowe (1811–1896), was published in 1852. It describes the life of Tom, a Black slave and devout Christian, who is sold from one person to another and suffers greatly at the hands of white slave owners, finally dying a tragic death. It quickly became a bestseller in America, selling four hundred thousand copies. The novel contributed significantly to the movement for emancipation of slaves in the United States.

21 The Elsie Dinsmore Series by Martha Farquharson Finley (1828–1909) consists of twenty-eight novels centred on the character of Elsie, beginning with the book *Elsie Dinsmore*. At first, the books were ignored by critics and book reviewers, but their overwhelming popularity made them girls' literature classics.

Chapter 3

22 From "Shizuka naru seishun" (My Quiet Youth), *Kaiteiban ikiru to iu koto* (To Live: Revised Edition).

23 Roka Tokutomi (1868–1927) was a Japanese novelist. The younger brother of the journalist Soho Tokutomi, he worked as a reporter for Minyusha before publishing his first novel, *Hototogisu* (The Cuckoo), and a collection of essays entitled *Shizen to jinsei* (Nature and Man), establishing his reputation as an author. He later came to idolize Leo Tolstoy. Other well-known works include *Omoide no ki* (Record of Memories), *Mimizu no tawagoto* (Ramblings of an Earthworm), *Fuji*, and *Kuroshio* (Black Tide).

24 Akiko Yanagiwara (1885–1967), daughter of Count Yanagiwara, was a poet who wrote under the pen name Byakuren. Her collections of tanka include *Fumie* (Trodden Images) and *Maboroshi no hana* (Phantom Flowers), and her collections of other forms of poetry include *Kicho no kake* (Shade of a Partition). She turned her back on wealth and position to spend her life with the socialist Ryusuke Miyazaki (see note 78). When he fell ill with tuberculosis, she supported them both by writing. After 1935, she became president of the tanka magazine *Kototama* (Word Spirits).

25 Although they worked in the red-light district, geisha were not prostitutes but entertainers skilled in dance, music, song, and conversation. They were often fashion setters as well. Although they took patrons, they did not sell sex to make a living. As for mistresses, as mentioned later in this chapter, men could legally register their mistresses as a relation in the second-degree equivalent to a wife. The practice of taking a mistress in this way was considered acceptable among the nobility. Akiko's mother, Ryo Okutsu, was the daughter of a prominent samurai and of a niece of the emperor, which made her the emperor's cousin. She became a geisha after her father died and her family became destitute. Count Yanagiwara bought her contractual freedom when she was sixteen and took her as his mistress. At eighteen, she bore him Akiko but died a few years later. Akiko was raised as the daughter of Count Yanagiwara and his wife. Female offspring in those days were used to secure strategic alliances between powerful families, which is why Akiko was adopted into the Kitakoji family while still a child as the future bride of their son.

26 Lancelot is not in fact betrothed to Elaine, but this is how Hanako understood what she read in English.

27 Nobutsuna Sasaki (1872–1963) was a poet and scholar of Japanese literature. He founded the Chikuhaku-kai tanka society and published the journal *Kokoro no hana* (Flowers of the Heart). His motto was "Wide, deep, each his own," and he respected the individuality of each poet. Many people joined his society, drawn by his tasteful poetic style, and went on to become writers of note, including Chimata Ishikure, Jun Kawada, Rigen Kinoshita, Hiroko Katayama (see note 33), Takeko Kujo (see note 31), and Byakuren Yanagiwara (see note 24). He also made many contributions to the study of the *Manyoshu* and historical research on medieval *waka* poetry. In 1937, he was awarded the Order of Culture by the Japanese government. Publications include the poetry anthology *Omoi gusa* (Idle Thoughts) and an essay compilation *Kagaku ronso* (Essays on Tanka Poetry).

28 Ichiyo Higuchi (1872–1896) was a fiction writer. She studied *waka* at the Haginoya poetry school founded by poet Utako Nakajima and classical Japanese literature under fiction writer Tosui Nakarai. Higuchi wrote about the joys and sorrows of ordinary Japanese people, opening up new territory in Japanese literature. She was highly acclaimed by such writers as Rintaro Mori (pen name: Ogai Mori) and Shigeyuki Koda (pen name: Rohan Koda), but died of tuberculosis at the age of twenty-four. Her works include *Takekurabe* (Child's Play), *Nigorie* (Troubled Waters), and *Jusanya* (The Thirteenth Night).

29 Shigure Hasegawa (1879–1941), a playwright and author, was well-known for her series *Nihon bijin-den* (Lives of Japanese Beauties). She established the literary journal *Nyonin geijutsu* (Women's Arts) to nurture women authors and raise their status. Published from 1928 to 1932, the journal was closed down by the government. During the Second World War, Hasegawa participated in the Kagayaku Butai (Shining Corps) formed in 1939 to encourage and entertain Japanese troops with visits and performances. Her plays include *Haomaru* and *Sakura fubuki* (Cherry Blossom Blizzard).

30 Miyoko Goto (1898–1978) was called the "mother poet" for her poems lamenting the untimely death of her eldest daughter. She was awarded the Yomiuri Culture Prize for her work *Shinshu haha no kashu* (Edited Collection of Mother's Poems) published in 1957.

31 Takeko Kujo (1887–1928) was gifted with beauty and intelligence. The daughter of the head priest of Nishi Honganji, a Buddhist temple of the Jodo Shinshu sect, and the wife of a baron, she lived for a time in England, an experience that gave her keen insight. She engaged in many humanitarian projects through the Buddhist Women's Association, which she helped found, and also established

the Kyoto Women's Technical College (now Kyoto Women's University). Her poetry collections include *Kinrei* (Gold Bell).

[32] *The Improvisatore* (1835) is a novel by Hans Christian Andersen. Set in Italy, the story depicts the travels, friendships, and loves of the poet Antonio. The literary quality of the Japanese translation entitled *Sokkyo shijin* by Ogai Mori (1862–1922) was superb, and the work is considered a classic example of Meiji period romanticism.

[33] Hiroko Katayama (1878–1957) translated many works of Irish literature under the pen name Mineko Matsumura. She was friends with such famous Japanese authors as Saisei Muro, Ryunosuke Akutagawa, and Tatsuo Hori, and is considered to have been the model for Hori's novels *Sei kazoku* (Holy Family) and *Nire no ie* (Elm House). Katayama's works include the poetry collections *Kawasemi* (Kingfisher) and *No ni sumite* (Living in the Field), the essay collection *Tokasetsu* (Candlemas), and translations of Irish literature, such as *Airurando gikyokushu dai-ikkan* (Ireland: A Collection of Plays Volume 1) and *Shingu gikyoku zenshu* (The Complete Collection of Synge Plays).

[34] From "Shizuka naru seishun" (My Quiet Youth), *Kaiteiban ikiru to iu koto* (To Live: Revised Edition).

[35] Teiichi Sugita (1851–1929) was a politician involved in the democratic movement of the Meiji period (1868–1912). He later served in such positions as Speaker of the House of Representatives.

[36] The High Treason Incident (1910) was an alleged conspiracy to assassinate the Meiji Emperor that resulted in the mass arrest of Japanese socialists and anarchists. Twenty-four alleged conspirators received the death sentence; twelve, including Shusui Kotoku, a prominent socialist and founder of the Society of Commoners, were executed in January of the next year. Thereafter, the socialist movement was severely suppressed, and the conspiracy is considered to have been largely fabricated by the government as an excuse to crack down on dissidents.

[37] Inspired by the Woman's Christian Temperance Union that arose in the 1870s in the United States, a group of women led by Kajiko Yajima and others founded the Tokyo Woman's Christian Temperance Union in 1886. In 1893, the organization expanded beyond Tokyo and was renamed the Japan Woman's Christian Temperance Union. Its aims were world peace, human rights, gender rights, and the prohibition of alcohol and tobacco for minors. Renamed the Japan Woman's Christian Organization after it left the Temperance Union in 2000, the organization is currently involved in addressing such social issues as gender discrimination, sexual violence, and sexual exploitation. It continues to lobby for

change in a range of fields and to implement such social welfare projects as women's shelters (HELP, Kyofukai Step House). In addition, it addresses issues related to the so-called *ianfu* ("comfort women"), women mainly from other Asian countries who were forced into sexual slavery by the Japanese military before and during the Second World War.

[38] Kajiko Yajima (1833–1925) was an educator and the aunt of journalist Soho Tokutomi and his younger brother, author Roka Tokutomi. She became a teacher in her forties and, after serving as the dorm matron at Shinei Jogakko, a mission school for girls, was appointed the first principal of Joshi Gakuin in 1889. (Shinei Jogakko was the forerunner of Joshi Gakuin.) Yajima helped form the Woman's Christian Temperance Union while she was serving as a dorm matron, and was actively involved in the movement to abolish Japan's system of licensed prostitution.

[39] Ochimi Kubushiro (1882–1972) was a women's liberationist and the niece of Soho and Roka Tokutomi. After graduating from Joshi Gakuin, she married Reverend Naokatsu Kubushiro. Influenced by her great-aunt, Kajiko Yajima, she became a director of the Japan Woman's Christian Temperance Union in 1916 and lobbied for the abolition of licensed prostitution. In 1924, she formed the League for the Realization of Women's Suffrage (Fujin Sanseiken Kakutoku Kisei Domei) with Fusae Ichikawa. After the Second World War, she became the chair of the Committee to Promote the Codification of the Prostitution Prevention Law (Baishun Kinshiho Seitei Sokushin Iinkai) and devoted her efforts to lobbying for legal reform.

[40] Tsuneko Gauntlett (1873–1953) was a women's liberationist. Influenced by her uncle, a pastor and a physician, and his wife, both of whom devoted their lives to helping people with leprosy, Tsuneko was awakened to her faith and to social work from a young age. She studied under Kajiko Yajima at Joshi Gakuin and married Edward Gauntlett in 1898. She was the first Japanese to legally apply for and receive British citizenship. While teaching at Tokyo Women's Christian University and Jiyu Gakuen, she was also engaged in the Japan Woman's Christian Temperance Union. She worked hard for the rehabilitation of women who had been forced to serve as prostitutes and was involved in the movement to abolish licensed prostitution. She attended the international meeting of the Woman's Christian Temperance Union in London in 1920 and the Woman Suffrage Association Convention in Geneva. Upon her return, she contributed to the establishment of the Japan Woman Suffrage Association. In 1946, she was appointed president of the Japan Woman's Christian Temperance Union. She made significant contributions to the women's suffrage movement and to the movement to promote world peace. Her younger brother was the well-known composer and conductor, Kosaku Yamada.

[41] Azuma Moriya (1884–1975) was an educator, women's liberationist, and a social activist. After serving as a substitute teacher at Mannen Elementary School, which was established in Shitaya to serve disadvantaged children, she joined the Japan Woman's Christian Temperance Union and worked to promote abstinence from alcoholic beverages, leading to the enactment of the Act Prohibiting Underage Drinking (Miseinensha Kinshuho) in 1922. Moriya also devoted herself to such causes as the abolition of licensed prostitution. In 1939, she established Cripplled Heim Tosei Gakuen, Japan's first social welfare institution for physically disabled children, and promoted education for children with disabilities and the training of school nurses.

[42] In Japan, the movement for the abolition of the system of licensed prostitution was known as *kosho seido haishi* (licensed prostitution system abolition) and also *haisho undo* (prostitution abolition movement). In 1886, through the efforts of British feminist Josephine Butler and others, government regulation of prostitution was abolished for the first time in England, and the abolition of licensed prostitution became a central theme of women's movements worldwide. In 1872, the Ordinance Liberating All Geisha and Prostitutes (Shogi Kaihorei) was issued in Japan, temporarily abolishing the system of government regulated prostitution, but it was reinstated soon after. Many organizations, including the Japan Woman's Christian Temperance Union and the Salvation Army, continued thereafter to lobby against licensed prostitution. The movement faltered and stagnated after 1931, when the Imperial Japanese Army began forcing women and girls, mostly from occupied territories in Asia, to serve its soldiers as *ianfu* ("comfort women"), a euphemism for sex slave. Even after Japan's surrender, no serious attempts were made to curtail prostitution. It was not until 1956 that the Anti-Prostitution Law (Baishun Boshiho) was passed in response to the protests of women's organizations and the rising tide of public opposition to licensed prostitution. The law was enacted in 1958.

[43] The temperance movement sought to eradicate a variety of social problems caused by the consumption of alcohol. The movement came to prominence from the mid-nineteenth century to the early twentieth century, especially in America and England. Based on Puritan moral codes, it developed into a movement that sought legislative reforms to prohibit alcohol production and use. In Japan, the movement was established in the 1880s, and the Act Prohibiting Underage Drinking (Miseinensha Kinshuho) came into effect in 1922.

[44] Women's suffrage, the right of women to participate in national affairs, including their right to vote and be voted for, gained increasing recognition in the late nineteenth century in Europe and North America. Similarly, the woman's

suffrage movement in Japan was launched in the late nineteenth century. The League for the Realization of Women's Suffrage (Fujin Sanseiken Kakutoku Kisei Domei) was founded in 1924 by notable feminists such as Fusae Ichikawa. It was renamed the Women's Suffrage League (Fusen Kakutoku Domei) the following year. In 1945, after the Second World War, women's suffrage was finally recognized in Japan through the revision of the House of Representatives Election Law based on a directive from the GHQ occupation government. Japanese women participated in elections for the first time in 1946, resulting in the election of thirty-nine women to the National Diet.

45 Raicho Hiratsuka (1886–1971) was a feminist activist and critic. After graduating from Japan Women's College, she founded the women's literary journal *Seito* (Bluestocking) in 1911. In 1918, she drew attention for participating in the Motherhood Protection Debate (Bosei Hogo Ronso) alongside Akiko Yosano. Afterwards, together with other feminists including Fusae Ichikawa and Mumeo Oku, she formed the New Women's Association (Shin Fujin Kyokai), an organization that sought to improve the status of women and build a women's suffrage movement. After the Second World War, she was an active proponent of permanent peace.

46 Sumako Matsui (1886–1919) was a Japanese actress. After enrolling in the Literary Association's Centre for Theatre Studies (Bungei Kyokai Engeki Kenkyujo), she gained exposure with her portrayal of Nora in an adaptation of Henrik Ibsen's *A Doll's House*. She went on to form a theatre troupe with the director Hogetsu Shimamura, winning popular acclaim for her starring performances as Salomé and Carmen, among other roles. She died by suicide after Shimamura's death in November 1918.

47 "In Memoriam A.H.H." is a poem by the British poet Alfred, Lord Tennyson, published in 1850. Written as a requiem for Arthur Henry Hallam (1811–1833), a close friend from Tennyson's days at Cambridge as well as his sister's fiancé, the poem charts Tennyson's meditations on the questions of life and death over the seventeen years following his friend's death.

Chapter 4

48 *Fukuin shinpo* (The Evangelical News) was a weekly evangelical magazine founded by the Christian pastor Masahisa Uemura (see note 69). It served as the journal of the United Church of Christ in Japan (Nihon Kirisuto Kyodan) and the Japan Church of Christ (Nihon Kirisuto Kyokai).

49 Hokkaido is the northernmost part of Japan, with freezing winters. Settlers were being sent in at this time to open up the land for farming. Life was extremely

hard and most farmers were very poor. Young women from other parts of Japan were recruited to marry settlers whom they had never met. These brides dreamed of making a better life in the north, and in many cases, their lives did gradually improve. Many others, however, continued to suffer extreme hardship and deprivation.

[50] From "Hina to demokurashi" (Dolls and Democracy), *Omina nareba* (Because I'm a Woman).

[51] Renzo Sawada (1888–1970) was a Japanese diplomat. After joining the Ministry of Foreign Affairs in 1914, he served as ambassador to various countries before becoming Japan's first ambassador to the United Nations after the Second World War. In retirement, he was appointed as an advisor to the Ministry of Foreign Affairs, in which capacity he contributed to the realization of Japan's accession to the United Nations in 1956.

[52] In Japanese anyone who is considered to be knowledgeable in a certain subject, such as an architect, a lawyer, or a politician, is called "sensei" (teacher) out of respect. Hanako, as a respected writer and translator, was therefore referred to as "sensei" by many different people, even though she was not a teacher in the literal sense of the word.

[53] From "Shizuka naru seishun" (My Quiet Youth), *Kaiteiban ikiru to iu koto* (To Live: Revised Edition).

[54] The First World War (1914–1918) was a global war that erupted against the backdrop of tensions between the Triple Alliance (Germany, Austria-Hungary, and Italy) and the Triple Entente (involving Russia, France, and Great Britain). Ignited by the assassination of the heir presumptive to the throne of Austria-Hungary in Sarajevo in June 1914, the war embroiled Turkey, Bulgaria, and other nations on the side of the Alliance, as well as Belgium, Japan, Italy (having withdrawn from the Triple Alliance), the USA, and China on the side of the Entente. Japan participated under the Anglo-Japanese Alliance (1902–1923) between Japan and Great Britain which the two nations entered into in 1902 and renewed twice to protect their respective interests in China and Korea. Fought primarily on European battlefields, the First World War continued for more than four years, finally ending with the surrender of Germany in November 1918. The Treaty of Versailles was signed the following year at the Paris Peace Conference.

[55] Nobuko Yoshiya (1896–1973) was a Japanese novelist. After her debut in 1916 as an author of adolescent girls' fiction, she built a female readership with novels such as *Onna no yujo* (Women's Friendship) and *Otto no teiso* (A Husband's Chastity). In 1952, her abilities were widely recognized after she was awarded the

Women's Literature Prize (*Joryu bungakusha-sho*) for her novel *Oni-bi* (Demon Fire). In 1965, she published *Toki no koe* (The Voice of the Times), a history of the movement to abolish prostitution. Her epic historical novel *Tokugawa no fujintachi* (Tokugawa Women), which shed light on women's history, became a bestseller after its publication in 1966 and excited a surge of public interest in the O-oku, the inner sanctum that served as the ladies' chambers at Edo Castle.

56 From "Kare to kanojo" (He and She), *Kaiteiban ikiru to iu koto* (To Live: Revised Edition).

57 Miyoko Kobashi (1883–1922) was a journalist and a member of the first cohort of students to graduate from Japan Women's College. In 1915, she became the publisher and editor of *Fujin shuho* (Women's Weekly), a journal that advocated the necessity of vocational training for women and which sought to raise men's awareness in order to advance the social status of women. Kobashi worked actively to create a Women's Press Club and also took part in efforts on the part of the Japan Woman's Christian Temperance Union to end licensed prostitution in Japan.

58 The Japan Women's College (Nihon Joshi Daigakko) was founded in 1901 by Jinzo Naruse, an educational reformist and Christian who studied in the United States in 1890 and promoted the education of women in Japan, as a forerunner of institutions of higher education for women. It is now known as Japan Women's University (Nihon Joshi Daigaku).

59 Jinzo Naruse (1858–1919) was an educational reformist and Christian who studied in the United States from 1890 to 1894 and promoted the education of women in Japan.

60 Fusae Ichikawa (1893–1981) was a feminist activist and politician. A graduate of the Aichi Normal School for Women, she worked as an elementary school teacher and newspaper reporter before helping to establish the New Women's Association (Shin Fujin Kyokai) in 1919 alongside Raicho Hiratsuka, after which she became an active proponent of women's suffrage and the emancipation of women. She advocated the ideal of fair elections free from corruption, winning election to the House of Councillors over five terms from 1953 and contributed significantly to the enactment of the Anti-Prostitution Law and the fight against political corruption.

61 The titles of the pieces in the original Japanese are as follows: "The Need for Higher Education for Women," (Josei koto kyoiku no hitsuyosei) "Licensed Prostitution Represents Barbaric Thought," (Kosho wa yaban shiso no daihyo nari) and "The Future of Japanese Women" (Nihon fujin no shorai).

[62] *A Girl of Limberlost* (1909) is a novel by Gene Stratton-Porter (1863–1924). The novel was translated into Japanese by Hanako Muraoka, who also translated Stratton-Porter's earlier novel *Freckles* (1904), which was published as *Sobakasu no shonen*.

[63] From "Zuihitsu natsu no omoide" (Essay: Summer Memories) in the magazine *Fubo kyoshitsu* (Parents' Classroom), published by the All Japan Parents' Council on Education (Zennihon Kyoiku Fubo Kaigi) July 1964.

[64] *Mother Carey's Chickens* (1911) is a novel by the American author Kate Douglas Wiggin (1856–1923), who won popular acclaim for her book *Rebecca of Sunnybrook Farm* (1903). Muraoka's Japanese translation of *Mother Carey's Chickens* was later published as *Kere-ke no hitobito* (*The Careys*).

Chapter 5

[65] The social activist Haru Kagawa (1888–1982) became involved in volunteer work after learning of Toyohiko Kagawa's efforts to alleviate poverty in the slums of Kobe (see note 66). She married Kagawa in 1913. While living in the slums and continuing her daily work as an itinerant nurse, she became infected with malignant trachoma and lost her vision in her right eye. Nevertheless, she engaged in relief activities for workers as the chair of the Society of Awakened Women (Kakusei Fujin Kyokai) during the labour disputes that erupted in 1921 at the Mitsubishi and Kawasaki shipyards in Kobe. She was also involved in relief efforts to support victims of the Great Kanto Earthquake of 1923. She assumed supervision of her husband's various projects after his death in 1960.

[66] The social activist Toyohiko Kagawa (1888–1960) was one of modern Japan's leading Christian figures. A graduate of Meiji Gakuin University, the Kobe Theological Seminary, and Princeton University, he worked to spread Christianity among the poor while attending the seminary in Kobe. In 1921, he was a leading figure in the labour disputes at the Mitsubishi and Kawasaki shipyards in Kobe and was active in settlement housing (social welfare facilities established in areas challenged by problems such as poverty or environmental issues) in Tokyo's Honjo neighbourhood. At peace with his lifelong poverty, he played pioneering roles in Japan's labour movement, farmers' movement, consumers' cooperative movement, and peace movement. His autobiographical novel *Shisen o koete* (Before the Dawn) became a bestseller.

[67] Kyobunkwan is a publisher and bookseller founded in 1885 by American Methodist missionaries including Robert S. Maclay and Irvin H. Correll, who were founding members of the Anglo-Japanese College (now Aoyama Gakuin).

At the time, Methodists regarded publishing as a potent method for evangelism. Today, the organization continues to publish books relating to Christianity while operating a bookstore complex in Tokyo's Ginza district that also features a café and conference hall. A floor dedicated to children's literature is home to the "Kingdom of Narnia," a section that features an assortment of high-quality children's books and which hosts lectures and exhibitions on a regular basis.

68 The Salvation Army is a Protestant Christian organization founded in 1865 by the British Methodist pastor William Booth. Originally known as the East London Christian Mission, it was reorganized as the Salvation Army in 1878. The organization was established in Japan in 1895 under the leadership of Gunpei Yamamuro, since which time it has been engaged in a variety of charitable endeavors.

69 Masahisa Uemura (1858–1925) was a protestant pastor and theologian. Baptized in 1873 under the influence of James Hamilton Ballagh, he went on to study at the Brown Preparatory School in Yokohama. After establishing the Fujimicho Church and Tokyo Shingakusha seminary, he continued to train evangelists and pursue his theological studies. He also founded the *Fukuin shinpo* (The Evangelical News) (see note 48). He was a leading figure in the evangelical movement in Japan and the author of *Shinri ippan* (An Aspect of Truth).

70 Gunpei Yamamuro (1872–1940) was the founder of the Salvation Army in Japan. After being inspired by a street preacher to convert to Christianity, he enrolled at the Doshisha School in Kyoto. With the arrival of the British Salvation Army in Japan in 1895, he enlisted as a member and devoted himself to improving social welfare, supporting the movement to abolish prostitution and helping the poor to obtain employment referrals and medical care. He introduced charity-kettle (*shakai nabe*) fundraising, served as the editor of the Army's magazine *Toki no koe* (The War Cry), and authored *Heimin no fukuin* (The Common People's Gospel).

71 Yuriko Mochizuki (1900–2001) was a journalist for *The Yomiuri Shimbun* before deciding to go abroad to study in France. After returning to Japan in 1925, she applied herself to writing critical essays and translations as an anarchist while also devoting her energies to the women's liberation movement. In 1938, she moved to northeastern China with her husband to become a reporter with the *Manshu shimbun* (Manchuria Newspaper). She remained active as an author and translator in the postwar period.

72 Shigeri Yamataka (1899–1977) was a feminist activist. Through her work as a magazine reporter, she helped found the League for the Realization of Women's Suffrage (Fujin Sanseiken Kakutoku Kisei Domei-kai) alongside Fusae

Ichikawa and others, supporting the movement as an influential member until its dissolution in 1940. Meanwhile, she was also active in the Motherhood Protection Movement (Bosei Hogo Undo) and went to great lengths to support the enactment of the 1937 Mother and Child Protection Law. After the Second World War, she became the founding chair of the National Federation of Regional Women's Organizations (Zenkoku Chiiki Fujin Dantai Renraku Kyogikai, usually abbreviated Chifuren), which sought to encourage women's social participation at the grassroots level. After 1962, she won election to the House of Councillors on two occasions, and in her later years argued in favour of the consolidation of movements to ban nuclear arms.

[73] The Yoshiwara licensed quarters was a legal red-light district during the Edo period, located in what is now northern Taito Ward in Tokyo. At its height, Yoshiwara was Edo's largest and most prosperous pleasure district, housing thousands of prostitutes. Most of these were young women from impoverished families. Indentured to their brothels, some died before they could buy back their freedom. Yoshiwara was shut down after Japan's Prostitution Prevention Law came into force in 1958.

[74] Institutes for Dutch studies, called *rangaku-juku* in Japanese, were privately run academies in the Edo period (1603–1867) devoted to the Dutch-language study of Western culture and scholarship. During Japan's period of national isolation (1639–1853), students were only able to access modern European science via Dutch-language sources.

[75] Temma Nobechi (1885–1965) was an author of children's literature, a Christian minister, and an evangelist.

[76] From "Kekkon o megutte" (Getting Married), *Kaiteiban ikiru to iu koto* (To Live: Revised Edition).

[77] In Japan, when a couple has a child, it is common for them to begin calling each other *okaasan* (Mother) or *mama* and *otosan* (Father) or *papa* instead of their names. Often the people around them do as well. This lasts until the couple has grandchildren, when they start calling each other *obahchan* "Grandma" and *ojiichan* "Grandpa." It is also common for younger children to refer to their older siblings by their relationship to them rather than by their names, i.e. *oneesan* (older sister) and *onisan* (older brother). The older children call the younger ones by their given names.

[78] Ryusuke Miyazaki (1892–1971) was an attorney-at-law and social activist. He first met Byakuren (see note 24) when he visited Akagane Goten, the "Copper-Coloured Palace" that served as the Ito family villa in Beppu, Oita prefecture, to

ask for permission to stage a performance of her play *Shiman doren* (The Heretic Angulimala). Later, as a founding member of the Tokyo University Shinjinkai (subsequently suppressed by the government as a seditious organization), he also served as the editor of the journal *Kaiho* (Liberation). In later life he devoted his energies to the popular movement to defend the constitution (*goken undo*) and to building friendly relations between Japan and China.

Chapter 6

[79] Japanese numbers are also used to make words. In this case, 8 = hachi, 7 = nana, 0 = maru (which means round or circle). Combining the first syllable of 8 (*ha*) with the first syllable of 7 (*na*) makes the word *hana*, which means flower, and is also Hanako's name. When *hana* is combined with the sound of 0 (*maru*), it makes the word *hanamaru*. The word *hanamaru* is a synonym for "excellent" or "perfect score" because teachers draw a circle (*maru*) around a good answer and then draw petals around the outside of that circle to make a flower (*hana*). This *hanamaru* mark on children's test papers means they have done well.

[80] From a collection of memorial poems *Michio o naka ni shite* (Revolving Around Michio).

[81] From "Uroko no gotoki mono" (Things Like Scales), *Wakaki haha ni kataru* (For Young Mothers).

Chapter 7

[82] Daisetsu Suzuki (1870–1966), also known as D.T. Suzuki, was a Japanese author and translator into multiple languages. He was instrumental in popularizing Zen philosophy in the West.

[83] From "Tomo o kataru" (About My Friends), *Kaiteiban ikiru to iu koto* (To Live: Revised Edition).

[84] The novelist Fumiko Hayashi (1903–1951) wrote children's stories and poems while waitressing in cafés, working in factories, and doing other menial jobs. She made her literary debut with the publication of the autobiographical novel *Horoki* (Diary of a Vagabond) in the literary journal *Nyonin geijutsu* (Women's Arts). A common thread running through her oeuvre is her sympathetic portrayal of the lives of common people. Other notable works include the novels *Seihin no sho* (A Record of Honorable Poverty), *Ukigumo* (Floating Clouds) and *Meshi* (Repast), as well as a collection of poetry, *Aouma o mitari* (I Saw a Pale Horse).

[85] Tomeko Watanabe (1882–1973) studied haiku and Japanese poetry under Nobutsuna Sasaki. She was the fourth daughter of the Japanese field marshal Iwao Oyama. Namiko, the protagonist of Roka Tokutomi's novel *Hototogisu* (The Cuckoo), was modelled on Tomeko's older sister.

[86] Novelist Otokichi Mikami (1891–1944) was the author of many historical novels written for a general readership, which earned him widespread popularity. These include *Katakiuchi jitsugetsu soshi* (Tales of Vengeance), *Yukinojo henge* (An Actor's Revenge), and *Oshidori jumon* (Charms for Wedded Bliss). After devoting his energies to establish the Japan Writers' Association (Bungeika Kyokai), he founded the monthly arts journal *Bungei shunju*. He also contributed to improving the social status of artists by establishing literary prizes such as the Akutagawa Prize and the Naoki Prize.

[87] Kan Kikuchi (1888–1948) was a popular author and playwright known for such works as *Onshu no kanata* (Beyond Love and Hate) and *Shinju fujin* (Madame Pearl). He helped establish the Japan Writers' Association (Bungeika Kyokai) and the magazine *Bungei shunju*, and later also contributed greatly to raising the social status of writers through the establishment of the Akutagawa Prize and the Naoki Prize.

[88] Akiko Yosano (1878–1942) was a poet. In 1900, she became involved with the New Poetry Society (Shinshisha), a poetry circle founded by Tekkan Yosano, and began publishing her tanka in the group's journal *Myojo* (Morning Star). The following year, she attracted notice with the release of the tanka collection *Midaregami* (Tangled Hair). She married Tekkan the same year. Her antiwar poem "Kimi shinitamou koto nakare" (Thou Shalt Not Die), written during the Russo-Japanese War, caused a major controversy. Her *Shinyaku Genji monogatari* (Newly Translated Tale of Genji) was a translation of the classical *Tale of Genji* into modern Japanese. During the Taisho period (1912–1926), she was active in the women's liberation movement and the critique of social issues. She was also involved in the founding of Bunka Gakuin, a school that aspired to provide a liberal education.

[89] Kuniko Imai (1890–1948) was a poet and an active member of the Araragi school of poetry under Akahiko Shimagi. Her poems also appeared in *Seito* (Bluestocking). She founded the poetry magazine *Asuka*. Her published collections of poetry include *Henpen* (Fragments) and *Murasakigusa* (Purple Grasses).

[90] After her marriage, Chiyo Uno (1897–1996) won successive newspaper-sponsored short story prizes. In 1921, although still married, she moved on her own to Tokyo where she began living as a writer. Prior to the Second World War, she was best known for her novel *Iro zange* (Confessions of Love). In 1957, she

was awarded the Noma Literary Prize for the novel *Ohan*. She is also known for her romantic entanglements with well-known figures such as Shiro Ozaki, Seiji Togo, and Takeo Kitahara.

91 Taiko Hirabayashi (1905–1972) was a novelist. Moving to Tokyo after developing an early interest in socialist movements, she was recognized as an author of proletarian literature with the publication of *Seryoshitsu nite* (In the Charity Hospital). Her postwar publications include *Ko iu onna* (This Kind of Woman), *Chitei no uta* (Song of the Underworld), and *Sabaku no hana* (A Flower in the Desert).

92 The word "Koshi" is the old name for a region along the Japan Sea in northwest Honshu that includes Niigata, where Hiroko's husband came from. According to the author, Hiroko used the word Koshi-ji (the name of the main road running through Koshi) in a poem she wrote after her husband's death. It's believed that Akutagawa used the word Koshibito for Hiroko because of this poem. Although Koshibito literally means "Person from/of Koshi," the word Koshi-ji used in Hiroko's poem has the double meaning of "border." Through the word Koshibito, Akutagawa thus may also have implied the feeling that Hiroko was beyond his reach and that his love for her in that sense was sacrosanct.

93 From "Chiisaki hikari" (Small Light), *Boshinsho* (Excerpts from a Mother's Mind).

94 The Imperial Diet was Japan's legislature until after the Second World War and consisted of the House of Representatives and the House of Peers. After the Second World War, it became the National Diet and is now composed of the House of Representatives (lower house) and the House of Councillors (upper house).

95 *Sister Sue* (1920) is a novel by Eleanor Hodgman Porter (1868–1920), best known as the author of *Pollyanna*. Muraoka's translation of the novel was serialized under the title *Choshi monogatari* (Tale of an Elder Sister) in the Seiransha magazine *Katei* (Home; later *Seiran*), then published in its entirety in 1932 by Kyobunkwan as *Ane wa tatakau* (Older Sister Fights). After the Second World War, the book was reissued by Kadokawa Bunko as *Sue nee-san* (Sister Sue), the title by which it is best known in Japan.

96 Manchukuo (the State of Manchuria) was a puppet state founded in 1932 following Japan's occupation of the northeastern region of China in the wake of the Mukden Incident (also known as the Manchurian Incident). Under the nominal rule of Pu Yi, the last emperor of the Qing dynasty, the country's capital was established in Ḥsinking (Changchun). The country became an empire in 1934 with Puyi's accession to the throne, and was later dissolved in 1945 with Japan's defeat at the end of the Second World War.

[97] The actor Ryo Ikebe, who at the time was living in Omori, recorded his memories of this couple called the "uh-huh beggars" in "Kuzumochi," an essay in his autobiographical collection *Soyokaze toki ni wa tsumujikaze* (Zephyrs and Sometimes the Whirlwind).

[98] The author believes that one reason Hanako wanted to adopt Midori was to preserve her husband's family line (a common reason for adopting and Midori's husband took the Muraoka name). Because Hanako and Keizo had rescued Umeko and taken care of her, Umeko would have given them Midori willingly and gladly, seeing this as a natural way to repay them for all they had done. Of course, as they lived next door, Umeko would see Midori every day. Hanako continued to financially support not only her immediate family and Umeko, but also her parents. In that sense, she was a much-loved godmother figure who took care of everyone who needed it.

[99] The Constitution of the Empire of Japan (also known as the Meiji Constitution) was Japan's pre-war Constitution. It was promulgated on February 11, 1889, and came into effect on November 29, 1890. Although the separation of powers and the guarantee of subjects' rights and freedoms were included after a fashion, in principle sovereignty was vested in the person of the sacred and inviolable Emperor descended from the unbroken Imperial line. The Meiji Constitution was abolished when the postwar Constitution of Japan came into effect on May 3, 1947.

[100] Established in 1901, the Patriotic Women's Association (Aikoku Fujinkai) was founded primarily to provide relief to disabled veterans and the bereaved families of war dead. In 1942, the association was integrated with the Greater Japan Women's Association (Dai Nippon Fujinkai) under the umbrella of the Imperial Rule Assistance Association (Taisei Yokusankai). It was abolished after the end of the Second World War.

[101] The Greater Japan National Defense Women's Association (Dai Nippon Kokubo Fujinkai) was established in 1932. Under the slogan "national defense begins in the kitchen," the organization arranged sendoffs for troops leaving for the front, provided assistance to disabled veterans and bereaved families, and conducted air-raid defense exercises. In 1942, the organization was rolled into the Greater Japan Women's Association (Dai Nippon Fujinkai).

[102] From "Boshin zuiso" (Thoughts on a Motherly Mind), *Haha to ko no mondai* (The Problems of Mothers and Children).

[103] The membership of the Women's Literature Society included Chiyo Uno, Fumiko Hayashi, Kuniko Imai, Tama Morita, Taiko Hirabayashi, Fumiko Enchi,

Sakae Tsuboi, Ineko Kubokawa (Sata), Tsuseko Yada, Tsuneko Nakazato, and Shizue Masugi.

Chapter 8

[104] The American architect and educator William Merrell Vories (1880–1964) arrived in Japan as a missionary in 1905. He designed as many as sixteen hundred buildings across Japan, including churches, schools, and hotels, and was active in a wide range of fields, from architecture to healthcare, education, and social work. Vories Memorial Hall still stands on the grounds of the Omi Brotherhood (formerly the Omi Mission) in Omihachiman in Shiga Prefecture.

[105] "Reverence" is a word that symbolizes the founding spirit of Toyo Eiwa, grounded in the teachings of the Bible and the ideal of a Christian education. It is the spirit running through Mark 12:30, "Love the Lord your God with all your heart and with all your soul and with all your mind and with all your strength." The message of the teaching is for followers "to be aware that [they] are precious and loved by God and to love and respect Him through worship, lessons, observances, and acts of service."

[106] "Service" is a word that expresses the founding spirit of Toyo Eiwa. Mark 12:31 instructs followers to "Love your neighbour as yourself." The phrase is interpreted to mean love not only yourself but also your neighbours (i.e. other people) and treat them kindly, for they too are loved by God.

[107] Among nationalists of the late nineteenth and early twentieth centuries, the term *kokutai* meant the Shinto-Confucian idealization of the Japanese nation-state. Japanese society was compared to a large family, with the emperor at the head as the benevolent guiding hand and patriarch. As such, the imperial throne served as the focus for the patriotic, nationalist fervour of the period prior to the Second World War.

[108] The author, Eri Muraoka was unable to verify with complete certainty exactly when Miss Shaw gave Hanako the copy of *Anne of Green Gables*. Based on an essay by Hanako in which she wrote, "I read *Anne of Green Gables* in 1939," the author stated in the original Japanese edition of *Anne's Cradle* published in 2008 that Hanako received the book in 1939. Content subsequently discovered in issues of the *Japan Christian Year-Book*, however, suggests there is a high possibility that Miss Shaw left Japan between 1936 and 1938. References to the timing of this incident have therefore been revised in this English edition to leave the date unspecified. If anyone who reads this book has further information on when Miss Shaw left Japan, the author would be grateful if they would inform her through the publisher.

[109] The English is copied verbatim from the March 1936 *Kyobunkwan Bulletin* and was provided by the author Eri Muraoka from the Toyo Eiwa Jogakuin Archives.

[110] From "Mukashi no sensei-tachi" (Past Teachers), *Kono sensei-tachi* (These Teachers).

[111] Banzai literally means "ten thousand years." After the reinstatement of the emperor as the ruler of Japan from 1868, it was used to mean "Long live the emperor!" During the Second World War, it was used to cheer on soldiers going to the front and as a battle cry. Since the end of the war, it has become similar in meaning and use to "Hooray" in English.

[112] From *Yumeharuka Yoshiya Nobuko* (Distant Dreams: Nobuko Yoshiya) by Seiko Tanabe, The Asahi Shimbun Company.

[113] In 1944, the Supreme Council for the Direction of the War was established to more fully coordinate the civil and military branches of the government, replacing the Liaison Conference between the Imperial General Headquarters established in 1937.

[114] "Shogakusei no haha" (Mother of a Primary School Student), *Kuinaki kekkon no tameni* (For a Marriage with No Regrets).

[115] Led by General MacArthur (except for the final year 1951–1952), the GHQ directed the Japanese government's transition from a totalitarian state to a democracy.

Chapter 9

[116] Elizabeth Saunders Home was opened in 1948 as an orphanage for biracial children by the social activist Miki Sawada (1901–1980), who used her own capital together with donations to repurchase the former Oiso residence of the Iwasaki family, which had been requisitioned by the occupying Allied Forces. The building was named in honor of the English woman who became the orphanage's first donor. Today, the institution continues to operate as a foster home for children unable to live with their parents.

[117] Gaiters are protective coverings for the legs, like puttees. The wearer winds a long cloth around the lower leg from the ankle to just below the knee then ties it off. In Japan they were worn during the Russo-Japanese War, and during the Second World War not only in military uniforms but also by men in the general populace. Various fabrics were used, such as thick cotton, woollens, or leather.

[118] *Hara Takashi kankei bunsho* (Documents Related to Prime Minister Takashi Hara).

[119] From "Katasumi kara no kotoba" (Words from an Obscure Corner) by Akiko Yanagiwara published in *Nippon hyoron* (Japan Review) April 1951.

[120] Books by Kiko Koike include *Yanaka kara kita hitotachi Ashio kodoku imin to Tanaka Shozo* (The People of Yanaka: Shozo Tanaka and Villagers Displaced by Ashio Copper Mine Pollution), *Kusarizuka: Jiyuminken to shujin rodo no kiroku* (Kusarizuka: A Record of Prison Labor and the Right to Freedom), *Hokkaido no yoake: Jomon Tonneru o horu* (The Dawn of Hokkaido: Digging the Jomon Tunnel), and *Heiminsha nojo no hitobito: Meiji shakai shugisha no roman to ikizama* (The People of Heiminsha Farm: The Romance and Way of Life of Meiji Socialists).

[121] From "Sono koro watashi wa: Michio bunko no koto" (Me, Then: About Michio's Library), by Shigeo Watanabe, from the Japan Board on Books for Young People Magazine.

Chapter 10

[122] Hisato Ichimada (1893–1984) was a Japanese politician and businessman of the Showa period (1926–1989). He served as the eighteenth governor of the Bank of Japan and Minister of Finance in the cabinets of Prime Ministers Ichiro Hatoyama and Nobusuke Kishi. His tenure at the Bank of Japan, which lasted 3,115 days, is the longest in history. He had the reputation of being the only businessman able to deal with the GHQ on his own terms and he wielded great influence in postwar financial and business circles. With his piercing eyes and high cheekbones, his features resembled those of the pope of that time, earning him the nickname "the Pope."

[123] Aiichiro Fujiyama (1897–1985) was a Japanese politician with a background in the business world. He held numerous positions of importance in the business community, including as president of the Dai Nippon Sugar Manufacturing Co., chairman of Japan Airlines, and chairman of the Japan Chamber of Commerce and Industry. In 1957, he was appointed Foreign Minister in the Cabinet of Prime Minister Nobusuke Kishi and entered politics after winning election the following year. He devoted his energies to the negotiations to revise the US–Japan Security Treaty and the restoration of political relations between Japan and China.

[124] Hisakichi Maeda (1893–1986), a businessman and politician, was the founder of the newspaper company, Sankei Shimbun, and the developer of Tokyo Tower.

[125] Shidzue Kato (1897–2001) was a Japanese feminist activist and politician who advocated for women's liberation. In 1919, she travelled to the United States and met Margaret Higgins Sanger, who inspired Kato to launch a Japanese birth-control movement upon her return to her native country. In 1931, she founded the Japan Birth Control Women's Union (Nihon Sanji Chosetsu Fujin Domei) and opened a birth-control clinic (*sanji seigen sodansho*) in 1934. She became one of the first women to be elected to the House of Representatives when women gained suffrage after the Second World War. In 1954, she formed the Japan Family Planning Federation (Nihon Kazoku Keikaku Renmei) and received the United Nations Population Award in 1988.

[126] The title of the second book, *Heren Kera no sukuinushi Ani Sariban* (Anne Sullivan: Helen Keller's Savior), is found in the afterword Hanako wrote for her biography of Helen Keller. However, the afterword did not give any details of when it was published or the publisher, so it is unclear whether it was originally a Japanese book or an English book.

[127] The movement was launched to coincide with Keller's visit. Badges were designed with a bluebird motif inspired by Maurice Maeterlinck's play *The Blue Bird*, which is about two children finding true happiness. In Japan, people with disabilities and their families often felt ashamed. The Blue Bird badges were sold to raise awareness that they can also be happy. The movement still sells the badges to raise money and awareness for their cause of helping children with disabilities.

[128] Although this letter was likely written in English, it no longer exists. The author quoted the Japanese version that Hanako had published at the end of her translation of *Kilmeny of the Orchard* (published under the Shincho Bunko label of Shinchosha Publishing Co., Ltd.), which the translator has here translated into English.

[129] Abegweit is the name by which Prince Edward Island is known by the Mi'kmaq Nation, the Indigenous people who have been fishing and hunting on the island for almost two thousand years. The word Abegweit means "cradled on the waves," a reference to the island's shape as well as the fertile soil that nourishes its natural abundance. In the sixteenth century, the island became embroiled in the colonial struggle between Great Britain and France, forcing the Mi'kmaq into a tenuous position. The island became a British territory in 1763 and was named Prince Edward Island in 1799 in honour of Prince Edward, the fourth son of King George III and the father of Queen Victoria. In 1873, the year before Lucy Maud Montgomery was born, Prince Edward Island joined Canada's Confederation to become a province.

[130] "Hanamori no ki" (Account of a Flower Guardian), *Kaiteiban ikiru to iu koto* (To Live: Revised Edition).

[131] "Osaka no kyujitsu" (A Holiday in Osaka), *Kaiteiban ikiru to iu koto* (To Live: Revised Edition).

[132] Hanako's favourite hymns were Hymns 7 and 277, which she herself had translated into Japanese.

Bibliography

Main References

Akage no An no shima prinsu edowado to no rekishi (The History of Anne of Green Gables' Island, Prince Edward Island; originally published in English as *Land of the Red Soil: A Popular History of Prince Edward Island*), Douglas Baldwin, translation by Kazuo Kimura, Kawade Shobo Shinsha Publishers Inc., 1995.

Bessatsu rekishi dokuhon Meiji Taisho wo ikita jugonin no onnatachi (Historical Reader: Fifteen Women Who Lived Through the Meiji and Taisho Periods), Shinjinbutsu Oraisha, 1985.

Bessatsu Taiyou kindai renai monogatari 50 (Extra Issue Sun: Love Stories of Modern Times), Heibonsha, 1979.

Byakuren musume ga kataru haha Akiko (Byakuren's Daughter Speaks of her Mother, Akiko), Reiko Miyajima, Association for the Preservation of the Former Ito Denemon Residence, 2007.

Gendai fujinden (watashi no ayunda michi) (The Lives of Contemporary Women: The Road I Took), Kiyoshi Kanzaki, Chuokoron-Shinsha, Inc., 1940.

Ginza monogatari rengagai wo tanpo suru (Ginza Story: Exploring Brick Town), Koichi Noguchi, Chuko Shinsho Label, Chuokoron-Shinsha, Inc., 1997.

Hayashi Fumiko (Fumiko Hayashi), Taiko Hirabayashi, Shinchosha Publishing Co., Ltd., 1969.

Hayashi Fumiko Uno Chiyo Koda Aya shu (Fumiko Hayashi, Chiyo Uno, Aya Koda Collection), Gendai Nihon Bungaku Daikei 69 (Outline of Modern Japanese Literature—Volume 69), Chikumashobo Ltd., 1969.

Hokkaido no yoake jomon tonneru wo horu (The Dawn of Hokkaido: Digging the Jomon Tunnel), Kiko Koike, Kokudosha Co., Ltd., 1982.

Hoso yawa zadankai ni yoru hoso shi (Broadcasting History through Round-table Talks: Bedtime Stories), Japan Broadcasting Corporation, 1968.

Ibara no mi (Seed of Thorns), Akiko Yanagiwara, Shinchosha Publishing Co., Ltd., 1928.

Joryu bungakushakai kiroku (Record of the Women's Literature Society), edited by the Japan Women's Literature Society, Chuokoron-Shinsha, Inc., 2007.

Kaiteiban ikiru to iu koto (To Live: Revised Edition), Hanako Muraoka, The Anne Memorial Room/Hanako Muraoka Study Room, 2004.

Kanagawa-ken insatsugyo-shi (History of the Printing Industry in Kanagawa Prefecture), Kanagawa Printing Industry Association, 1991.

Kindai nihon shakai undoshi jinbutsu daijiten (Encyclopedia of Leading Figures in the History of Social Movements in Modern Japan), Nichigai Associates, Inc., 1997.

Kindai nihon shiso annai (A Guide to Modern Japanese Thought), Masanao Kano, Iwanami Shoten, Publishers, 1999.

Kokubo fujinkai hinomaru to kappogi (National Defense Women's Association: The Japanese Flag and Aprons), Tadatoshi Fujii, Iwanami Shinsho Series, Iwanami Shoten Publishers, 1985.

Manshu no kiroku manei firumu ni utsusareta Manshu (Records of Manchuria: Images of Manchuria from Manei Film), Shueisha Inc., 1995.

Me de miru Toyo Eiwa jogakuin no hyakujunen (Pictorial History of Toyo Eiwa Jogakuin 1884-1994), Toyo Eiwa Jogakuin, 1995.

Meiji gakuin gojunen-shi (A Fifty-Year History of Meiji Gakuin), Meiji Gakuin, 1927.

Meiji kaijo den watashi wa watashi yo (The Lives of Amazing Meiji Women: I Am Me), Mayumi Mori, Bunshun Bunko Label, Bungeishunju Ltd., 2000.

Meiji kirisuto-kyo no ryuiki – Shizuoka bando to bakushin tachi (The Meiji Christians' Catchment: The Shizuoka Band and Shogunate Retainers), Aito Ota, Chuko Bunko Label, Chuokoron-Shinsha, Inc., 1992.

Meiji shakaishugi shiryo sosho 1 shakaishugi kyokaishi (Documentary Literature Concerning Meiji Socialism Volume 1: A History of the Socialism Association), Shinsensha, 1973.

Monogatari no musume Soei wo sagashite (Women of Stories: Searching for Soei), Minato Kawamura, Kodansha Ltd., 2005.

Nanatsu no tsubomi (Seven Buds), Keiko Matsuda, Himawari-sha, 1949.

Nihon hoso shi (The History of Broadcasting in Japan), Japan Broadcasting Corporation, 1951.

Nihon kirisuto-kyo kaishi (A History of the Japan Presbyterian Church), Japan Presbyterian Church Office, 1929.

Nihon ni okeru kirisuto-kyo to shakai undo (Christianity and Social Movements in Japan), Tatsuo Morita, Ushio Shobo, 1950.

Nihon no fujin mondai (Women's Issues in Japan), Nobuhiko Murakami, Iwanami Shoten, Publishers, 1978.

Nihon no kodomo no bungaku ten (Japanese Children's Literature Exhibition), Kanagawa Literature Promotion Association, 1985.

Nihon no sozoryoku – kindai gendai o kaika saseta yonhyaku nanajunin (Japanese Creativity: 470 People Who Contributed to the Flowering of Civilization in Modern and Contemporary Japan), NHK Publishing, Inc., 1993.

Nomura Kodo Araebisu to sono jidai (Kodo Nomura Araebisu and Those Times), Aito Ota, Christian Literature Society of Japan, 2003.

Okasan dowa no sekai e Tokunaga Sumiko no sokuseki (Mother Enters the World of Children's Stories: Traces of Sumiko Tokunaga), Reiko Watanabe, Bungeisha Publishing Co., Ltd., 2003.

Omina nareba (Because I'm a Woman), Hanako Muraoka, The Anne Memorial Room/Hanako Muraoka Study Room, 2004.

Sankeigakuen gojunen-shi (A Fifty-Year History of Sankei Gakuen), Sankei Gakuen Head Office, 2005.

Seitan hyakujunen Yoshiya Nobuko ten (Exhibition Commemorating the 110th Anniversary of Nobuko Yoshiya's Birth), Kanagawa Museum of Modern Literature, 2006.

Sengo ni okeru minpo kaisei no keika (Revising the Civil Code in Postwar Japan), Nippon Hyoronsha Co., Ltd., 1956.

Senkusha tachi no shozo asu o hiraita joseitachi (Portraits of Pioneers: Women who Paved the Way to the Future), Tokyo Women's Foundation, 1994.

Shashin de miru puru gakuin no hyakujunen (Poole Gakuin: The Way It Was), Poole Gakuin, 1990.

Shinko sanjunen kirisuto-sha retsuden (The Lives of Christians Who Converted Thirty Years Before), Keiseisha Shoten, 1921.

Shinpen kindai bijinden (ge) (The Lives of Modern Beauties: New Edition, final volume), Shigure Hasegawa, Iwanami Bunko Label, Iwanami Shoten Publishers, 1985.

Shinpen tokasetsu (New Edition: Candlemas), Hiroko Katayama, Getsuyosha Limited, 2007.

Shizuoka Eiwa jogakuin hyakunen-shi (A Hundred-Year History of Shizuoka Eiwa Jogakuin), Shizuoka Eiwa Jogakuin, 1990.

Shosetsu Tosaborikawa josei jitsugyoka Hirooka Asako no shogai (Tosabori River – The Novel: The Life of Businesswoman Asako Hirooka), Chieko Furukawa, Ushio Publishing Co., Ltd, 1988.

Showa bungaku seisuishi (A History of the Rise and Fall of Showa Literature), Jun Takami, Bunshun Bunko Label, Bungeishunju Ltd., 1987.

Showashi 1926–1945 (A History of the Showa Period 1926-1945), Kazutoshi Hando, Heibonsha, 2004.

Showashi sengohen 1945-1989 (A History of the Postwar Showa Period: 1945-1989), Kazutoshi Hando, Heibonsha, 2006.

Taisho modan kara sengo made (From the Modern Taisho Period to the End of the Second World War), Sekai Bunka Publishing Inc., 2006.

The History of the Church Missionary Society, Church Missionary Society, 1916.

Tokasetsu (Candlemas), Hiroko Katayama (pen name Mineko Matsumura), Getsuyosha Limited, 2004.

Tokyo daikushu/sensaishi dai yonkan (The Great Tokyo Air Raid: History of War Devastation, Volume 4), Tokyo Daikushu o Kiroku Suru Kai (Association to Record the Great Tokyo Air Raid), 1973.

Toyo Eiwa jogakko gojunen-shi (A Fifty-Year History of Toyo Eiwa Jogakko), Toyo Eiwa Jogakko, 1934.

Toyo Eiwa jogakuin hyakunen-shi (A Hundred-Year History of Toyo Eiwa Jogakuin), Toyo Eiwa Jogakuin, 1984.

Tsukiji gaikokujin kyoryuchi (The Tsukiji Foreign Settlement), Seiro Kawasaki, Yushodo Co., Ltd., 2002.

Tsukiji kyoryuchi 1-3 (The Tsukiji Foreign Settlement 1 to 3), The Tsukiji Foreign Settlement Research Society, 2000-2004.

Wagatsuma koishi Kagawa Toyohiko no tsuma Haru no shogai (My Beloved Wife: The Life of Toyohiko Kagawa's Wife Haru), Shige Kato, Banseisha, 1999.

Watashi no fujin undo (My Feminist Movement), Fusae Ichikawa, Akimoto Shobo, 1972.

Yamanashi Eiwa ishizue no toki wo ikite (Founders of Yamanashi Eiwa: Our Living Mission), Yamanashi Eiwa Alumni Association, 2006.

Yokohama no ayumi (The History of Yokohama), Association for the Dissemination of Documents Concerning Yokohama Port, 1986.

Yokohama no hon to bunka bessatsu (Yokohama Books and Culture: Supplementary Volume), Yokohama Central Library, 1994.

Yokohama seiko meiyokan (reprint) (Biographical Dictionary of Successful Yokohama Citizens), Yurindo Co., Ltd., 1980.

Yumeharuka Yoshiya Nobuko (jo/ge) (Distant Dreams: Nobuko Yoshiya, Volumes 1 & 2), Seiko Tanabe, The Asahi Shimbun Company, 1999.

Zuikan hitsushu (Random Thoughts and Essays), Renzo Sawada, Association for the Posthumous Publication of Renzo Sawada's Manuscripts, 1990.

Magazines

Fujin shinpo (Women's News), Japan Woman's Christian Temperance Union

Fusen (Women's Suffrage), April 1933 Issue, Women's Suffrage League, reprinted edition, Volume 8, Fuji-shuppan Co., Ltd., 1992-1994.

Josei tenbo (Women's Prospects), January 1940 Issue, Women's Suffrage League, reprinted edition, Volume 19, Fuji-shuppan Co., Ltd., 1992–1994.

Katei bunko kenkyukai kaiho (Home Library Research Society Bulletin), Home Library

Research Societies

Kyobunkwan geppo (Kyobunkwan Bulletin), Kyobunkwan Publishers

NHK hoso bunka (NHK Broadcasting Culture), Japan Broadcasting Corporation, 1961.

Nupunkeshi 62-go (Nupunkeshi No. 62), Group for the Compilation of Kitami City History, Planning Department, Kitami City, 2003.

Sankei Gakuen, Otemachi Sankei Gakuen

Shokoshi (*Little Children of Light*), Kyobunkwan Publishers

Yokohama Hodo (Yokohama Sidewalks), No. 78 April Issue, Izumi Tsushinsha, 1968.

Research Paper

"Muraoka Hanako-ron/Taiheiyo senso mae o chushin ni" (On Hanako Muraoka: Focused on the Period Before the Pacific War), Hiroe Suzuki, 1995.

Japan Christian Year-Book (1937–1941)

Index

Eri Muraoka, granddaughter of Hanako Muraoka, graduated from Seijo University in Tokyo in 1990, majoring in literature and arts, and subsequently worked as a writer for a women's magazine. In 2014, her celebrated biography of her grandmother, who translated *Anne of Green Gables* into Japanese, *An no Yurikago Muraoka Hanako no Shogai*, became the basis of a highly acclaimed six-month TV drama series on NHK, Japan's public television station. In 2019 she published the biography of Tokiko Iwatani.

Skye Hohmann

Cathy Hirano graduated from International Christian University in Tokyo in 1983 with a BA in cultural anthropology and has been translating professionally since 1984. Her translations of YA fiction and fantasy have won several awards, including a 2020 Michael L. Printz Honor award for *The Beast Player* by Nahoko Uehashi. Her translations of *The Life-Changing Magic of Tidying Up* and its sequels by Marie Kondo are international bestsellers. She lives in Shikoku, Japan.